Critical Muslim 41

Bodies

Critical Muslim is published quarterly by C. Hurst & Co. (Publishers) Ltd. on behalf of and in conjunction with Critical Muslim Ltd. and the Muslim Institute, London.

All editorial correspondence to Muslim Institute, CAN Mezzanine, 49–51 East Road, London N1 6AH, United Kingdom.
E-mail: editorial@criticalmuslim.com

ISBN: 9781787387164 ISSN: 2048-8475

To subscribe or place an order by credit/debit card or cheque (pounds sterling only) please contact Kathleen May at the Hurst address above or e-mail kathleen@hurstpub.co.uk

Tel: 020 7255 2201

A one-year subscription, inclusive of postage (four issues), costs £50 (UK), £65 (Europe) and £75 (rest of the world), this includes full access to the *Critical Muslim* series and archive online. Digital only subscription is £3.30 per month.

Critical Muslim

Subscribe to Critical Muslim

Now in its eleventh year in print, *Critical Muslim* is also available online. Users can access the site for just £3.30 per month – or for those with a print subscription it is included as part of the package. In return, you'll get access to everything in the series (including our entire archive), and a clean, accessible reading experience for desktop computers and handheld devices — entirely free of advertising.

Full subscription

The print edition of *Critical Muslim* is published quarterly in January, April, July and October. As a subscriber to the print edition, you'll receive new issues directly to your door, as well as full access to our digital archive.

United Kingdom £50/year
Europe £65/year
Rest of the World £75/year

Digital Only

Immediate online access to *Critical Muslim*

Browse the full *Critical Muslim* archive

Cancel any time

£3.30 per month

www.criticalmuslim.io

CM41

WINTER 2022

CONTENTS

BODIES

Nadeem Baghdadi, 'Sit and Think', mixed media on paper

ARTS AND LETTERS

REVIEWS

ET CETERA

BODIES

INTRODUCTION: BODY HORROR

C Scott Jordan

It has been almost ten years since I cut up a human body and I still wonder why we were so compelled to begin by praying over the corpse. This requires some unpacking.

First, I have found my personal theology to be quite peculiar when compared to others. While I do appreciate and respect the discipline that ritual prayer offers to us humans, at the mercy of time and physics, I am not into ritualised prayer. Prayer is a communication, yes, but not in the traditional sense. For me, prayer is beyond language. Rather, it is lived action, even a lifestyle. It has a resemblance to a dialogue or even a polylogue – lest we let it become a monologue. It does not really end or begin much as our correspondences with parents, loved ones, or dear friends are all just continuations of one long script. For God, who is beyond all, direction and quantity are arbitrary. It does come with a degree of awareness (which we all ought to seek in our own time). But to reduce it to some specialisation, another woefully human propensity, reduces the overall sanctity of it. Asking for prayers or specialising prayers for one or something feels mildly abusive and renders me ever so uncomfortable. As if prayers were an Amazon Wishlist that if we all vow to be good little humans then at the end of the year, we will get an invoice stating our loved ones are in paradise, happy, and Timmy got into his first-choice uni. For me prayer is also quite personal, intimate. And I am as comfortable in an assembly of praying persons as I am in a communal shower. Exposed and strangely ashamed of any deviating thoughts that spring into my head.

Second, the bodies before us, I was assured, were expired. Definitely deceased; they were no more. Plumage notwithstanding, they were ex-living people. And regardless the eloquence of our prayers, I did not realistically think we could do anything about such a permanent condition.

The prayers we were to offer were more of a giving thanks. An appreciation. As it were, a beautiful gesture similar to how indigenous American peoples would give thanks to the Earth and all its spirits and creatures for the sustenance allowed before each feast or how the Australians have inculcated the thanking of the aboriginal community, whose land they conveniently occupy, before certain events. So, why was I so bent out of shape about praying over dead bodies amongst my student peers? Well, you see, the whole thing felt a bit redundant, we had technically already done this.

Every year around the delightfully inappropriate holiday season, the Saint Louis University School of Medicine, in conjunction with the Center for Anatomical Sciences and Education, hosts a sort of gala to thank the families of those who donate their bodies to the school for overly optimistic youngsters to carve up over the course of a semester. The evening includes a beautiful service, now made interfaith, at the St. Francis Xavier College Church where families open up old wounds to again re-eulogise the deceased while first year students smile, most blissfully ignorant of how far medical education has come in terms of body procurement. Only a couple of hundred years ago, dopey smiles and awkward dinner talk would be replaced with shovels, lanterns, and, preferably, someone keeping watch. The acts, which out of context could be described as 'grotesque', we would soon commit in that laboratory on the top floor of the ancient (by American standards) School of Medicine building would connect us to greats like Leonardo DaVinci or William Burke and William Hare. As American college students, we were just happy to have a free meal.

My mind tends to over think when I find myself in the middle of tasks that must be done, regardless of how pointless I find them to be. First comes comedy. How fitting we all are weeping in our prayers. Within stainless-steal sarcophagi, the bodies before us lay in body bags that, while airtight (to preserve the moisture, we are told), did little in the way of keeping the aromatic formaldehyde molecules from wreaking havoc on our eyes and airways. Thus, streams of tears fittingly run down our cheeks. Then comes reasoning. You can sell me on the logic of praying over a human regardless of my personal belief, but these are not humans, they are just bodies. Finally comes the ultimate irony. This opening prayer completely betrays the veneer put up to dissociate us as objective scientific practitioners-to-be from the antithetical act of what is effectively dismembering a fellow human. Great measures are taken for us to mentally be aware that these are bodies, husks – no longer the persons that used to inhabit, or if you prefer, *be* them. Their names are withheld from us, they are anonymous (though, be nice to the right people and ask the right questions and inquiring minds are always fed). We were given a story about a young female med student who, prior to the strict anonymity policy, came to discover she had been dissecting her grandmother. Never given a proper ending to the story, the assumption was that she went mad over such a revelation and had to therefore be interred at a mental facility for the rest of her days. Otherwise, we would have no reason to fear breaking the policy!

But really think about it. We were trained to use an entirely new vocabulary, they say for respect, but really it is all sugar-coating. They are not bodies, they are *cadavers*. Or maybe it was all to get us ready for HIPAA (Health Insurance Portability and Accountability Act of 1996), a set of regulations put in place to keep private the sacred medical history of others. In other classes, this would present in our case studies where patients would be referred to by broad (and quite racially charged) generalisations instead of by name. But is the point to keep private other's deep secrets or to save ourselves from the legal repercussions. Lesson one of medical school is save thy self first, then save that patient, and make sure they cannot sue you! So much for the Hippocratic Oath (or as I call it, the Hypocritical Oath). And so, you see the roots of why I excised myself from any love or desire to be a part of the American medical establishment.

But let us return to this veil of ignorance. A cloth was even draped over the faces of the cadavers, that is, until it came time to dissect the muscles of the face and finally extract the brain (easier said than done, I assure you!). As that lesson tends to be saved to the end, there is not much left of the body by that point, suspending any humanity we may cling to the flesh. The less human they were, the easier it would be on us.

But prior to standing in that laboratory, I was acutely aware that dead bodies were not human. I was fortunate to never have lost anyone close to me, at least since I can remember, until I was in university. My Uncle Tony passed away my freshman year of university, from cancer only after making a rather miraculous recovery after suffering severe burns incurred by a horrendous car accident almost a decade before. Jordans, as members of my family would often like to restate, are not an easy people to put in the ground. And while the human my uncle was has lived on in the eulogia and photographs, and of course the memories, what rested in the coffin at the Nebraska City funeral home was not my uncle. And I take comfort in that. Released of the limits and the pain.

Less than a year later my grandfather would pass away. And while both my Uncle Tony's and my grandfather's preparations, it must be said, were carefully and masterfully done, what lay in the casket was just a body, a relic.

Before too long, this became sort of a recurring thing. I have these hardened memories of attending funerals with my father. It was as if it was the thing to do when I was too old for things that entertain kiddies but too young to simply go to the pub and have a pint with my dad. My father did not do what your stereotypical American father does. He did not teach me to shoot a gun (and I continue to retain no interest in that skill), he did not teach me to drive a manual transmission (which I do deeply regret), he did not even teach me to shave (my mother did at my impassioned behest over the horror of pubescent whiskers). But, he did teach me to deal with death.

Like a horse teaches its foal to take its first steps that become the mad dash that only ends one way, I learned to always speak in whispered tones, to listen, to give condolence, and then to present yourself to the body. Before the host you could speak, offer a prayer, recant a memory, you could even touch the body respectfully with a pat on the shoulder, a compassionate hold of the hand, or even a kiss on the forehead. All depending on whatever helped. Admittedly, it is a rather one-sided affair. I recall going to three funerals over the course of a year for people I did not know. They were connections to my dad's work and whenever we showed up the bereaved families were always happy to see us. And my dad would walk with me to see the body and as if he knew I was just standing there overthinking the pointlessness of standing next to a body who was not a person, he would begin complimenting the funeral staff's preservation techniques and then filling my head with stories about the person who used to be this body.

When it came time to be present over my own father's body, he was unfortunately not there to fill my overthinking and wondering mind, but instead confirmed that in the end, we just become bodies. This point was driven home by the state I found my father's body in. Prior to the funeral I was shown my father's body to give the final okay, all looks good here. As I looked upon him, I could not help but burst out in laughter. His face was adorned with Elvis Presley's mutton chop sideburns that he wouldn't be caught dead in, but, well. While the nurses at the hospital he spent his last moments with did a relatively good job of keeping him cleaned up – he had kept the same clean-cut moustache and haircut since his time in the Navy three decades prior – the way the apparatus that assisted his breathing was fastened to his face allowed for that curious facial hair to grow as if groomed that way. No matter, this was an easy fix and did not require the ever-so-sorry funeral director's apologies. My father had gotten the last laugh, and this was just a body, an imitation. The human that was, certainly now in a better place. The freezing cold December day we put him to rest prevented doubt of this and the chaotic madness that was the preceding year, 2020, certified it.

Admittedly, I had it easy. Regardless my history with corpses. My group's cadaver had belonged to a woman who lived well into her eighties who, as a quick extracurricular investigation determined, had died from 'natural causes'. Existential conundrums were overshadowed by our fear that what organs remained within this well-lived body would be in considerably less than 'textbook' condition. The cadaver in the group next to us was that of a fit and healthy male, aged twenty-five who had passed away from testicular cancer – one top ranking fear throughout my twenties. The faculty rightly feared for our fragile little psyches, faced with such an existential crisis inducing mirror.

Or, were we supposed to be praying, 'Please God, do not let me become this.' But a prayer against what we all know to be an inevitability seemed problematic as well. Bodies are scary. And the difference between the thing in the bag and those of us in our scrubs could be one simple decision. A drunk driver, inclement weather conditions, sleep deprivation, ignoring for too long that one thing that seems off, or simply going down the wrong path at the wrong time – any or all of these could put us in the stainless-steal sarcophagus. We had one professor, a lung specialist, who said statistically if it is not the heart that gets you, it will be the lungs, and neither are particularly pleasant, so pray for getting hit by the bus. It is not clean, but it is quick. But aside from being the only real evidence we all eventually leave behind there must be more to the body.

I want to believe that the body is more than just a shell for the soul. There must be something different between what I feel experiencing a dead human body and encountering a rotting piece of fruit. Perhaps there is an instinct to cringe at death rooted in an inability to square the circle of expiry as a living being or perhaps it is just one of our survival feedback loops. I cannot be sure either way. The macabre of a dead body fills us with dread. But horror becomes me when I see a dead squirrel on the other side of an automobile's encounter (a common occurrence when walking or jogging along Midwestern American roads). Is it just as when I see a body in preparation for a funeral? But what I see is not that individual, but a body. I do not fear the individual, I fear the corpse. This is why the dread is so compounded when we see images of 'walking corpses' such as in old photos and films documenting the Holocaust. We look upon piles of bodies or mass graves and feel sad for what humans can be capable of, but there is a different horror when bodies that look like they should not be capable of bearing life, walk on. More contemporaneously we see starving children roam the Horn of Africa, or the pulsating bellies of maimed innocents in the real horror-show that everyone has seemed to have forgotten now taking place in Yemen, Syria, and Afghanistan.

Two photos from my primary education are burned into my memory.

The first image was published on the front page of the *Chicago Defender* and was the cover of *Jet* magazine depicting the body of Emmet Till after his brutal murder in 1955. It is hard to say what killed fourteen-year-old Emmet Till as he was lynched, his body mutilated, and shot several times. His mother insisted on an open casket funeral stating, 'there was just no way I could describe what was in that box. No way. And I just wanted the world to see'. Organic matter twisted in ways once thought impossible, an image that reasonably makes onlookers ill to their stomachs. This was the punishment for his interacting with a white woman in Mississippi. No one living could say for sure, but Till could have done anything from whistling at her (he was trained to whistle to himself to assist with his mild speech impediment) to grabbing her by the arm in an attempt at playful flirtation. Because the body was so badly mutilated, a defence could not, without a reasonable doubt, indicate that the body recovered was, in fact,

Tills, and no justice was handed down by a court of law, including that concerning the charge of kidnapping, which the white woman's husband and his half-brother admitted to having done during the trial.

The second photo forever pasted in my head depicts a large crowd of white Omaha denizens gathered in jubilant victory. Perhaps the Cornhuskers had taken home the National Football Championship, or it is one of the many autumn festivals. Centred before the posed mob is what appears to be a statue, perhaps they are about to set it in place. A memorial? On closer examination, one notices odd flashes around the statue. It is not a statue, it is a body, still smouldering in the flames that have turned it into an ash cast of an individual that had recently been lynched from a traffic signal. The remains were once William Brown, a black man. The Omaha police had arrested Brown on suspicion of raping a nineteen-year-old white girl. Trials can be very slow and this was the Red Summer of 1919, where over twenty race riots took place all across the US. A mob, possibly ignited by an old crime boss and an alliance of poor white union labourers, demanded a swift act of justice. The mayor at the time would not allow his city to fall to mob rule and barricaded the Douglas County Courthouse in preparation for a siege with himself and Brown inside. Today that courthouse still stands, now with a statue of Martin Luther King Jr. in the front yard. The mob quickly grew out of control and had at one point drawn out the mayor who declared if anyone would hang tonight, it would be him first. The mob kindly obliged. Luckily a couple of journalists, with the aid of an automobile, cut the mayor down and trafficked him off out of town. After the courthouse was doused in petrol and set aflame, the remaining alliance of black and white police and prisoners agreed to hand over Brown to secure their own safety. The mob lynched Brown, used his body for target practice, then dragged his body by chains from the back of a car that made several laps around the streets of downtown Omaha, all this before the body was unceremoniously burned. Years later, it would come to light that the girl who was raped never made a definitive identification that William Brown was indeed the man.

An interesting insight I have taken away from my time in the anatomy lab is that the fixing process used for our cadavers gives the skin a sort of iridescent opaqueness and ethnicity does not shine as bright without oxygenated blood flowing in under the surface. And even if your brain must seek the racial identity of your cadaver, once you get past the skin (a layer thicker than you'd think that can be a hell of a job to cut through even with a fresh scalpel) we are all the same colourless heaps of bones and guts. The insides of bodies are February, endless grey, unless you are lucky enough to have gotten one of the bodies where the veins are filled with blue wax and the arteries with red. Alas, even medical schools work on tight budgets (which was hard to believe based on what they were making us pay for this joy) and only a couple of the bodies got this treatment, which in the long run feels like a cheat. The amount of time spent deciphering veins from arteries without the indication of colour makes you want to rip apart every colour-printed anatomy textbook you come across. The aggravation grows when you reason that just as your undergraduate education does little to prepare you for graduate education, this practice is rather futile as we are parsing through worn and lifeless flesh. The real thing must be a whole new world.

The truth behind that assumption is yes and no. The beauty you learn in dissecting a cadaver is that while yes, we all have our little differences and may miss *this* or have a more present *that*, we are almost nauseatingly similar. It really takes the mystique out of medicine. Medicine has an artistic element to it, but very quickly resembles maths. When you hold a human heart in your hands and see, wow, it really is the size of one's closed fist (and if it is not, then you have one serious condition on your hands), the magic may be lost, but hope is somewhat reignited. The differences, which everyone is so eager to let define humans, are truly surface level or existent in the depths of the brain. Jeremy Henzell-Thomas discovers this in his quest to reconcile the saying 'men are from Mars and women are from Venus', which he comes to find out is far more programmed than we may be tempted to believe. The Patriarchy lives indeed, but only in our educations and development. The gendered roles can be unlearned or even rewired. Since our course director was a neuroanatomist, we had the privilege of a healthy dose of neurology. And you would think that everything concerning the brain and neurons is incomprehensibly complex, but it can at times be relatively simple. If you can interpret circuit charts, you can trace back and deduce many neurological ailments.

Medical school application essay templates would make you think everyone goes to medical school to fill some past trauma over some family member's sickness. If only there had been a doctor who understood more about Alzheimer's or whatever. But, truth be told, I was a knowledge junky and discovery was my motivation. The only family history I had was my dad's unseasonably young heart attack and the heart was boring to me. We almost understand every little detail about the thing. So much so that we are within grasp of 3-D printing the things, and what's more, I just read that a heart transplant using a genetically modified pig's heart was successfully completed. Since I have a crippling fear of the vastness of outer space, the brain was my final frontier. So, you can imagine my disappointment when I learned that a great deal of neurological disorders can readily be diagnosed by looking at the face, the eyes, and how people walk.

A psychological theory is proposed which has been adopted by certain artists to explain what is at play here from the reduction of the human to a body as machine as well as to explain the feelings evoked through the photographs of massacred bodies. It is referred to as abjection and is at the heart of the abject art movement. Objectification of the body, or breaking the complexity of life down into compounded, simple processes, fulfils the notion of abjection, detaching the subject from the many other objects. The self becomes lost in the other or even in just things. I explore this theory with trepidation as it is rooted in a lot of Freudian psychology that I feel has created more problems than it has solved. The root of the idea is found in the phenomenon that occurs when a child first looks into a mirror, it sees itself as something independent of its environment, particularly the mother. Often motherhood is the emphasis of abject art pieces. The pain as well as the gross bodily display that is the reality of childbirth serves as subject. The human body is frequently portrayed in all its gore as object. More frequently the female body, particularly the breasts and vagina, the mysterious internal genitalia – an unknown to be feared – replace common objects or are replaced by other objects. Religious icons are also free game for the abject artist to give bodily disgust or to soil in the biological. Though the point is not transposition, but to blur the lines between object and subject, inside and out, animate and inanimate, the sacred and the profane. But what is it saying about the body?

Here I do not wish to go too far into it, as a whole host of philosophies, dipping transdisciplinarily, can provide almost as many answers as one desires. My fear in abjection is that while it forces the audience to face a reality, it does nothing in the way of navigating them towards resolution. So, we are left to say the body is an object which we possess, on one hand the ultimate metaphor for empowerment and agency or, on the other hand, we can let others possess it on our behalf or find our bodies repossessed.

Seeing the body as a thing to simply be possessed leaves a bad taste in the mouth. Far too easily dialled into the capitalistic business-as-usual approach to simplifying everything down to exchanges. The ease with which this mentality consumes everything in its sights makes me at the very least long for the body to be something greater than a piece of capital on which God sends us forth to make profit. Sins and saintly deeds just debits and credits. At the final judgement you are given the bill and pray your card does not get declined. The invasiveness of capitalism is experienced first-hand when Themrise Khan reflects on her umrah. While in Medina, she notes the unabashed acceptance of an H&M and a Starbucks right across the street from the iconic *Masjid-e-Nabawi*. These contradictions were only the beginning for Khan who, with her mother and two aunties, embarked on the journey once Saudi Arabia reformed their policy to allow women above a certain age to travel without a male guardian. Khan's introspective quest takes on the contradictions within Islam alongside of those which need not be, but constantly are, thrown into conflict between tradition and modernity. Across the Holy Land she rages against the patriarchy that dominates the religion, even limiting not only what a Muslim woman is, but how a Muslim woman can be in relation to the world and God. The hope, a valiant hope ripe amongst a great deal of other changes demanded in the wake of the Covid-19 pandemic, is that a space can be created for women to have the same relationship with God as men.

Khan's recounted normalcy of Western capitalism in the Holy Land strikes a chord with the brutality of normalised domestic violence in India uncovered through Chandrika Parmar's raw headfirst plunge into how deeply the notion of property can be corrupted. When India, like most of the rest of the world, went into lockdown, the globally trending message of 'Stay Home, Stay Safe' was stretched beyond parody or farce. Home, that owned safe place, became a prison for victims already suffering the abuse of a spouse or parent. And in the accounts of abuse, it is not just the surface level husband's ownership of the wife's body – stripping the wife down to the level of duty-free property – but the possession stretches to encompass her whole identity and dignity in some cases. Old laws resist reform in India where spousal rape continues to be unrecognised while lack of education or will for public discourse on matters of sex, mental health, and family maintains an atmosphere of complacent normalcy – a truly threatening global trend that lurks in just the right places to prevent progress or change where it is needed most.

Khan and Parmar's articles call for a break from convention. Ultimately, you could tie their aims together as a decolonising endeavour, but this is not a simple repossession of the body or gaining of the space desired. It is breaking, once and for all, broken systems. Wiping the board clean and starting anew does not quite accomplish the trick. Reform and recovery are needed so that a society can, together, become something new.

Samia Rahman grapples with similar issues in her analysis of Salman Rushdie's novel *Shame*. Interesting here as Rushdie expands the metaphor of the body to represent an entire nation or is it the state, the difference here is the people or the borders. Overall, the novel speaks of a system, and a fragile one at that. The body is a limiting structure, much as a state's borders are, but the transformation depicted in *Shame* strikes at the transformation of the people, this new nation, which is largely seen in an ebb and flow of identity crises. Shame then is the result of having one's identity space denied or even othered. *Shame*'s main character, Sufiya Zinobia transforms into a great beast, unable to find a space for herself in not only a misogynist world, but one bearing the alienating double indemnity of being both a woman and a person of colour, or of being a Muslim woman. In pairing *Shame* with the blogs of Mona Eltahawy, Rahman identifies emotion, something strongly tied to woman, also a weakness, but as something which ties the body to the mind or soul, what makes one a living human. 'If emotions are what enable people to construct national identity, the irony is undeniable, because emotionality has long been associated with women, the same women who are consistently denied their rightful place in nation-building', writes Rahman. Emotion, something established as requiring a body, allows us to become. If hindered, it can be contained or haunted by shame, but if embracing the shame or even becoming shameless there is little limit to what constructions it can be capable of.

In reflecting on his own Malay-ness, Shanon Shah looks at how this becoming force can be subverted by bad, yet strongly perpetuated, narratives. Stereotypes cast Malays as 'lazy' and incapable of higher intellect and creative prowess. Yet while these stereotypes may have been forged by outsiders and colonisers, it did not stop elite powers within what is modern day Malaysia from using such narratives to maintain a status quo. Such narratives are engrained in culture through film and even enshrined in constitutions. The danger today is that their continued existence allows for serious crimes and corrupt practices to proceed unchecked as possession of the mind allows for possession of the body and resources, meanwhile the whole planet suffers and the same communities that have always been victims of such extractions are now the first to suffer from the climate fallouts.

Shah's essay shows how narratives, often purported in films, solidify stereotypes and fears into the form of phobias and -isms. I would name them here, but I am bound to forget your favourite. Shah cites the classic monster film genre as one way these graft onto the subconscious. I think this can be taken a step further. Where abjection presents with a certain passiveness beyond the initial shock factor, the genre of body horror forces an interaction.

Body horror as a genre is quite an unwieldy beast when you really consider what it encompasses. The genre is so broad it can include classic monster films with basic cinematography all the way to the seizure-inducing hyperbolic cyberpunk posthuman nightmares of science fiction. And even if the film can be categorised under a variety of other genres, elements of body horror can always be sneaked in to assist with worldbuilding or give a new challenge to an overly flat character. Body horror also spans almost the entire history of human storytelling. Ancient civilisations the world over are filled with myths and legends of beings capable of transforming between various species and states. So, to keep the body of this piece from becoming its own pulsing, tumorous Akira-esque monstrosity, clarification will be necessary.

The body horror I will speak of here is generally broken down into two categories. First is the type of body horror brought about through biological transcendence. This would be films that involve people transforming through a mutation, disease, pregnancy complication, or curse that sees the body do 'unnatural' things. The second type of body horror is that provoked by technological intervention. This deals with all matters of cybernetics and posthumanism, even promiscuous and killer robots or automobiles. But, the best body horror synthesises the two. In so doing, an interesting revelation is surfaced.

The first name that often comes to mind when considering the body horror genre in film is The Baron of Blood himself, The King of Venereal Horror, David Cronenberg. His most mainstream and accessible film (though of course, as goes for all body horror, not for everyone) is 1986's remake, *The Fly*. It should be noted that David Cronenberg does a remake as they ought to all be done. Not a simple copy-paste job. In fact, the only thing in common with Cronenberg's *The Fly* and Kurt Neumann's 1958 version is the use of a molecular transmission device, a common house fly, and they both give credit to the short story 'The Fly' by George Langelaan which of all places was first published in a 1957 issue of *Playboy*. In Cronenberg's version, scientist Seth Brundle is molecularly fused, down to the level of DNA, with a house fly when transporting himself via his invention the telepod. At first, Brundle notices peak physical condition only to see himself rapidly degrade into a horrifying fly-man. While this lies more in the realm of the biological transcendence body horror category, since a piece of technology instigates the mess (and at one point his hybrid body again is hybridised with the machine itself) you get all the wonderful modernist hubris added to the package of themes.

But Cronenberg's true all-in-one body horror masterpiece is 1983's *Videodrome*. We follow Max Renn, the president of a sensationalist television station on his quest for the future of television. Desensitised to violence and pornography, Renn stumbles upon a show called Videodrome, which is simply the live feed of people being tortured, believed to be being broadcast out of the most lawless and random place Cronenberg could think of – Malaysia. In his quest to gain the rights he learns that Videodrome carries a broadcast signal that causes its viewers to develop a brain tumour that instigates hallucinations and, eventually, death. But a man found to have died years prior to the film's storyline, kept 'alive' only by thousands of pre-recorded VHS tapes, explains that the death is only of the old flesh. The hope is that television will replace every fascette of human life. 'Long live the new flesh' is hailed numerous times throughout the film. The film is chalk full of sexual inuendo, blurring the lines between the biological and the technological, and constantly keeps you asking what is real and what is not. After a viewing one could not be blamed for desiring a CT scan.

Cronenberg's son Brandon has shown promise in his filmography and that the rein of Cronenberg shall be long indeed. His most recent contribution is 2020's *Possessor*, when a team of assassins use a machine to enter the consciousness of seemingly random people to carry out their hits. After each assassination, the host commits suicide, releasing themselves from the mind of the possessed and hiding any hint of their involvement. Such work requires its assassins to cut themselves completely from their humanity to make sure the process can run seamlessly and the assassin keeps their psyche separate from those they imitate. The heart of the story is a woman, Tasya Vos, attempting to keep her work life separate from her domestic life with her husband and son. This all goes wrong when an assassination is botched, and the host Vos has possessed begins fighting back for control of his body.

This particular example is interesting as the expectation is flipped. A woman possesses a white male to use him to carry out her will. Although it is unclear whether or not her employer is using this all to convince her to give up her last links to her humanity. Honestly, the whole thing could have been in Vos's head and the film simple a metaphor for choosing between one's family and one's career, which in the hyperbolic consumerist reality of the day, is not much of a choice at all. Kafka's *Metamorphosis* anyone? But the idea holds, which reaffirm's Parmar and Khan's desire for the body, particularly those of minorities and disenfranchise individuals, to be more than an object of possession, but powerful spaces.

Some of the greatest body horror has come out of Japan. Katsuhiro Otomo's 1988 classic *Akira* is often hailed as the gold standard and required watching of the body horror genre. But, Shinya Tsukamoto's low-budget, underground, indy, almost experimental, sixty-seven-minute *Tetsuo: The Iron Man* raises the bar on what body horror cinema can do. Two male characters cross paths when one hits the other with his car. The first, known in the script as the Metal Fetishist, inserts a metal rod into his leg, that after festering causes him to run into the street where he is struck by the Salaryman. The Salaryman, accompanied by his Girlfriend believe the Metal Fetishist to be dead, so they dump his body in a nearby wooded area. The Salaryman and the Girlfriend, racked with guilt, hide out at their home where they give in to carnal desires to take their mind off the whole ordeal. Slowly the Salaryman notices metal pieces overtaking his body. From their meals to their sexual encounters, first the soundtrack — all normal bodily sounds are replaced with the sounds of metal on metal, then slowly the Salaryman transforms into the Iron Man. This reaches a head when the Salaryman reveals a massive drill to have erupted from his pelvis region. As the Salaryman continues to transform, it is revealed that the Metal Fetishist has also transformed and that the two, finding themselves presumably in a town only big enough for one Iron Man, engage in battle. As those familiar with the trope in anime know, when two mighty forces fight for a while without defeating each other, they are destined to become best friends. This time the Salaryman and the Metal Fetishist transform into one massive metal tank, one man mounted upon the other, with a free arm, now wielding a massive gun. They then set off on a mission to 'rust the world into the dust of the universe', creating their own 'new world'.

What is most fascinating about the best of the body horror genre is that at their root, they are all simple stories when you get past the guts and bolts. *Possessor* is just about a woman trying to find a work/family balance in an advanced consumerist society. *The Fly* is just the timeless tale of a man attaining ultimate success and it costing him everything. *Videodrome* is a story of addiction and the futile road to sate it. *Tetsuo: The Iron Man* is a story of two men learning that their sexuality is, since it can be considered rude to ask, let us just say 'generally socially unacceptable'. So, faced with the existential threat of sexually transmitted disease, they seek to make a new world where they can be accepted. Though, it should be reiterated, since the last line of the film is roughly translated as 'our love can destroy this whole fucking world', that militant apocalypse probably is not the best strategy to go about changing the world.

Body horror is even becoming increasingly common in post pandemic cinema, though I think the pandemic only added to a world already suffering from a series of identity crises concerning racial tensions, gender and sexuality considerations, and a long overdue updated discussion of fundamental human rights. The 2021 Cannes Film Festival gave its top award, the Palme d'Or, to not only a body horror film, but one that expands upon the ideas and themes of *Tetsuo: The Iron Man*, Julia Ducournau's French-Belgium feature *Titane*. *Titane* has it all, technofetishism, cyborgs, sex with cars, impregnation by cars, gender subversions, themes of motherhood and parenting, religious iconography, and all the body horror your heart would desire. Although the film is rather gory, there is very little blood as most of the blood is replaced with black motor oil. The story opens with a series of scantily clad women dancing erotically on top of muscle cars as onlookers gawk and request autographs. The whole scene reminds me of Dionysian ritual where the gods are replaced with sports cars. We learn that one of the dancers, Alexia, is a serial killer who as a child was involved in a car accident that required a titanium plate to be put in her skull. After having sex with and becoming impregnated by one of the sports cars, Alexia proceeds to burn her parents' house down and run away. Unable to run too far, she cuts her hair and breaks her nose to resemble a boy who had gone missing ten years prior. A delusional father accepts Alexia as his long-lost son as she attempts to blend in by cutting her hair and taping down her breasts and increasingly pregnant belly. Aside from being a fresh take on the gender-swap trope, and also almost seeming to intentionally group as many trigger warnings into one film as is humanly possible, *Titane* presented the human body as an incredibly tough thing. Something enduring and capable of defying assumed limits.

The expansion of limitations is an interesting theme that resonates in almost all body horror. In fact, in reviewing a lot of body horror films (more than I would recommend to the casual viewer) I noticed an obsession with the perception of an evolutionary step forward. It is the posthumanist thesis but usually said with less foaming at the mouth than what you hear from the fanatical devotees to that particular -ism. Wendy Schultz explores this idea in her survey of developing body enhancement techniques. But, with the exception of a few who drank the high dose postmodernism Kool-Aid, each of these films falls short. The real theme is that the expansion of the limitations we perceive on the body is not overcome through a literal evolution into a new species, but through a doubling down on what is important and essential towards the ever so precious idea — what is human? Indeed, certain limits can be bent, but humanity must remain.

Three profound, reflective essays in this issue explore the concept of the body as a limit. Aamer Hussein, finally free to travel for the first time since the lockdowns of 2020, finds his body less than cooperative in such freedoms as a luggage mix up results in his being without essential medication. As a small army of friends attempt to assist him in his quest for his medicine and a fresh change of clothes, he comes to terms with an unwelcomed hunter that lingers inside his body. Hussein will decide if the body in which they are both contained is destined to be a prison or a home. Robin Yassin-Kassab reflects on his memories, trying to make sense of his body's history of interesting and awkward medical encounters, how his beleaguering migraines may have actually saved him and his son's lives, and finally philosophises on the self and body asking, 'if the body is limitless, am I limitless too?' Naomi Foyle seeks greater understanding of a condition she had recently been diagnosed with. Though to call it a condition presumes the darker narratives that have twisted public perception of those with autism. In her study and critical reflection, Foyle wonders if we may have it all wrong about what is medically normal and abnormal, for the abnormal could also present with extraordinary abilities.

In the anatomy lab, I learned, hands on, the fragility, limitations, and frank toughness of the human body. When you attempt to carefully dissect the pancreas you learn why pancreatic cancer is nearly impossible to remove. Like an ash structure, when touched it crumples away to dust, you'd never be able to remove the whole thing without allowing the cancer to get into the blood stream. Again, restricted by budget, while a bone saw was available for opening the skull and the rib cage, we all had one to share amongst us; and so we were encouraged to begin with a chisel and hammer. It was hard work and I had chosen my group for reasons other than strength, so found myself the strongest member of my group and thus delegated to bone cracking. The whole semester was a constant struggle between being gentle out of respect and applying the necessary muscle and brutality to break open a human body. While it may seem counter intuitive, in the end my worries subsided and I learned to love the body even more.

I see scars in a different light after my time in the anatomy lab. Often, we think of them as blemishes, but really they are proof of the power in bodies. The power to heal. I am fortunate that I have a quality of skin that allows for scars to fade into nigh invisibility. One thin white line remains on my inner wrist. I was in primary school, somewhere around the age of ten and had earned the trust-based responsibility of a key to the house, so that I could come home after school until my mother got off work. These were the days of 'stranger danger' so I was not allowed to talk to anyone I did not know, nor answer the door for anyone other than my mother, especially if there was a man claiming to be Jesus at the door. On one of these journeys home I inserted the key, twisted the nob and not minding my surroundings neglected the torn and exposed metal in the door frame as I push the door inward, slicing open my right lower arm. I remember there being a lot of pain and a lot of blood, but I knew I had to quickly shut the door to prevent home invaders from taking advantage of the situation. Door shut, deadbolt locked, I then proceeded to the telephone to dial my mother's work number, to be dialled only in the most extreme of emergencies, I reasoned this should qualify. But my mother was in a critical meeting and beyond anyone in the office's reach. Woe to the days before mobile ubiquity. Through, what I assume was, a high-pitched voice accented with hysterics and strained by uncontrolled sobbing, I must have gotten someone's attention, for after hanging up, resigned to what I could not imagine as anything but the cruel end of yet another innocent boy's life, I heard the phone ring. In defeat and shame I uttered a pitiful 'Hello' into the phone. To my surprise, on the other end of the line was my grandmother, a nurse. She was not one for indirect communication. 'No one is coming to help you, but I am here, and I am going to walk you through this,' she said. So, we talked and I explained what had happened. The tears dried up and she told me that I needed to clean the wound and dress it. The time that passed with her on the other line probably lasted tops thirty minutes before my mother was located and made a mad dash home to check on me, but my childhood memory compares the event to the cliché scene in an action movie where the hero removes a bullet from his shoulder, stitches the wound closed, and cauterises the wound with an iron. In the end, no stitches were needed.

I always had a special bond with my grandmother. We graduated from the same university exactly sixty years apart from one another. She was one of the few intellectual members of my family who I could look up to and gain support from. She read everything I managed to get published. And in 2021, that grim and dastardly sequel to 2020, she passed away when I was stuck on the far side of the world, something she always thought was so cool that I had a chance to see. And I, along with a world of others was not able to see my grandmother off to her final resting place which is such a critical part of saying goodbye. Not only supply chains, but cycles of mourning were also victims of this global calamity. Also in 2021, I attended my first Muslim and Malay funeral and quite frankly would be happy to never attend another one again. We were fortunate the body we were putting to rest was Covid negative, or else, detached men in hazmat suits would be dumping the lifeless body into a hole to be buried as quickly as possible. And even as someone who can readily dissociate the living from the dead, there's just something wrong in that and whatever a body may be, it breaks my heart for it to be given that sort of a farewell.

Suddenly I hear my mother singing/spelling along with Aretha Franklin's 1967 classic, R-e-s-p-e-c-t, a song my mother was always ready to belt out regardless of the feelings of my brother and I, and whether or not we found ourselves in crowded public places. Embarrassment notwithstanding, it remains an essential lesson. While my father taught me how to deal with death my mother taught me how to deal with the living. Easier said than done indeed! My mother, a trained nurse, was always very open about the human body with us and no topic was taboo. Bodies come in all shapes, sizes, colours, with a little more *this* and a little less *that* but nevertheless earning your utmost respect and admiration. They always change, sometimes breakdown, but never any less beautiful. Something worthy of the same appreciation you give to a storied forest or a majestic mountain. We were to respect the beauty of the body and maybe if we spent less time concerned with how we looked, we could get ahead on real issues.

The body, whatever it may be, makes us human. And in exploring our bodies and reaching deeper understandings of their limits and their powers, we can grow to live better with one another. And that, I would say, is worthy of a prayer or two.

THIS BODY: A HISTORY

Robin Yassin-Kassab

1.

This may be my very first memory. I'm standing in a square space between four doors — one in front of me, one behind, and one to either side. One by one I close the doors. The shade increases as I go, until, closing the last door, I am enveloped in utter darkness. It's comfortable and warm. Then I open the doors, one by one, until I'm so bathed in light, so surrounded by space, that I can't see where my limits end.

I feel this action was often repeated, so for a long time I was sure the memory was a genuine recollection of a game I used to play, but then I interrogated the details. For a start, I remember the door handles being at the level of my waist, where door handles are today, but given my tiny stature at the age of three or four, the handles should have been much higher up. Next, and crucially, there was no space in the house we lived in then that fitted my remembered position between four doors. I've checked with my mother, and anyway, what kind of architect would design a room the size of a stand-up coffin?

I've read that all early childhood memories are unreliable, so I reluctantly accept that I've invented this one. Nevertheless, the memory persists. It feels real, and meaningful. So, what does it mean? Surely it contains some metaphorical truth. Was it about opening and closing my eyes, rather than doors? Was it about inhaling and exhaling? I've also read that babies are, at first, incapable of distinguishing between their body and the body of their mother, which indeed they were absorbed in for a timeless nine months. So, does the memory refer to establishing my body's borders, the private inside and the public world without?

Nothing in the realm of the sensorium is simple. To start with, it seems that an account of a body's life will be more comprehensible, less ambiguous, than a mental biography. The body is more amenable to statistical explanation. In theory, if I'd recorded and kept the requisite figures, I could list the weight of the body at monthly intervals, or its height, or its shoe size, and the results would be indisputable – but I could never write an indisputable account of my inner life. Yet even on the physical level, easy comprehensibility is an illusion. For comprehensibility, I'd have to establish boundaries and definitions. That is, I'd have to answer questions that I am incapable of answering. Such as: Where do I end and the rest of the world begin? What is body and what is self? What mind and what matter? What soul and what spirit? (Or if you like, what *rooh* and what *nafs*?) Can these categories be neatly separated, or are they always ultimately one?

Next memory. My mother at this stage was certainly a separate entity, because I had to shake her to wake her up. 'Mummy,' I whined. 'Mummy, wake up. I can't get the last sweetie out of the packet.' She woke up, slowly and then, suddenly, very fast. In the slow moments she took the sweet packet from my hand, fumbled it in her fingers, squinted at what it was. Then she leapt from the bed, threw on some outer garments, and dragged me to the car. This was because the sweet packet was in fact a large and now empty packet of pain killers. Fortunate that the last pill had stuck.

We drove as they drive in Hollywood films, screeching the tyres and scattering the innocent before us, until we arrived at the children's hospital. I remember huge, shiny metal vats brought before me and then replaced with others as each rapidly filled with vomit. Vat after vat. So much vomit. Was it possible that I contained all that?

A lot of the first memories involve bodily catastrophes. This, I suppose, because the shock fixes them in the mind. Less dangerous events are less important for survival-learning, and less worthy of the effort required to forge new neural pathways.

I remember splitting my lip, and the scene on the bloodied steps. A little girl was present. Perhaps we'd been playing when suddenly the concrete reared up and struck. I remember, slightly later, running with another little girl (was I chasing her? or was she chasing me?) round and round a sitting room, a frenzied hysterical loop, until the sharp arm of an armchair stopped me, cutting into my brow. There was a waterfall of blood, and thereafter a scar which lasted until it was covered by another, this one won while walking with my children on an Omani mountainside, watching their steps rather than my own position, and walking into a thorn tree.

But I am getting ahead of myself.

I was a little older when my appendix nearly burst. The pain, I think, was seriously agonising, but it wasn't accompanied by fear. I must have assumed I was immortal. Besides, my mother was a doctor. I trusted her and those of her profession. There were doctors all around.

This episode introduced me to the marvels of chemistry, or in other words, to the interconnectedness of body and spirit. Arrived in hospital, the body was pierced by a needle, an opiate was dispatched into the bloodstream, and consciousness was transformed. The body on a trolley was floating along corridors, the mouth grinning as explosively as the appendix was throbbing.

In the anteroom to theatre there was another needle to spike the back of my hand.

'How long will it take to go to sleep?'

'Count, and you'll see.'

I think I reached five by the time I was reached by the anaesthetic. Under its effect, I vanished entirely.

But wait — it gets stranger. At the age of nine or ten I had an out of body experience.

I was in the kitchen helping, or getting in the way of, my mother making jam. A fat pot of red viscous gloopy stuff bubbled on the stove. Time was moving as it's supposed to, and the other human basics — space and self — were behaving in the manner appropriate to each. But then suddenly, and seemingly before the pain hit (or didn't hit), the gears changed, and prosaic reality sped into the distance.

First the scene before me became a film reel playing in freeze frame mode. The pot tipped, and stopped. The jam lurched over the side, and stopped. A gloop of it leapt into the air, and stopped, hanging there flashing red. This gloop descended, and stopped. It descended a frame further, and attached to the skin on my belly (I'd taken off my T-shirt), and stopped.

Then I was somewhere else entirely. Where was I? I wondered it softly with a gentle, curling, delighted curiosity. Had I been embodied, a smile would have played on my lips. Where? I was just beyond the kitchen, in the hall, high up, bobbing against the ceiling. And from this vantage, I could hear a strange sound. What kind of sound was that? I wondered. What could it possibly be? Soon I worked it out, with a pleasure both elated and intellectual: it was a scream, a screaming. Somebody was screaming. So here was another lovely puzzle. Who was screaming? Who? It was ......me. And with that understanding I was jolted back ungainly into my twisted shrieking body.

For a while, I believed this meant I'd met experiential proof of the disembodied soul, but much later the notion was complicated, to say the least, by reading Thomas Metzinger's account of out of body experiences (OBEs) within his larger description of all first-person experience as a 'complex form of virtual reality'. Metzinger quotes Susan Blackmore arguing that OBEs are 'models of reality created by brains that are cut off from sensory input during stressful situations and have to fall back on internal sources of information'. Which seems like part of what happened to me.

Whatever it is, there's a compassionate mechanism at work. I've met a man whose legs were wrecked in a car accident. It took him many minutes to believe it, though the legs were wrapped misshapen right over his head, because he felt so healthy and peaceful. And somewhere I read reports given by the survivors of mauling by lions. They described feeling a light and disembodied bliss as they were tossed and torn.

My own experience of temporarily leaving the body brought home in a fresh way the old puzzle of location. The mystery, that is, of being where I am.

I think I remember asking the question in my earliest childhood. Why am I located in this body, in this skull, and not in any of the others? Why here and not there? Why this name, and why this form? And ever since, beyond the strange specificity of being located here and now, I've found it unutterably strange, utterly bewildering, to be a consciousness, to be a body, at all.

2

Soon after, with the passage into early adolescence, an anxiety set in which was less existential and more narcissistic, certainly more social. That is, I had a problem with my face. Not with any particular element of the face, but with them all together. There was too much crammed in, I decided, too much intensity and movement.

The thing is, simply put, I had a somewhat Arab face, too lively in comparison with the north-western European faces which made the overwhelming majority of those around me, in school, in the streets, and on the television. These were the common problematics of the body-in-public. To experience them, you didn't need to be somewhat Arab. All around me, everyone was worrying. They were too fat, or too skinny, or too spotty, they had the wrong-coloured hair or the wrong-coloured skin, or their teeth looked bad, or their ears were too small, they were flat-chested or embarrassingly buxom, they wore glasses, their voices were pitched too high or too low, their bums looked big in whatever they were wearing, they were too ugly to be seen, or conversely, too beautiful (because those considered beautiful are targets for resentment and lechery, and therefore not as lucky as we might think).

But adolescence brought a further, greater torment, one lasting much longer than the worries concerning my face. This was the ongoing curse of migraine.

How to describe the pain to those who don't know? It is indescribable in ordinary terms, because it is both sharp and dull. It aches, and throbs, and shoots, and stabs, and burns. It does any other pain-related verb you choose. It is full spectrum pain.

It shocks with thrumming electricity, makes a violent vibration, launches an assault of light and perverted colour. During the migraine attack, the victim is convinced of the seamless nonduality of body and mind, for they are all pain altogether, all swirling nausea, and can be read in any language available, physical, emotional or mental. A panoply of extreme negative emotions – fear, agonising sadness, fury, panic – arrive like colliding waves, each collision increasing the general amplitude. There is a seizing up of cerebral functioning. The IQ tumbles. The victim is incapable of simple mathematics, of producing grammatical sentences, or of walking in a straight line.

The migraines, whatever else they are, are a curse inherited from my ancestors. Both my mother and my maternal grandfather suffered them. Indeed, when I search for my first memory of one, I come up instead with an episode of my mother in pain. Migraine had knocked her down, so I was sent to the neighbours' house. Here I was sat before a screen on which a terrible, heart-rending, tragic, traumatic film played out. It showed a noble elephant set upon by dogs (or tigers – I forget). These cruel beasts swarmed the elephant, leapt on its aged back, bit and ripped and scraped until it fell to its knees bellowing, and then to its side, glancing desperately about as if for help, for fairness, for mercy, which never came, until finally, and in the lowest indignity, it expired.

When my mother had recovered sufficiently to be a mother again, she came to collect me. 'He had a lovely time,' the neighbours reported. I promptly burst into unquenchable tears.

So, my first memory of migraine doesn't involve my own head, but the painful injustice and bottomless sorrow of life itself. Which means it's a very apt memory.

They began for me at secondary school, like a hammer blow to the temple. In the episodes since I have suffered flashings in the visual field, a tunnelling of vision, a darkening until near blindness. Once, miraculously, I prayed one away. More usually they've led to wailing and weeping, crawling about on the floor, and other forms of temporary insanity.

Once, I found myself seasick in the streets of Rabat, too afflicted to stop a taxi or even move in a specific direction. I stumbled in circles and eventually sat down, clutching the pavement in case I fell off. Passers-by probably assumed I was drunk.

Someone once picked me up off a bathroom floor and took me to hospital, despite my garbled protests. I'd been vomiting for hours, was now spitting bile, and couldn't stand up, so their alarm was understandable. The doctor sedated me and waited for the attack to pass. There's nothing else to do.

The ultimate causes of migraine may be genetic, atmospheric, dietary, or stress-related. Science has never managed to firmly pin the thing down. What is sure, however, is that migraine is a means for the body to order itself to stop whatever it's doing, to remove itself from the current situation, to cease, desist, or at least interrupt the ongoing activity.

And so, a migraine may have once saved my life. This was on 26 December 2004. The day before I'd taken my son camping on an unpeopled desert beach a couple of hours south of Muscat. We'd made a fire, cooked food, gone to sleep happy. But in the morning, I woke up gripped by savage pain. I massaged my skull, to no avail. I vomited and washed my head in the sea. After I'd vomited again, I was reduced to my hands and knees, scuttling crab-like in the sand, throwing up repeatedly, then raising my face to my son in fake-cheery rictus. 'Don't worry, Baba,' I gasped. 'I'll be fine!' But would I? I was so violently ill, and weakening so rapidly, I was worried I might lose consciousness. Ibrahim was only five years old. I couldn't leave him by himself. So, counter-intuitively, we packed the car and drove home. I drove very slowly, squinting to see the track. I had to stop every twenty minutes or so to do some more retching, but eventually we did arrive home. As I tumbled towards bed, I was informed that a tsunami was battering the shores of the Indian Ocean. Worst hit, of course, were Indonesia, Sri Lanka, and Thailand, but the waves reached as far west as the African coast. People were killed in Somalia. A ship capsized off Salalah, in the south of Oman. And when I next visited the beach where we'd camped, I noted that several metres of sand bank had been sliced away.

Experts expected the elephant population in the low-lying south of Sri Lanka would have been wiped out, but the elephants, remarkably, had started walking uphill hours before the wave. Likewise, the people of the Jawara and other tribes in the Andaman Islands had moved inland, for mysterious reasons, and so saved themselves. Was my migraine a similar phenomenon? Was it a hyper-sensitive response to vibratory disturbance, which forced Ibrahim and me from our vulnerable position towards safety? I have no proof of it, but I prefer to think so, because it justifies the decades of otherwise useless pain.

3

A justification, then. A happy outcome. Though my stories of the body are still tending towards the catastrophic, or the tormenting, or at least the annoying. And for good reason – because when we're experiencing life, the body is usually transparent. We see and act through it, barely conscious it's there. We notice it only when it malfunctions (I had no idea I had an appendix, until the appendix bulged with poison). Otherwise, we take it for granted. Yet its smooth functioning is at the root of a great deal of our pleasure, even if we fail to credit it. When climbing mountains, I shine my eyes on the mountains themselves and attribute my pleasure to them, but happiness owes in more concrete terms to unseen physical operations. Like the righteous luxury of soaking in endorphins during exertion, of air pouring through the lungs, of blood circulating freely. Like the bliss of a body deservedly exhausted, which is indistinguishable from satisfaction. Or the glory of the youthful, well-working body, of power and ease conjoined, which is inseparable from bright self-confidence.

The body brings an abundance of pleasure and orders us to seek still more. Through its brain structures and hormones and sexual organs, it directs us to a fascination with the bodies of others. A fascination, and the consequent urge to fasten, which structures our social lives and governs so much of our behaviour. In my case, it focused me on the loving delighting female body, on certain specific specimens of the category. Enhaloed by fizzing excitement, the woman's body was a refuge from everything harsh and ugly; it was a better planet, a fuller dimension, somehow deeper and more real than its measurable, merely physical characteristics.

The act of fastening elicited sperm from my body, and thereby another occasion for bewildered wonder — that millions of these tiny things leave the body and behave as little bodies in their own right, committed to their goal, fighting off hindrances, until the winning homunculus arrives...

4

And now I have become a father. My body has shared in the production of two more, and our story has leapfrogged many years of bodily transparency until its arrival here: in the Arabian Gulf.

In the Gulf the heat wraps the body like a blanket. It's as if the atmosphere is embracing it tightly, which made me feel as if I were really at home here on this planet. I used to go jogging in the heat. The body poured sweat, and passengers stared from their air-conditioned cars at my eccentric behaviour. I went swimming and hiking too, which I suppose saved me from total rotundity.

Because, for the first time in its now not-so-short life, the body had begun to swell at the belly. It didn't need to. It shouldn't have fallen in the trap. In general, it adapts to its environment. In the heat, its walking style alters, its breathing changes, its pace relaxes. And it requires less food – but oh the body likes to eat. This body does anyway. (Or is it me who likes to eat? In which case, the body is innocent. The responsibility isn't clear cut; and again, the boundary between I and it is ambiguous.)

The body likes to eat – or I do – plus the joys of consumption are particularly pronounced in the Gulf. They are perhaps the whole point of the Gulf. Consumption is what people generally do in the Gulf whenever they're not working or sleeping. They stroll the shopping malls, from shawarma stall to ice cream parlour. They browse the Pakistani, South Indian, Filipino, Yemeni or Thai restaurants, and swim supermarket aisles which brim with the vegetables and fruits of Africa and Asia. From freezer trays laden with the swimming creatures of the Arabian Sea, and butcher slabs groaning under New Zealand lamb, Australian beef, Saudi camel, Omani ostrich, they take their pick.

At least I did. Or my body did. It also drank endless cans of non-diet cola, as if the climate had given permission.

There is a brain mechanism which commands the body, when it finds salt or sugar and fat conjoined, to graze until the food source is exhausted. This made sense for our hunter-gatherer ancestors, who rarely found such dainty pickings, but produces quite different effects when the stuff is mass produced. Hence the diabetes crisis in the Gulf, and the obesity crisis across the fully-integrated capitalist world.

And hence what, for me, felt like a fateful transitional moment: the swelling of my belly. Because I hadn't known it contained the possibility of swelling. For as long as I could remember the mouth had gobbled and the belly remained slim – not a belly at all really, just a slope from the ribcage to the hips. So now the spreading waistline and rising kilos tolled a bell: the body was entering its middle age.

I renounced the cans of sugared liquid. I pulled myself back from three piled plates of oily Indian fare each university cafeteria lunchtime. I pulled the body back. It pulled itself.

I sought to remember the Prophet's exhortation to fill a third of the belly with food, a third with water, and a third with air. Exhortations were now necessary.

Vulnerable to risk and time, the body had passed a peak and was declining. Serialised misfortune wore it down. The most grievous misfortune of those years was surely the episode of the necrotic foot, when I returned to Oman from a holiday in Sri Lanka with a blistered toe, a tiny wound invaded by a mighty infection.

I'd been feverish and sore on the journey, so went straight from airport to hospital. I'd expected an injection and then to go home, but I was kept in for the next fortnight. In the time I stayed, Bill Clinton's quadruple bypass surgery was announced, then performed, and then the president left the hospital. I watched it all on TV from my hospital bed. Each morning the South African doctor stood at the foot of the bed and gazed wordlessly at my foot and leg. He consulted the university hospital and he consulted colleagues in central African hospitals, where he'd worked for a few years. 'This is a tropical thing,' he muttered often. He had me hooked up intravenously to four different antibiotics. There was a constant taste of metal in my mouth.

The leg was raised, black and bulging at the ankle, and red inflammation was advancing up the calf, a little further every day. Until one day it began to retreat. 'You were twelve hours away from an amputation above the knee,' the doctor told me then.

Despite the danger, or perhaps because of the danger, I enjoyed my sojourn in the Muscat Private Hospital. Physical threat woke me up a little more. The smiling Keralan nurses had such names as Baby, Girly, and Shiny. I read Saul Bellow's Augie March. I made notes for what would become a novel.

I was lucky. Before antibiotics I'd have died, and rather horribly. (Though I'd have already been dead – of the childhood appendicitis.)

But I wasn't always lucky. For example, when I decided to have a vasectomy – to halt the miracle of the homunculi – a series of scrotal disasters ensued.

I found myself in a different private hospital, seated before a German doctor.

'I'd like a vasectomy,' I said.

The doctor nodded. 'How long have you had this problem?'

'There's no problem,' I said. 'I just want a vasectomy.'

'I see,' said the doctor. 'And how long have you had this problem?'

At that point I should have found another doctor, another hospital, but I batted the miscommunication away. Once I felt sure we'd agreed on what the word 'vasectomy' meant, we set a time for the operation. Finally, I was careful to ask how long the doctor was planning on staying in the country, in case any follow-up consultations became necessary.

'O,' he said breezily, revolving his hand. 'I'm here indefinitely.'

A local anaesthetic was administered. A blanket was piled at my neck to discourage my eyes from looking down. I was reduced to a head therefore, a face composing sober expressions in its attempt to maintain dignity, as if it had nothing to do with the body below.

I'd been told the operation would last about fifteen minutes, but time ticked on. I could see a clock on one of the walls. After half an hour the anaesthetic was wearing off. I could feel strings being pulled down in the groin, in the abdomen.

'It's been going on a while,' I said.

'Well, there's a lot of fat,' said the doctor.

At last, the tricky surgeon held a ragged thread aloft. 'Here we have it,' he announced. I breathed a deep sigh of relief. Half an hour later, I was on the way home, expecting a recovery period, as promised, of a couple of days.

Four days later, far from being recovered, I was swollen and so sore I could hardly walk. I returned to the hospital and asked to see my indefinitely-remaining doctor.

'He's gone back to Germany,' I was told.

Somehow, I wasn't surprised. I asked for another doctor, anyone vaguely qualified. This request was granted. Someone vaguely qualified turned up to examine me, then told me not to worry, everything was fine. The recovery period would last a couple of days.

I didn't believe it. I drove straight to the Muscat Private Hospital, where someone properly qualified told me what I already knew – the groin was infected. Antibiotics sorted it out, but discomfort verging on pain persisted for a long time afterwards. Years later, in Scotland, I discovered a couple of extra little pellets in my scrotum. These were water cysts –

thoroughly benign, thank God — most likely the belated result of vasectomy-related trauma.

The cysts required surgical removal. This time the anaesthetic was general. I vanished again and was reborn shivering and gibbering.

Still today, I sometimes feel internal strings being tugged. I'm never sure if the pain refers to a present physical event or if it's an expression of stored trauma, for the body remembers damage, and will transmit pain even after the damage has healed.

Also in Oman, I lost a molar. The Keralan dentist who persuaded me to have a probably unnecessary root canal, and botched it, joins the German doctor as a villain of the piece.

5

But the chief villain is Time, with a capital T.

In late middle age, I need glasses to read, to see the food I eat, to appreciate the close-up details of my wife's face. My scalp is bald in patches. My skin has lost much of its elasticity. Creased and folded in all the ways it's been used, all the smiles and scowls, it provides a record of past dramas and accumulated harms. The body in general, like the skin in particular, no longer bounces back to its pristine state. This stage of life has brought the dawning, and then the persisting, of chronic complaints.

Case One: a viral infection of the sinuses blocked the inner left ear, disrupting my balance for a couple of weeks. I adapted to that, but the inner ear never properly unblocked, and the sinuses flare up in stormy weather.

Case Two: something snapped in the lower back while I was swinging an axe. This injury never healed but expresses itself in a continuing diversity of ways, shifting up and down the spine, from left to right, to hip and thigh.

Oh, but I am lucky, or blessed, to have reached this far in reasonable general health. I have friends who have not been as lucky. Some have died, whereas I still live. And age even has its benefits. The migraines, for example, are diminishing in both intensity and frequency, and I can now look forward to their complete cessation. The migraines of my grandfather and my mother both eased in their fifties, and had finally ended by their sixtieth birthdays.

Moreover, I grow wiser in relationship with my body. Better put, I am fortunate enough to live in circumstances that allow for health and wisdom. I live in the countryside and work with the land. I breathe clean, quiet air and eat unprocessed food. Increasingly I follow the 'weak' or unreliable (but nonetheless excellent) narration, usually attributed to Ali: 'Do not make of your stomachs a graveyard of animals.'

I treat the body more gently than I used to. No longer assuming immortality, I fear the bodily torments to come. In particular, I fear breathlessness, because of regret over my many years of smoking, and because of the dark panic connected to choking. And I fear the cruel degeneration of mental capacity that afflicts so many of those who achieve long life. But I can't predict what ailments will strike. There are very many terrible ways to decline and die.

At least in this I'm not alone. We all become victims of the body, sooner or later. Everyone goes through it. Not only humans but everything that can feel experiences it. There is some solace in this unspoken solidarity of all living things – we all must suffer the pains of bodily disintegration.

Our common vulnerability should produce a common recognition of the body's prerogatives. 'Your body has a right over you,' says the hadith. Islam demonstrates its respect for the body by forbidding intoxicants, recommending frequent ablution, and prescribing movements of prayer so that body and mind act in concert. Fasting recognises the interconnection of body and soul. But Islam punishes the body too, and the inhabitants of the Muslim world often do far worse things to bodies than what their religion permits. Muslim-world police forces punch and kick with casual ease. For the dictatorships, abuse of citizens' bodies is a central means of governance. Over the last decade, for instance, tens of thousands of Syrians have been murdered slowly in the most mind-explodingly brutal ways. Torturers make an art of turning the body into a weapon, into a Trojan Horse by which to storm a person's soul.

This reminds me of a conversation I once had with the excellent Iraqi novelist Ali Bader. The Arabs, he said, should forget about whether we want a secular or Islamic system, or a Sunni or Shia dispensation, or a capitalist or socialist economy. We should leave ideologies out of the debate entirely and demand instead, solely and simply, respect for the body. If the Arabs learnt to respect the body, he said, to refrain from beating it, torturing it, raping it, imprisoning it, forcing it to wear certain garments, and so on, then everything else would follow from that.

6

If we paid enough attention, we could understand the body as sacred.

I have meditated regularly over the last two years. This is a demonstration of respect for the body, making the effort to see it and feel it. And the closer I look, the more there is to see. The more I feel, the more I find, the more the mystery deepens.

Sometimes I meditate on the sensations of the body, region by region. At first, crossing through, for example, the upper arm, I felt nothing much, more an idea than a feeling, just a recognition that, yes, it's there. Gradually though, more experience arose, until the upper arm became a surging mass of tingling sensation. Now it seems that each area of the body presents itself for examination when I turn to it, each inch rising to meet consciousness, and any moment of stasis involves pricklings of the scalp, burnings of the lips, the intensely hot firing of nerve endings in the fingertips. I feel the pulse everywhere. Mind and matter distinctions break down, so I experience thoughts as vibrations and emotions as waves.

Meditation helps me to understand how the mind pictures the body. Once my wife came home while I was meditating. She climbed the stairs to see where I was. Quietly she opened the door and saw me. At the same time, eyes closed, I saw myself from her perspective. The image was just a flash passing over my inner screen. It would have remained subliminal if I hadn't been paying such close attention. (In cases of psychosis such images may be clearly, externally seen, and are then called heautoscopic, or doppelganger, hallucinations.)

I'm sure the body exists beyond my perceptions of it, but the body I perceive is inextricable from my mind. This is obvious when you think about it, yet still endlessly bewildering. The body disappears in refracting mirrors, and carries me with it...

Most of the time when I meditate, I focus solely on the breath at the nostrils, on the interface of in and out. Slowly the perception has developed from breath as concept to breath as sensation to something stranger still. Now if I'm careful, if I'm attentive enough, one breath deconstructs into many trembling dots of light. This numinous experience is of the body interacting with the larger body, its environment. It takes in oxygen and emits carbon dioxide continuously, without interruption. It seeks inspiration until it expires.

So where do the body's limits end? It includes the atmosphere. Its elemental atoms were formed in exploding stars, so it also includes outer space.

If the body is limitless, am I limitless too?

Well, not necessarily. Because I am not it. In several ways it is foreign to me:

It precedes me. I have photographic proof of its existence from years before I have any memory of my own.

I can't control it. I don't understand its operations. I don't regulate its blood pressure or temperature or metabolic rate. I wouldn't know how. It does those things, not me.

It remains present when I disappear. When it is deeply asleep, for instance, I am nowhere to be found.

It serves as a clock, it measures time – it ages – whereas I do not. I feel no time passing, though I draw maps of time with memories and numbers.

Here's the most fundamental difference – the body can be said with reasonable certainty to exist; it can be proved, that is, in empirically measurable terms. While I certainly can't. Can anyone see me, or feel me? Can you measure my consciousness, or weigh my soul?

I oscillate between limit and limitless.

I close then open the doors, one in front, one behind, one to either side.

SHAME AGAIN

Samia Rahman

There is a scene in Salman Rushdie's novel *Shame*, published in 1983 before his work became synonymous with the infamous *Satanic Verses* affair, which will remain forever etched in my mind. A female character, Sufiya Zinobia, experiences a wild and savage splitting, culminating in a grotesque human-beast transformation: 'The edges of Sufiya Zinobia were beginning to become uncertain, as if there were two beings occupying that air-space, competing for it, two entities of identical shape, but of tragically opposed natures.' Sufiya's splitting, driven by her role as the embodiment of the narrator of the novel's response to real-life incidents and how they manifest and take form in his own imagination, is utterly beyond her control. Her body is a mere vessel for these responses, which seep from the subconscious to the conscious, eventually locating in her physical being; after all, what else are bodies but socially constructed sites of difference.

To articulate a feeling of difference, such as shame, is not the same as struggling to define a concept. Emotions that are internalised do more than manifest deep within the recesses of our psyche, they locate themselves on these socially constructed sites before burrowing into visceral flesh and blood, expressing themselves in jarred and faltering mechanisms that malfunction in the body. We know that the catastrophic trajectory from shame to violence is mapped, or should we say seared, onto human beings. With the former inevitably leading to the latter, as is the case with Sufiya Zinobia, who 'had been given to understand that she embodied her mother's shame'. Starved of love or affection from a mother who, wishing her daughter had been born a boy, declares 'she is my shame'. Desperate to please her husband who had 'wanted a hero of a son' and, most significantly, had fallen out of love with her, she attempts to ingratiate herself back into his affections in the only way society normalises female agency – through her capacity for reproduction. But even this attempt ends in failure, 'I gave him an idiot female instead' and in place of a hero son, Sufiya Zinobia is born blushing, imbibing all of the suppressed emotions of unhappiness, injustice, and discontent that provide the context for her entry into the world.

If shame as an emotion transcends the physical body, body politics invite us to consider which bodies are unthinkingly included or excluded in what we might regard as the polity. Rushdie's novel itself is or is not a fictionalised satire of the burgeoning young nation Pakistan, and dancing across its pages are the fortunes of two prominent dynasties, the Hyder and Harappa families, who may or may not be based on two former presidents of Pakistan and their tribes – the Bhutto clan and the family of General Zia-ul Haq. It is through these families that Rushdie charts a government's inadequate response to the political demands of those bodies that harbour ideas, thoughts, ideologies, or desires that transgress what society regards as acceptable boundaries. The body, it is often argued by feminist intellectuals such as the late bell hooks and Audre Lorde, is simultaneously socially shaped and colonised. And in *Shame*, physical representations of difference come alive in the characters' fortunes; pawns in the crossfire of power relations that impact them and push against the hierarchies of authoritarianism, whether military or theocratic, that they challenge. The consequence is a loss of individual autonomy and what we see in Sufiya Zinobia is the expression of the crushed guilt of her father, Raza Hyder, a military dictator who imposes authority on a population through the violence meted onto their physical bodies and collective psyche. She is both victim and tyrant in this tale of magical realism that throws upside down everything we ever understood of both fictional and historical narrative, to explore shame and violence as they are visited upon a cast of chimerical characters.

Moral perspectives and virtues dictate how bodies must be regulated and protected. Perhaps it is no coincidence that the punjabi word for woman is *janasi* or *zamani* which can be translated as 'life-giver'. Meanwhile, in Urdu, the official language of Pakistan, one of the words for woman is *aurat*, which, deriving from the Arabic word referring to private parts or something to be concealed, certainly symbolises shame. Pockets of struggle remain, however, as women defy the dominant discourse by opposing prevailing ideologies that have marked their body with meaning. In Rushdie's novel, three sheltered and illiterate sisters are restricted to the women's quarters of their bleak and isolated mansion built on faded memories and unspoken secrets by their unyielding father. When he dies having squandered the family wealth and leaving them destitute, the unworldly sisters find themselves adrift in a society they have no experience of. It is no surprise therefore, that, on their first foray out of their bubble of ignorance, the sisters host a ball attended by colonial Britishers 'the Angrez sahibs' and somehow an 'immaculate conception' occurs. The trio quickly retreat back to the comfort of their isolated world and together experience the phenomenon of pregnancy, each beset with identical symptoms of morning sickness and food cravings, the agony of childbirth, and the joint responsibility of bringing up the child they have borne, Omar Khayyam Shakil.

Twentieth century philosophers such as Pierre Bourdieu or even Michel Foucault, argue that the body is a text upon which representations of power are politically inscribed by practices of precarity and suppression. This social management of the body differs from the body politic, yet both concepts are synonymous with the impact of shame. A small child languishing in a claustrophobic mansion littered with treasures from a forgotten past, Omar's indistinguishable three mothers revisit their childhood upon their son, so that he does not step foot beyond the grounds until his twelfth birthday. Shut out by the intense intimacy between the three women, he wanders alone from room to room discovering trinkets and antiquities from which he weaves together the fragments of a family history no one else will tell him about. The discovery of a library proves a haven of riches as he devours books and teaches himself language, literature, and history. He also finds a manual from which he learns to hypnotise the workers in the house, but his new-found skill only uncovers more shameful secrets that compound his loneliness. Despite this dysfunctional existence, his mothers reject society's inevitable judgement of his illegitimacy and teach Omar that he is not a source of shame, instilling him instead with the idea that shame is an emotion to be rejected. This is entirely in keeping with the postmodern theories in vogue at the time of Rushdie's writing of *Shame*, but in Omar's experience, what the late sociologist Zygmunt Bauman would describe as his individualised upbringing, experienced by his mothers' before him, does not lead to liberation from shame. It is in fact his reconnection with society and the liberty that comes from the desire to be part of something that came before him and will continue after his demise, which has the potential to actualise his freedom, even if that means freedom from shame is not the answer.

Deficient in any understanding of shame due to his isolated childhood, Omar acts heinously towards others, until the moment his shamelessness comes face to face with the embodiment of shame, Sufiya Zinobia, herself. Absorbing the shame ignored by those who are shameless, she and Omar Khayyam, now a doctor, are married and he unwittingly feeds her intolerable burden that causes her to eventually, horrifically be taken over by the beast of shame that resides and grows within the many selves that constitute her identity.

There is unorthodoxy in the way that the volatility of self is played out through the character of Sufiya Zinobia. Perhaps it should not be any surprise that social conditioning and normalisation incorrectly assume a stable nature of identity and power relations when it comes to women. The assumption is that shame detracts from individual agency and creates what could be uncomplicatedly described as the plight of subjectivity. Yet marginalised bodies such as hers – unwanted and despised, have the potential to skew power dynamics, creating space for a context to emerge, a wider understanding of how they are constructed or understood. Shame is an exercise in power, or disempowerment, and does not present itself in any singular form or manner. Resistance to shame marked Omar Khayyam's journey but it ominously denied the body as a site where power is inevitably contested and negotiated. His is an ignorance of the way in which the body is subjected to systemic regimes such as authoritarian governments or misogynistic societies, and perpetuates the containment and control of bodies by agents of oppression.

Yet, there are contexts in which resistance to shame can lead to liberation from agents of oppression in the body politic. When the Egyptian-American writer and activist Mona Eltahawy wrote of being sexually assaulted by security forces during the 2011 Arab Spring protests in Cairo, she railed at the shamed silence that rendered her and other female victims voiceless. There was not the widespread uproar or condemnation she anticipated, even within the protest movement itself, and the hushed tones with which the attacks were discussed, deeply infuriated her then and now: 'The trifecta of misogyny is the misogyny that connects the state, the street and the home. So unless we take the rage that the revolution directed at the state and direct it at the street and at home, our revolution is nothing.' In a social media post she articulated how the brutality had caused her to re-evaluate the role of bodies and shame in resistance. 'What happened to me... was the first time I felt consequence so harshly on my body. This was putting my body on the (front) line. This was understanding it deep in my bones.'

In *The Cultural Politics of Emotions*, Sara Ahmed discusses the refusal to comply with societal norms when there is a complacency that feeling shame is enough expiation for wrongdoing by the state. Eltahawy expected the Egyptian state to be shamed by its failure to treat its citizens, particularly women, with dignity and respect, but it wasn't. Even if the horrors visited upon protestors during the Arab Spring became a source of national shame in the same way that a once-colonising nation, reflecting on its colonial past, feels collective shame or regret for its historic wrongdoings, this would be akin to a papering over of the cracks. The national shame Eltahawy had expected, could never atone for the violence inflicted upon her body. The vocalising of shame by the body politic merely reconciles itself to an idealised form, through an act not dissimilar to virtue signalling. The passive witnessing of the pain of others re-inscribes the distinction between the sovereign national state and those who do not abide by the standard it claims to uphold. A nation advocating for shame on a national and social level, whether it is Rushdie's fictitious Pakistan or Eltahawy's Egypt, while simultaneously denying shame, participates in a circular affirmation that avoids stepping back and listening or responding to those who have been aggrieved. Instead, just as shaming has been used and is still used as a policing method to control societies, our increasingly individualised global context offers opportunities for the weaponising of shame as a method to control populations and undermine freethinking. Use by the Egyptian security forces of sexual assault, forced virginity tests and untold acts of humiliation proved a cynical attempt by the body politic to terrorise subjects into submission. Gendered violence is intended to break not just individual women but the families, movements, and communities they belong to – no less because women's bodies are inscribed with notions of honour and shame. The rape of women in war is a deliberate and abominable strategy that rips out the heart of communities, torturing and traumatising societies and destroying morale.

For Eltahawy, a rejection of shame must be unlike the denial of self that Omar Khayyam is embroiled in. Instead, rejecting shame requires building a platform upon which she may articulate and own shamelessness, thereby regaining ownership of her body and controlling the narrative of her journey from shame to shamelessness. Rushdie's exposition of shame blurs the line between fantasy and reality and subverts any notion of absolute truth, but his era, the postmodern era, is over. Eltahawy sees her truth as her transparency, or as Bauman would argue, symptomatic of our age of individualisation, whereby the ideology of the biographical narrative has the potential to obscure the web of interconnectedness that forms the context for our reality, and the role of the sociologist is to reveal this plethora of ways of living. Eltahawy's journey from shame to shamelessness is a presentation of her way of living, it is true, but it is a mystery to me how it precludes the possibility of other ways, or even the network of associations that are constructed and formed around experience. As I wrote in the Relations issue of *Critical Muslim*, Bauman views relations as a continuum of weak and ephemeral liaisons that require minimal commitment. Social attachments remain brief and are characterised by self-interest and narcissism. The consequential heightened emotional anxiety and insecurity felt by your average millennial leads to a cycle of fragile entanglements that lack stability and trigger chronic retreat into isolation. Such detachment from society stifles the development of personal responsibility or collective interest, undermining social cohesion and any sense of community. The microcosm is instructive of the macrocosm, providing fuel to the catastrophic fire of hyper-reality and post-truth politics that renders facts obsolete when they dare to not reflect the designated acceptable reality.

Bauman's outlook is bleak but perhaps rather more pessimistic than it needs to be. After all, Mona Eltahawy uses social media as a space to build community and break free from the isolation that comes with discussing taboo topics. Her online newsletter *Feminist Giant* promises to 'Defy, Disobey, Disrupt'. She writes about undergoing two abortions, a source of great shame in many conservative or traditional societies and an issue not openly spoken about in the public or even private sphere. Her more recent blog series catalogues the departure of youth and the onset of menopause. In a world that prizes women in possession of youth and beauty, her ageing process is spat out on the page with stark honesty, deliberately indiscreet and immodest, because, 'when you are shameless you cannot be shamed'. In a blog post titled 'Moisturize Your Vagina', which extrapolates the trials of vaginal dryness in menopausal women, Eltahawy pulls no punches: 'Patriarchy deploys shame like a drone: it shadows you, ready to take you out any minute, exhausting you by keeping you forever aware of its presence to the detriment of all other things that you could be investing your attention in.'

Patriarchy as an act of violent osmosis is also Sufiya Zinobia's experience. And where she embodies a psychiatrist's expression of shame, Omar Khayyam offers a lesson in repression; the corrosive bliss of wilful ignorance. Freud defines shame as a feeling similar to self-loathing, a perception of being an unworthy and defective human being. Consistently experiencing situations that bring about feelings of shame create such intensity of pain for the individual that, according to Freud and many other branches of psychiatry, an unconscious rupture of the self occurs. The consequence for the individual's 'true' self is that it becomes shrouded and dominated by a 'false' self, as we see with Sufiya Zinobia's metamorphosis into the hideous creature. Repression is an instinctive response to the pain shame arouses, but serves to only exacerbate the eventual crisis within the body and mind. Ahmed draws on such Freudian concepts of shame to consider their role in constructing group identity. Shame involves a 'self-negation' propelled by a desire to peel out of our bodies and abandon ourselves because that is how much we despise who we perceive ourselves to be.

Here, shame is experienced when we fail to live up to the ideal. Sara Ahmed calls it an ideal other — an idealised person we look up to but fail to live up to. We care what the ideal other thinks because we are desperate for their validation and we love and wish to be all that they represent. Shame as a social force is often identified with less individualist societies or those who belong to religious communities. External judgement as well as the pressures individuals place themselves under to uphold what they regard as standards of behaviour and fulfil obligations to their religious authority, can cause debilitating feelings of shame. The explosive interconnectedness of social media has exacerbated this reality as liquid modernity is leading young people to form fleeting and insecure connections, sometimes sharing intimate images on the basis of the intensity of heightened but passing moments, only to find the bond of trust broken and the private images they shared in confidence, disseminated into the public sphere, causing them unparalleled shame and humiliation. The shame of being exposed, or having compromising private images revealed to family and friends, has caused many youngsters to become vulnerable to blackmail or even take their own lives. The agony of judgement based on rumour or the casting of aspersions or erroneous assumptions, has inflicted crippling censure within tight-knit communities. Equally harmful is the act of concealing scandal that has been uncovered in insular shame-based communities. It is often power dynamics and the multi-faceted impact of shame that causes communities to turn a blind eye to unspeakable acts among their members, leaving victims silenced, powerless, shamed even, and perpetrators free to continue. How many of us who grew up in shame-based communities have heard the rhetorical 'What will the neighbours say' or 'Don't bring shame upon the family'? Often an eldest daughter will endure the misery of an unhappy or abusive marriage purely because it would reflect badly on her younger siblings' marriage prospects if she were to leave.

Shame has long been a purveyor of injustice and a device to exert control within domestic spheres. It is unsurprising, then, that those who don't conform to Ahmed's ideal, or who face unfairness as a result of others' responses to shame, flee, seeking solace in the anonymity of urban spaces far from their place of origin, where they can reinvent themselves in forms that feel closer to their 'true self', or at least embark upon a journey towards whatever that represents to them. Eltahawy's subversion of shame challenges the concept of the idealised, young, fertile, and beautiful woman by celebrating her own story. The upshot is that those who are also not this ideal other but are taught by society to feel shame because they cannot live up to this same ideal, are finally able to find resonance with an alternative. Where there is no alternative except the ideal other to look up to, shame is fuelled, particularly among those who diverge from the norm. Self-identifying as sex-positive in a society that is scandalised by extra-marital sex or as queer in a community that disapproves of partnerships that do not fall into the narrow margins of

to be hard-wired in their brains. It stands to reason that various social, cultural, technological, and environmental factors may hasten its degradation. It is doubtful map-reading is included as standard in our school curriculum, not to mention identifying constellations in the night sky, which is in any case rarely dark enough to make them out given the widespread artificial light pollution.

There are other fixed ideas about gender-based differences that are very common, such as men really cannot do more than one thing at a time while women are natural multi-taskers, that women talk so much but men say so little, and that women show more empathy. Those who hold to these stereotypes will often assume that they are hard-wired in the brain, such that men and women are born with radically different brains.

Recent cutting-edge neuroscience research is urging us to go beyond the binary view of the brain typically expressed in the title of Louann Brizendine's book *The Female Brain* (2006) which was so comprehensively debunked by Rebecca M. Young and Evan Balaban in their review of this book in *Nature*. In the same way, cognitive neuroscientist Gina Rippon claims to have consummately shattered 'the myth of the female brain' in her recent book, *The Gendered Brain*. The painstaking analysis of thirty years of research on human brain differences by experienced neuroscientist Lise Eliot has also led her to conclude that none of the alleged brain differences actually explains the familiar but modest differences in personality and abilities between men and women.

Nevertheless, it is well to acknowledge that belief in the existence of hard-wired differences between male and female brains still has a loyal following which might suggest that this is still a hotly contested field, even if the weight of evidence is increasingly stacking up in support of the view that gender related differences are not hard-wired in the brain. If you google 'sex-based brain differences', it is striking that the two top hits after the obligatory Wikipedia entry on the 'Neuroscience of Sex Differences' reflect the opposing camps. The first is Lise Eliot's review in *Nature* from 2019 of *The Gendered Brain*, entitled 'Neurosexism: the myth that men and women have different brains', and the second is an article by Bruce Goldman in *Stanford Medicine* from 2017 entitled 'Two minds: The cognitive differences between men and women' in which he refers to 'the growing pile of evidence that there are indeed inherent differences in how men's and women's brains are wired and how they work.'

Goldman relates that 'when Nirao Shah decided in 1998 to study sex-based differences in the brain using up-to-the-minute molecular tools, he didn't have a ton of competition.' Shah's objective was to find and explore neural circuits that might explain sex-associated behavioural differences in mating, parenting, and aggression. 'These behaviours,' he claimed 'are innate rather than learned – at least in animals – so the circuitry involved ought to be developmentally hard-wired into the brain. These circuits should differ depending on which sex you're looking at.' At the time, the idea of gender-based differences was not a universally popular idea. Neuroscientists had largely attributed any observed sex-associated differences in cognition and behaviour in humans to social and cultural influences. Goldman notes, however, that in the fifteen years up to the publication of his article there had been a sea change, such that the seventy-article January/February 2017 issue of the *Journal of Neuroscience Research* was the first-ever issue of any neuroscience journal devoted entirely to the influence of sex differences on nervous-system function.

In 2013, science journalist Steve Connor reported on some research carried out by Ragini Verma and colleagues at the Department of Radiology, Perleman School of Medicine, University of Pennsylvania. This study, based on 949 individuals (521 females and 428 males) aged between eight and twenty-two, claimed that such differences 'could explain why men were "better at map reading" and why women were "better at remembering a conversation".' Using a special brain-scanning technique called diffusion tensor imaging, which can measure the flow of water along a nerve pathway, it mapped the level of connectivity between nearly a hundred regions of the brain, creating a neural map called the 'connectome'. Connor reports how this showed 'for the first time that the brains of men and women are wired up differently', in that 'many of the connections in a typical male brain run between the front and the back of the same side of the brain, whereas in women the connections are more likely to run from side to side between the left and right hemispheres.' According to the study, these differences 'occur during adolescence when many of the secondary sexual characteristics, such as facial hair in men and breasts in women, develop under the influence of sex hormones.' The researchers contend that such differences in the architecture of the human brain help to provide a neural basis for understanding the findings of many psychological studies that men tend to outperform women in spatial tasks, muscle control, and motor skills, while women tend to do better in memory tests, such as remembering words and faces, verbal skills, intuitive tasks, and social cognition tests, which aim to measure empathy and emotional intelligence. 'The only part of the brain where right-left connectivity was greater in men than in women was in the cerebellum, an evolutionary ancient part of the brain that is linked with motor control.'

A contradiction immediately springs to mind, one that reveals all to clearly how difficult it is to pin down supposed differences to a gendered brain. Women talk a lot, while men are generally taciturn? Author Nancy Kline, in her book *Time to Think: Listening to Ignite the Human Mind,* compares a 'Thinking Environment' with what she calls 'Male Conditioning'. In the thinking environment, people listen; in the environment controlled by male conditioning, they take over and talk. Familiar territory? Have you ever been to a conference where, despite the request of the chairman that people restrict themselves to short comments or concise questions, someone, usually a man, stands up and launches into a twenty-minute monologue? The myth of the man who is economical with words. And that reminds me that at seminars at the Centre of Islamic Studies, University of Cambridge, the director used to open the Q&A sessions with the instruction 'No *haya* please', a plea to Muslim women present not to hold back and keep silent because of any patriarchal conditioning that such reserve was an essential aspect of the 'modesty' traditionally expected of women when it came to public discourse.

Let's explore the other dichotomies Nancy Kline sets out. Here they are: Ask Incisive Questions/Know Everything; Establish Quality/Assume Superiority; Appreciate/Criticise; Be at Ease/Control; Encourage/ Toughen; Humanise the Place/Conquer the Place; Create Diversity/ Deride Difference. It's pretty obvious which pole of each dichotomy belongs to the 'thinking environment' and which to 'male conditioning'.

Kline's exposure of 'male conditioning' raises the whole question of the extent to which differences associated with 'gender' should indeed be attributed to conditioning, whether male or female, rather than hard-wired in our brains. Coming back to the oft-repeated claim that men tend

to perform better in tests requiring spatial ability, Margaret Tarampi, a
post-doctoral research fellow at the Center for Spatial Studies, University
of California, Santa Barbara, and the lead author of a 2016 study on 'sex
differences in spatial ability' in *Psychological Science*, suggests that this isn't
an innate difference, but something that manifests as a result of social
influences. Commenting on the study, Penn Collins, a writer for *Good*,
clarifies that the claim that men read maps better than women 'isn't true
at all.' Tarampi's results suggest that 'negative reinforcement may have
been the sole factor in the gap.' In short, if people are repeatedly told that
they are inferior at something, they tend to match the lowered
expectations and perform poorly as a result. 'Women only performed
worse than men at map reading when they were informed of the age-old
stereotype. Those who weren't scored as well as men. That said, the test
also found that women's abilities increased when the task was tied to a
social component, like helping a stranger or incorporated a human
dimension such as relying on faces as milestones.' As Tarampi concluded,
'when we tell participants that this is a test of perspective-taking, and
perspective-taking is about empathy, then in that case women perform the
same as males.' So, this study serves as an important reminder of how
self-fulfilling prophecies powerfully condition the human mind.

The 2019 publication of *The Gendered Brain: The new neuroscience that
shatters the myth of the female brain* by Gina Rippon, a distinguished emeritus
professor of cognitive neuroimaging, created quite a stir, and one can see
why. Hailed by Rachel Cooke in the *Observer* as 'revolutionary to a glorious
degree' and 'a brilliant debunking of the notion of a "female brain" [that]
could do more for gender equality than any number of feminist
manifestos', it was also praised in *The Sunday Times* as 'a book that will
force you to confront your own prejudices, biases and beliefs.' This is
wholly consistent with Rippon's role as an expert advocate for initiatives
to overcome the under-representation of women in Science, Technology,
Engineering, and Mathematics (STEM), her membership of the European
Gender Equality Network, and her international work in contributing to
the public communication of science, for which she was made an Honorary
Fellow of the British Science Association in 2015. In the headline of her
review of the book in *Nature*, Lise Eliot pointedly uses the word
'Neurosexism', first coined by psychologist Cordelia Fine in *Delusions of*

Gender, to distil Rippon's central message that 'a gendered world will produce a gendered brain.' She explains clearly how Rippon's rigorous scrutiny of cutting-edge neuroscience reveals that 'the hunt for male and female distinctions inside the skull is a lesson in bad research practice,' for 'the history of sex-difference research is rife with innumeracy, misinterpretation, publication bias, weak statistical power, inadequate controls and worse.' As Rippon shows, although 'the hunt for brain differences has been vigorously pursued with all the techniques that science could muster' and, with the advent of magnetic resonance imaging (MRI), has exploded over the last three decades. Yet, 'conclusive findings about sex-linked brain differences have failed to materialise.'

Rippon provides telling examples of the way in which highly questionable research has been given overblown attention to confirm existing biases. She describes, for instance, one of the numerous brain studies heralded as 'finally' explaining the difference between men and women. This was an MRI analysis from 2005 of only twenty-one men and twenty-seven women by researchers at the University of California. As Lise Eliot comments, 'tiny by today's standards, this brief communication nonetheless went on quite a publicity tour, from newspapers and blogs to television, books, and, eventually, teacher education and corporate leadership conferences.' The attention it attracted was clearly out of all proportion to its miniscule significance as a piece of research. Eliot confirms this shocking imbalance in her own recent article in *The Conversation* in which she points out that stereotypes about male and female brains 'hold surprising sway over the way actual brain science is designed and interpreted, and since the dawn of MRI neuroscientists have worked ceaselessly to find differences between men's and women's brains.'

Manipulative selection of data is another way in which existing frames and biases are confirmed. Rippon refers to a highly touted MRI study of adolescent participants at the University of Pennsylvania conducted by M. Ingalhalikar in 2014 entitled 'Sex differences in the structural connectome of the human brain.' In Eliot's words, this study 'seared into the public imagination a picture of men's and women's brains as diametrically opposed subway maps with the connections in women mostly between hemispheres, and those in men within them. However, the map omits the vast majority of connections that did not differ; nor did it control either for puberty-related maturation or for brain size, all of which reduces apparent male–female difference.'

We might not be too surprised by Rippon's quote from social psychologist Gustave Le Bon, who used his portable cephalometer to declare in 1895 that women 'represent the most inferior forms of human evolution', but what are we to make of a 2017 blog to co-workers by Google engineer James Damore attributing the dearth of women in technology and leadership roles to 'biological causes'?

As Genevieve Fox writes in her review of Rippon's book in *The Guardian,* 'the neat, binary distinctiveness' of the male/female labels is being challenged. 'The brain is no more gendered than the liver or kidneys or heart. While most of us remain confined in the biosocial straitjackets that 'divert a basically unisex brain down one culturally gendered pathway or another, we are coming to realise that nature is inextricably entangled with nurture.'

Returning to the debunking by Rebecca M. Young and Evan Balaban of Louann Brizendine's book *The Female Brain* (2006), the title of their review in *Nature* speaks for itself: 'Psychoneuroindoctrinology'. As they point out, 'despite the author's extensive academic credentials, *The Female Brain* disappointingly fails to meet even the most basic standards of scientific accuracy and balance. The book is riddled with scientific errors and is misleading about the processes of brain development, the neuroendocrine system, and the nature of sex differences in general'.

Their conclusion lays bare the abiding problem of intransigent confirmation bias: 'ultimately, this book, like others in its genre, is a melodrama…that obscures how biology matters; neither hormones nor brains are pink or blue. Our attempts to understand the biology of human behaviour cannot move forward until we try to explain things as they are, not as we would like them to be.'

In popular communication of research, data is often translated in careless and stereotypical ways. I'm reminded of the statement by the philosopher Friedrich Nietzsche that 'sometimes people don't want to hear the truth because they don't want their illusions destroyed.' I tried to address the problem of popular or dominant 'narratives' in my essay entitled 'Simple Stories vs Complex Facts' for the issue of *Critical Muslim* on *Narratives.* In discussing the widespread Sinophobia in Victorian

England, I pointed out that a populist narrative such as the 'clash of civilisations' is by no means confined to the vulgar mob heated up by populist rhetoric. If Sherlock Holmes, the epitome of observational powers, forensic science, and logical reasoning, can succumb to it then we can infer that the conditioned beliefs, fixed ideas and mindsets, the cognitive macro-structures referred to as 'schemata', 'frames', 'scripts' and, indeed, 'narratives' can be highly resistant or impervious to modification, even within the scientific community.

We might add other synonyms for the loaded narrative that have been generated by the present discussion, such as 'myths' and 'stereotypes', even 'illusions', or, indeed, 'indoctrinologies', to paraphrase Young and Balaban's neologism as a pointed variant of 'ideologies.' And we could also include within their semantic field the broader canvas of 'worldview' and 'paradigm'. A particularly useful notion is the 'narrative fallacy', which Nobel Prize winning economist Daniel Kahneman refers to in his book *Thinking, Fast and Slow* as 'flawed stories of the past' which 'shape our views of the world and our expectations for the future'. They are simple (even simplistic) but alluring and compelling explanatory stories which arise from our continuous attempt to make sense of the world.

The popular myth about male and female brains is just another top-down narrative based on stereotypical expectations that facilitate rapid thinking and obviate the need for laborious bottom-up factual analysis, meticulous evidence-based inquiry and careful assimilation of complex information. To refer to my previous explanation in the *Narratives* issue, 'As a simple conceptual framework that is easy to digest, often inherited or received rather than individually constructed,' a narrative 'also acts as a handy meme for the transmission of cultural ideas, symbols, or practices from one mind to another'. This helps to answer the pressing question as to why myths and stereotypes persist in this way, why outdated ideas and obsolete paradigms can hold such sway, and why confirmation bias is so rife, even amongst the scientific community which prides itself on its 'objectivity'. But beyond even that, we might want to ask the more pressing question as to how we are to avoid being imprisoned by such narratives, so that we can approach ever-nearer to the 'truth', always bearing in mind that every renewed conceptualisation or re-imagining of the truth is always going to be a provisional hypothesis capable of refinement.

To do so, we need to be aware that changes in terminology do not necessarily reflect a meaningful paradigm shift. The myth of the 'female brain' has not really been modified to any great extent by the apparent change, noted by Rippon, that the hunt for proof of women's inferiority has more recently shifted to the more 'respectable' hunt for proof of male–female 'complementarity'. As Eliot comments, 'so, this line goes, women are not really less intelligent than men, just "different" in a way that happens to coincide with biblical teachings and the status quo of gender roles. Thus, women's brains are said to be wired for empathy and intuition, whereas male brains are supposed to be optimised for reason and action.' Whatever the putative differences, they are still held to be 'wired'.

To my mind, the key strategy for avoiding crystallisation of any idea into an entrenched dogma does lie to some extent in the brain, but not in the immutability of hard-wiring, rather in the plasticity that enables the brain to change and adapt. As Genevieve Fox concludes in her review of Rippon, 'what used to be thought fixed and inevitable is being shown to be plastic and flexible; the powerful biology-changing effects of our physical and our social worlds are being revealed.' Psychology and mental health writer Kendra Cherry explains in a very recent article that while 'early researchers believed that neurogenesis (the creation of new neurons) stopped shortly after birth,' it is now understood that 'the brain possesses the remarkable capacity to reorganise pathways, create new connections, and, in some cases, even create new neurons as a result of new experiences – a concept called neuroplasticity, or brain plasticity.'

The fact is that there are many things we can do to promote neurogenesis within our own brains. Australian writer Thai Nguyen explores a battery of 'Proven Ways To Grow Your Brain' and they are well worth referring to as a practical conclusion to this essay. They are not 'lifestyle fads' by self-promoting 'self-help' gurus, but effective tools rooted in reputable research by neuroscientists properly referenced by Nguyen.

In summary, neurogenesis, neuroplasticity, and increased brain connectivity are promoted and enhanced by:

1. *Fasting*, which shifts the body to produce less fat, which signals for the brain to trigger neurons to produce more energy. Intermittent fasting can also promote synaptic plasticity, neuron growth, and resistance to neurodegeneration. Overall, it also improves cognitive abilities.

2. *Travelling,* which exposes the brain to new and sometimes complex and challenging environments that cause the brain to sprout dendrites, short-branched extensions of nerve cells.

3. *Exercise.* Nguyen mentions the importance of exercise, but he might have combined his recommendation for travelling with that of the physical exercise involved in taking trips into the natural world, including country walking, hiking, and trekking.

4. *Memory Training.* The use of mnemonic devices that combine visualisation, imagery, spatial navigation, and rhythm and melody promote 'connectivity in the brain's prefrontal parietal network.' I can vouch for the power of visualisation and imagery myself. I capitalised on the advantages of 'dual coding' within the brain by the mnemonic device of translating verbal into visual imagery (something I initially learnt from *The Art of Memory* by the sixteenth century Hermetic philosopher Giordano Bruno) and as a result was able to remember and reproduce very comprehensive and detailed material in my final B.A. examinations. I incorporated such techniques into the study skills curriculum I subsequently developed as a teacher and director of studies. I can also vouch for the way in which the use of both hemispheres of the brain in the rhythmic alternation of left and right steps in walking generates coherence and disentangles excessive complexity in thinking, as well as enhancing memory.

5. *Music,* including *Learning a Musical Instrument.* The neurologist Oliver Sacks, whose work has featured in a stream of best-selling case histories, one of which was adapted into the Oscar-nominated film *Awakenings,* fell in love with the music of Bach as a little boy. After a performance of one of Bach's Two-Part Inventions, an MRI revealed that his brain had 'lit up all over.' Petr Janata, a cognitive neuroscientist at the University of California, noted that 'our responses to music are widely distributed throughout the brain.'

6. *Creating Artwork.* Engaging in artwork promoted enhanced connectivity of the brain at a resting state known as the 'default mode network' (DMN) which influences mental processes such as introspection, memory, and empathy. Engaging in art also strengthens the neural pathway that controls attention and focus.

7. *Dancing,* especially free-style dancing and forms that don't retrace memorised steps. This increases neural connectivity by demanding that

you integrate several brain functions at once – kinaesthetic, rational, musical, and emotional.

8. *Reading fiction.* This has been proven to enhance brain connectivity, especially in the region that controls physical sensations and movement systems, probably because reading a novel can transport you into the body and soul of the protagonist and enable you to identify with another physical, mental, or emotional state.

9. *Expanding your vocabulary.* This activates the brain's visual and auditory processes and memory processing.

10. *Using your non-dominant hand* to do simple tasks such as brushing your teeth, texting, or stirring your coffee/tea can help you form new neural pathways. Such cognitive exercises are also known as 'neurobics'. Although I knew nothing about the neurological benefits of using my non-dominant hand, I practised this assiduously for a while as a young man since it was recommended by the spiritual teacher G.I Gurdjieff whose system of 'harmonious development' I was studying at the time.

11. *Sleep.* Researchers at the New York University School of Medicine have shown that 'sleep after learning strengthens connections between brain cells.'

12. *Diet.* Eating foods rich in flavonoids (cocoa and blueberries) and antioxidants (green tea) also helps with brain growth.

13. *Meditation.*

I would also add to this list the fundamental importance of *discussion* as a means of opening minds and hearts as well as engaging critically with alternative ideas and perspectives. It is through discussion, dialogue and dialectic that we are able to advance and refine our existing state of knowledge, and there needs to be much more dialogic teaching and learning in our schools.

We might want to look at how the Muslim communities fare in the skills that promote neurogenesis. Well, they do pretty well in fasting and also in meditation if they engage in contemplative practices such as *muraqaba* or *tafakkur*. They also score highly in memory training, although this is often associated with rote verbal memorisation rather than the use of mnemonics that involve visualisation, imagery, and other techniques. If they are Sufis, they may also score highly in music and dancing, especially if they are Mevlevi! I also have the distinct impression, borne out by my involvement with initiatives in nature education for minority ethnic communities, that younger Muslims, including intrepid Muslim women, are increasingly engaging in outdoor pursuits, so are ticking the 'exercise' box in the natural world. I am also heartened to see more and more Muslim parents giving their children the opportunity to learn a musical instrument and to explore the world of literature. As for the expansion of vocabulary, this will emerge from wider reading, and is also indicated by the great strides by the Muslim community in education, well surpassing the standards reached by the working-class white community. Eight Muslim faith schools were recognised among the top twenty schools in Britain for academic progress in the published GCSE league tables for 2019. We just need to take on board that it was reported in 2016 that young Muslim women have taken the lead over men in the race for degrees.

The signs are that a new adventurous generation of Muslims in the UK will embody a good many of the skills that will help their brains to transcend any patriarchal dogmas about immutable differences between the roles of men and women, whether or not those dogmas are generated by obsolete myths about hard-wired differences between male and female brains. May all their endeavours be blessed, and may they become role models for the ushering in of a new paradigm that vigorously questions all stereotypes in its hunger for truth that liberates and inspires.

'LAZY' BODIES

Shanon Shah

Thank God we grow up. And if we're lucky, we grow wiser.

I hope I'm one of the lucky ones.

When I was a child, I thought Malays were lazy. And stupid. And derivative. I thought they could not do mathematics and that they were incapable of producing great art, music, or literature. I also thought they were religious hypocrites – Muslims in name, but idle and untrustworthy gossips by nature. They were football mad, but when was the last time a Malaysian team even qualified for the World Cup?

Have I mentioned that, in Malaysia, I am officially classified as Malay? Never mind that my father's parents were Punjabi speakers who migrated to colonial Malaya from what is now Pakistan, and that my mother is Malaysian Chinese.

How does *this* make me Malay?

The Malaysian Federal Constitution defines a Malay as 'a person who professes the religion of Islam, habitually speaks the Malay language, [and] conforms to Malay custom' (Article 160). It also enshrines a 'special position' for Malays (Article 153). Successive post-Independence administrations have increasingly translated this as non-negotiable political, economic, and cultural supremacy at the expense of nearly 40 percent of the rest of the country's population. This is but one of the many legacies of British colonialism that have disrupted and reshaped widespread understandings of race and religion in Malaysia and the public policies that define and regulate them.

Yet I didn't ask to be classified as Malay, and neither did my siblings before me. In my case, the doctor who registered my birth casually listed my mother's race as 'Chinese' and my father's as 'Malay'. Perhaps he was being tactful – in the part of Malaysia I come from, the line between 'real' ethnic Malays and those with Indian ancestry is very blurry.

And so, while I never asked to be Malay, I still grew up trying to pass as Malay. I tried, for instance, to perfect my spoken Malay — formal and patois. As the youngest in my family, my siblings thought I was the one who 'passed' most convincingly. The joke was on us, though. Every single Malay person I have ever known in Malaysia has always been able to spot, pretty quickly, that I'm not a 'real' Malay. The giveaways, in order of obviousness, have usually been my name, my physical features, the occasionally odd phrasing or pronunciation in my spoken Malay, and my ignorance about deeper aspects of Malay culture. It's almost as though there was and is something in my physical body, or my subconsciousness, that has betrayed my attempts to adopt and perform 'authentic' Malay-ness.

I'm relieved to say that I neither despise Malays nor feel the need to pass as a 'real' Malay anymore. The antidote has been a no-brainer — the older I grew, the more meaningful friendships I developed with Malaysians of all ethnic backgrounds, including Malays. English-speaking Malays, Malay-speaking Malays, and bilingual Malays. Elite Malays and working-class Malays. Urban Malays and rural Malays. Secular Malays and piously Muslim Malays. 'Pure' Malays and Malays with mixed ancestry — Javanese, Tamil, Keralan, Yemeni, Gujarati, Chinese, and Eurasian.

Yet, to this day, I have heard Malays openly criticise their own race as lazy, backward, gullible, and superstitious, whether in informal conversations or high-level official events. A dismissive phrase I have often come across — usually rendered in English, even when the speaker is communicating in Malay — is that these are characteristics of the 'typical Malay'. By this logic, the traits that I always thought of as my failures at 'passing' are actually assets, including fluency in English, an overseas university education, and urbane taste in art and culture.

I don't mean that ethnic Malays are the only producers of this sort of rhetoric in Malaysia. The reason I grew up with so many negative stereotypes of Malays embedded in my mind is that they were held by many, many Malaysians of different ethnicities. Also, it must be said that there are some pretty nasty stereotypes about Malaysians of Chinese, Indian, Eurasian and Indigenous ancestry too.

Anyway, my subconscious simmered in this soup of slurs long before I set foot in London where I have lost count of the number of Brits I have encountered – white, black, and brown – who casually reproduce cringe-worthy racial stereotypes about Malaysia and Malaysians. Never mind that many of them probably cannot find Malaysia on a map or can barely tell the distinction between 'Malay' (a language and an ethnic marker) and 'Malaysian' (a national identity and marker of citizenship).

And here is the paradox about my identity. The more secure and comfortable I am about not being a 'real' Malay, the more I love and appreciate actual Malay culture and heritage. But the more affection I develop for Malay-ness, the more I discover a persistent residue of internalised racism – within myself and the many Malays I continue to meet. What is the source of this reservoir of externally imposed and deeply internalised racial insult? Does this dynamic exist in other contexts? Regardless of where it has existed, why is this particular aspect of racialised identity significant for us now and for the future?

The answer, unsurprisingly, is European colonialism. In his magisterial work *The Myth of the Lazy Native* (1977), the Malaysian social scientist Syed Hussein Alatas (1928–2007) traced the dominant colonial image of the 'natives' of the territories now known as Malaysia, Indonesia, and the Philippines from the sixteenth to the twentieth centuries. Alatas used the term 'image' in the singular – but why? Surely there were variations in the political and cultural circumstances of the different colonising powers and the people they colonised? Surely there were differences in the colonial encounters between Roman Catholic Spaniards and Christianised Filipinos, between Dutch Protestants and Muslim Javanese, and between the British (as later arrivals) and Muslim Malays?

Also, wouldn't these images – in the plural – have changed with time? Many Portuguese writers from the sixteenth century, for example, were charmed by how polished, well-bred and cultured the Malays of Malacca were. But there was a sting in the tail even during this period – Malaccan Malays were also seen as cunning, malicious, and potentially violent.

It is crucial to acknowledge these subtleties. This early balance of positive and negative assessments by Portuguese writers probably reflected the balance of power at the time. During the Portuguese conquest of Malacca in 1511, Westerners still did not rule the archipelago and there was still active and vibrant native trade.

Against this backdrop, Alatas suggests that it was during the height of Dutch expansion in the mid-eighteenth century that a dominant, singular image began to develop – that of the 'lazy' or 'indolent' native. This negative image was circulated and reproduced amongst colonial administrators and took on a life of its own. The negative colonial British image of the Malays in Malaya reached new heights in the nineteenth century.

Even so, it is possible to distinguish some crucial nuances between British attitudes from the earlier and latter parts of the nineteenth century. Thomas Stamford Raffles – the founder of Singapore and British Lieutenant Governor of Java and Bengkulen – first encountered Malays in 1810, when he became Agent for the Governor-General of Malacca. While Raffles developed several negative ideas about Malays, he often tempered these with subtler reflections. For example, while he found Malays 'rude', 'uncivilised', and 'simple', he recognised them as a 'nation' – a positive notion, compared to describing them simply as savages. According to Raffles, 'if they are to be termed savages, certainly they are the most polite of all savages: but in truth they are very far from being savages'. He also believed that the negative characteristics of Malays were not inherent or hereditary, but were the product of environment and circumstance.

Writing in 1820, John Crawfurd, a British Resident at the court of the Sultan of Java, echoed Raffles's conclusions about the situational rather than hereditary causes of the intellectual backwardness of the Malays:

Such a feebleness of intellect is the result of such a state of society, and such a climate, that we may usually reckon that the greatest powers of the native mind will hardly bear a comparison, in point of strength and resources, to the ordinary standard of the human understanding in the highest stages of civilisation, though they may necessarily be better suited for distinction in the peculiar circumstances in which they are called into action.

Notice the shift, however, by the time another British Resident, Frank Swettenham, published his observations about Malays in the early twentieth century, exemplified in this excerpt:

Less than one months' fitful exertion in twelve, a fish basket in the river or in a swamp, an hour with a casting net in the evening, would supply a man with food. A little more than this and he would have something to sell. Probably that accounts for the Malay's inherent laziness: that and a climate which inclines the body to ease and rest, the mind to dreamy contemplation rather than to strenuous and persistent toil.

Like Raffles and Crawfurd before him, Swettenham interpreted the disposition of Malays through a social and environmental lens. What changed, however, was that the Malays, in his eyes, were not just intellectually feeble – they were lazy, too. Inherently lazy.

These were not just isolated observations by individuals writing in their private diaries. According to Alatas, the idea of the 'lazy native' pervaded the writings of European colonial authors, administrators, missionaries, and travellers. This was not just true of European ideas of natives in the Malay world – it applied to many other parts of the Empire, too, as I will point out below. And they were not writing to or for the natives, who were largely unaware of these assessments – they were writing for audiences 'back home' to convince them of the laziness and backwardness of the natives. They added moral justifications to economic motivations – European domination was not just necessary to exploit the abundant resources of these exotic lands, but also to save the natives from their wretched selves. In the Malay territories, according to Alatas, such ideas were shared by British, Dutch, and Spanish colonial powers even as they vied with each other for political and economic superiority.

It must be acknowledged that the idea of the 'lazy native' did not go unchallenged. Even within the centres of colonial power, there were political liberals who opposed – or, at the very least, were uncomfortable with – imperialism and colonialism for a variety of reasons. But these voices never managed to gain much influence until after the devastating aftermath of the First World War.

The natives fought back, too. But they were defeated, by and large, through warfare or economic strangulation, or both. The native 'rulers' who continued leading their subjects were often those who were suborned, or who actively collaborated with colonial powers for their own political survival.

This is part of the reason why Alatas argues that the static image of backwardness, idleness and idiocy, and the notion of the 'lazy native', is a myth. And this myth obscures the opposition towards colonial expansion amongst colonising and colonised populations. It also downplays how such opposition was often violently quashed.

Yet this is not the main reason Alatas argues that the idea of the lazy native is a myth. Alatas holds that the terms 'lazy' and 'indolent' were overwhelmingly applied to those natives who refused to prop up colonial capitalism. If Malays were inherently 'lazy', how should we describe the fact that they planted and harvested crops, reared livestock, fished, traded extensively, built and sustained villages and townships, and created objects of refinement and beauty long before the arrival of Europeans? But with the onslaught of European expansion, many Malays refused to work for colonial powers. When they were eventually subjugated and had to work for their colonial masters, many did this half-heartedly and insolently. This, according to Alatas, was not laziness. If anything, it can better be understood as a form of 'silent protest'.

A useful contrast can be drawn with colonial depictions of the migrant Chinese and Indian labourers brought to Malaysia. They were variously caricatured as treacherous, lying, violent, wicked, and constantly drunk on toddy (for the Indians) and high on opium (for the Chinese). But they were rarely called lazy. Why? Because they toiled in the service of colonial plantations, mining, and the building of transport infrastructure. Never mind that they did not have a choice – most were brought to Malaya as indentured labourers. A system of debt bondage held them hostage to the whims of the colonial regime and the elites within their own communities – if they dared not to work, they were often beaten, tortured, or left to die in poverty.

We can summarise that according to colonial logic, a lazy body is a body that refuses to advance colonial capitalist interests. An industrious body is a body that can and will, even to its own death. The consequences of the interplay between these racialised images and the impacts of colonial capitalism have not only endured – they are having devastating impacts on our planet. But more on that later.

When I was younger, one significant reason I was secretly smug about not being a 'real' Malay was that, unlike them, I was not lazy. I worked hard – very hard – and therefore did well in school. I was *The Little Engine That Could*.

Thank God we grow up.

Or do we?

The myth of the lazy native transformed slightly in the twentieth century, but its basic premise remained deep and enduring. Most of the changes that did occur were adaptations to the shocks suffered by the colonial capitalist system. In Malaya, for example, British administrators realised that the exploitative working conditions imposed upon native and migrant populations were simply untenable. Poor sanitation and hygiene resulted in the spread of malaria and other diseases, which took a toll on the output of the indentured labour force. The terrible circumstances endured by workers provoked moral indignation even amongst colonial ideologues – this, and the fact that rising numbers of sick and dead labourers translated into vastly reduced revenues and profits. The horrors of the First World War were also a wake-up call for colonial administrators, especially in Asia. Twentieth century British rule in Malaya then became marked by the building of hospitals, transport systems, and other infrastructures to rectify the previous decades of colonial underdevelopment.

By the eve of the Second World War, the colonial civil servant and historian of Southeast Asia J. S. Furnivall was genuinely sympathetic towards the plight of the natives of the Malay territories. He even admitted, with sincere regret, that historical colonial rule was marked by profiteering and abuse. But Furnivall also opposed nationalist and pro-independence movements in the region. He was instead a proponent of 'enlightened' colonialism, an ideology that complements still-widespread sentiments amongst many people in Britain and Malaysia – that at least the British introduced 'progress' and 'infrastructure' to their colonial territories.

It was only in the aftermath of the Second World War, when struggles for independence spread like wildfire throughout the British Empire, that Furnivall reluctantly supported independence. Even this belated support was marked by nostalgic apologia – the necessity of granting independence was the unfortunate result of the British not doing more to win the hearts and minds of the peoples they colonised. For Furnivall, the granting of independence was the most pragmatic way to guarantee the post-war survival of Western civilisation and colonial interests. But the natives – still seen as lazy and intellectually feeble – needed 'training and preparation' for independence from their colonial masters. They were no longer the white man's burden but his understudy.

The Furnivall Variant of the myth of the lazy native is one of the more well-documented developments in the ideology of late colonialism in the twentieth century. Hollywood got hold of another aspect of the myth and gave it a historic twist.

To understand the Hollywood Variant, it's important to recall that the period of high imperialism in the nineteenth century was accompanied by scientific advancement, especially in the realm of 'natural history'. Darwin's *On the Origin of Species*, for instance, was published in 1859, two years after the Indian Rebellion of 1857. These scientific developments led to a thirst amongst colonial explorers for the discovery, among other things, of 'missing links' to the age of dinosaurs. Sci-fi novels such as *The Island of Dr Moreau* by H.G. Wells and *The Lost World* by Sir Arthur Conan Doyle epitomised the concerns and contradictions beneath the larger ethos of colonial scientific exploration.

Against this backdrop, the first written reports of giant lizards in the eastern Indonesian island of Komodo emerged in the early twentieth century. As a result, the Dutch colonial government panicked at the potential influx of adventurers and explorers and banned the collecting of all animals from Komodo. After the First World War, however, this ban was occasionally lifted to accommodate scientific expeditions. A turning point occurred in 1926, when the Dutch lifted this ban for a group from the Bronx Zoo in the US.

At this time, the US was already starting to assert itself as an imperial power, which partly found expression through the development of its zoos and natural history museums. The 1926 American expedition to Dutch-controlled Indonesia was led by Douglas Burden, an elite New Yorker with an intense desire for swashbuckling adventures in distant and exotic places. Burden had been on prior expeditions to Alaska, Central America and mainland Southeast Asia, but this Indonesian trip was to become a phenomenon 'back home' through the publication of a travel book, film footage of the giant lizard in its natural habitat, and coverage in several popular scientific and geographic journals. It is this combination of factors that transformed a lizard into a dragon – the Komodo Dragon.

Burden's writings are valuable, giving us a fascinating glimpse of the story of the transition of imperialism's centre of gravity from Europe to the US through the lens of zoology. For our purposes, his descriptions of the 'natives' he encountered are most germane. Burden's excitement about the near-naked 'little Malay girls' he met in Bogor, West Java, is obvious in his writings. He could barely believe that these 'dusky maidens' – 'immature Eves' – would so willingly pose nude for his pictures. On Bali – 'a lazy and languorous island' – Burden was again overwhelmed by 'women, women, everywhere, such round, plump partridges, yet so lithe and graceful, and exhibiting such perfection of form as to inspire the artist'.

The men, however, provoked a different reaction, such as the 'rather fat, lazy, unattractive' local ruler Burden had to convince about his need to explore Komodo. In other words, our intrepid American's quest for a pre-historic creature in a far-off land necessitated the overcoming of naked native temptresses and lazy native male rulers.

When Burden finally saw his first *Varanus komodoensis*, he wrote:

> The lizard was working his way slowly down from the mountain crags. The sun slanted down that hill, so that a black shadow preceded the black beast as he came. It was a perfectly marvellous sight – a primeval monster in a primeval setting – sufficient to give any hunter a real thrill. Had he only stood up on his hind legs, as I now know they can, the dinosaurian picture would have been complete.

Burden's scientific expedition was therefore nothing short of an adventure into the heart of a 'primitive', pre-historic world. The nubile native women and indolent, inept native men he met along the way were merely props for a grander, salvific narrative. His Holy Grail was the 'dinosaurian' Komodo Dragon which he had to hunt, subdue, and transport to captivity back in the Land of the Free. And this motivation was not solely personal or private – his stories were meant to inspire folks back home with his adventures beyond the realm of civilisation, in an ancient, savage world where dragons ruled.

Hollywood studios were quick to spot an opportunity to capitalise on the 'dragon fever' that eventually gripped zoo visitors and large sectors of the American public. Burden was friends with Merian C Cooper, the former Air Force man and adventurer who, with Ernest B. Schoedsack, directed and produced the 1933 horror classic *King Kong*. In a letter to Burden in 1964, Cooper said:

> When you told me that the two Komodo Dragons you brought back to the Bronx Zoo, where they drew great crowds, were eventually killed by civilisation, I immediately thought of doing the same thing with my Giant Gorilla. I had already established him in my mind on a pre-historic island with prehistoric monsters and I now thought of having him destroyed by the most sophisticated thing I could think of in civilisation, in the most fantastic way. My very original concept was to place him on the top of the Empire State Building and have him killed by aeroplanes. I made considerable investigation on how this could be done technically with a live gorilla.

The conceptualisation of the monster and the use of special effects made *King Kong* a gamechanger in Hollywood. It also introduced a racialised, colonial 'Beauty and the Beast' storyline that has recurred in many a Hollywood epic since. As Burden wrote in *Dragon Lizards of Komodo*, 'a fiery dragon in itself is a fascinating idea — so, also, is the thought of a beautiful, white-skinned maiden. Link these two ideas together, in some way or other, and you have a story which by its very nature would survive through untold ages.' Lack of space does not permit me to explore the Freudian possibilities for analysing this male desire to save 'white-skinned' maidens from primitive monsters originating from far-off uncivilised lands. Suffice it to say that this is basically the history of American cinema from D.W. Griffith's *The Birth of a Nation* (1915) to the present.

In post-independence Malaysia, the myth of the lazy native persistently endured through continued proliferation by a ruling party that supposedly represented the natives — the United Malays National Organisation (UMNO). In 1971, UMNO published an edited volume, *Revolusi Mental* *(Mental Revolution)*, that characterised Malays as dishonest, backward, cowardly, irrational, and weak.

But what of the authors of the volume? Were they not Malay, too? This is where the Janus-faced nature of the myth of the lazy native was laid bare. The authors, and Malays like them, were modernised, educated, and progressive — to use the terminology that I have heard repeatedly in my lifetime, they were not 'typical Malays'. As Alatas described it, '*Revolusi Mental* is a distorted ideology of a Malay ruling party sharing the false consciousness of colonial capitalism.' And yet, UMNO, as the ruling party in Malaysia, was the guardian of special privileges for Malays. To explain this paradox, Alatas observed that UMNO combined self-assertion and self-degradation to justify the rule of the Malay political elite: 'they operated with colonial categories of thought despite their anti-colonial pronouncements.'

Another influential work that emerged around this time was *The Malay Dilemma* by Mahathir Mohamad – first published in 1970, when Mahathir had been expelled from UMNO. Mahathir rejoined UMNO soon after the publication of the *Malay Dilemma* and became prime minister in 1981, remaining in this position until his retirement in 2003. He returned to politics more than a decade later to join forces with the coalition of opposition parties that toppled the UMNO-led government in the historic 2018 elections. He became prime minister yet again at age 92, only to leave office in March 2020 amid a change of government that was triggered by a series of confusing and convoluted political defections.

I was three years old when Mahathir became Prime Minister. I had never read *The Malay Dilemma* but, given how ubiquitous it became, I absorbed much of its 'wisdom' by osmosis. It drew its power from the way that Mahathir appeared to derive his insights from empirical evidence, for example in this excerpt about the influence of crop cultivation and the environment on Malay character:

Rice cultivation, in which the majority of the Malays were occupied, is a seasonal occupation. Actual work takes up only two months, but the yield is sufficient for the whole year. This was especially so in the days when the population was small and land was plentiful. There was a lot of free time. Even after the gathering of other food-stuffs, there was still a lot of leisure time left. The hot, humid climate of the land was not conducive to either vigorous work or even to mental activity. Thus, except for a few, people were content to spend their unlimited leisure in merely resting or in extensive conversation with neighbours and friends.

On capacity for hard work, Mahathir wrote:

Malay leaders have been known to say that Malays are not suited for business or skilled work. They are agriculturists. Money does not mean the same thing to them as it does to the Chinese. They do not have the wish or the capacity for hard work. And above all they cannot change.

Yet Mahathir's 'evidence' is often simplistic, involving sweeping generalisations and the reproduction of dodgy stereotypes. It is virtually impossible to tell where the thinking of colonial writers such as Raffles, Swettenham and Furnivall ends and that of Mahathir's begins. To be fair, Mahathir and other pro-UMNO writers were also explicitly critical about the ills of British colonialism. Yet, like the colonialists who preceded them, they still laid the blame on Malay *character* for social and political problems – poverty, underdevelopment, and lack of education. At the time of writing, Mahathir has gone on record to say, in effect, that he *still* holds this position about 'lazy' Malays.

Alatas argued that this anti-Malay Malay nationalism had become an ideology of the Malay ruling class to mask how *it* had profited from colonial capitalism. Alatas observed this in the 1970s, and his diagnosis is infuriatingly relevant more than four decades later. The repeated and pervasive negative characterisation of Malays in post-independence Malaysia was and still is a way of blaming them for UMNO's – or any other party's – failures in government. To be clear, this racialised scapegoating of Malays co-existed – and still co-exists – alongside the politicised demonisation of other minority groups, including ethnic Chinese, Indians, Christians, and now queer and trans people. Mahathir has also accused Malaysian Chinese of stubbornly refusing to assimilate – because they continue using chopsticks to eat.

In my experience, this racism is felt and expressed not just in the mind and soul, but in the body, too. The different parts of *my* body were constantly engaged in a tug-of-war between passing as a 'real Malay' whilst wanting desperately not to be a 'typical Malay'. My brain was happy when my hands held posh-looking literature in English which my eyes hungrily devoured, but knew the same eyes had to read texts in Malay, too, to survive. My lips, teeth, and tongue alternated between trying to perfect the accents of urban English speakers in Malaysia and mimicking authentic, colloquial Malay. Even my taste buds were not spared. Much as I loved the sumptuous variety of foods in Malaysia, I grew up genuinely wondering if scones, Victoria sponge, and steak were actually superior by default.

This is why the stuff of everyday life – like the food we put into our bodies and the clothing we cover our bodies with – can become such vicious sites of colonial and anti-colonial struggle. But instead of the 'colonial/anti-colonial' binary, the oppositional terms that might be more familiar now are 'conservative/liberal', 'anti-Western/Western', or – in some instances — 'religious/secular'. And these struggles go beyond food and clothing. When the Kenyan writer Ngugi wa Thiong'o stopped writing in English and turned almost entirely to his native language, Gikuyu, this was intellectual and cultural resistance rooted in the choice to stop his physical body from reproducing what he regarded as a 'cultural bomb' in Africa.

Maybe this is too obvious — pointing out that racism and anti-racist struggles are not just fought on structural and ideological levels, but on a physical, bodily level as well. Maybe humanity has outgrown such irrational and nakedly offensive stereotypes about race. But then how else can we explain occurrences such as the visual depictions — made as recently as 2019 — of tennis legend Serena Williams as an aggressive *ape*? It seems like wilful ignorance to deny the direct or indirect connection between such enduring stereotypes and the legacy of King Kong or other Hollywood monsters.

What is less obvious is not just the connections between racism, colonialism, and capitalism, but how climatic and environmental explanations were the building blocks of racialised, capitalist colonial ideology. This is where the legacies of the past intrude upon the present, globally and urgently, most obviously in the crisis of climate change.

No matter what certain corporate interests or wealthier nations might claim, the climate crisis is not simply an environmental problem requiring technical or scientific fixes. It is a crisis borne of social and economic inequality and has social and political causes — mostly rooted historically in extractive and exploitative colonial capitalism. It will require social and political solutions, including the payment of reparations by rich nations and corporations for the damage they historically wreaked upon the territories they impoverished. But the idea of reparations and historic responsibility are anathema to states such as the US, the UK, the EU, Canada, and Australia, who continue to dodge meaningful international negotiations around these issues.

Climate and environment were embedded in the DNA of colonial capitalism. The examples provided by Alatas are only part of a larger story of modern colonialism in many different lands. European explorers, soldiers, medical officers, missionaries, and, later, administrators, often took thermometers, barometers, and other bits of meteorological kit to make sense of the new terrains and territories that they needed to colonise. These early efforts laid the groundwork for more institutionalised and organised endeavours to coordinate global meteorological observations. In the nineteenth century, for example, Alexander von Humboldt – the German naturalist, geographer and explorer – urged the Royal Society to make better use of Britain's imperial coverage for scientific advancement. Imperial Japan, too, actively pursued its own programme of scientific colonialism.

As with the colonial writings studied by Alatas, however, there was a shift between the attitudes of earlier and later colonial scientists. While earlier naturalists were critical of colonial mismanagement of famine and environmental stress, later figures sought to 'naturalise' famine in the colonies, for example, in India. In other words, the Empire could be absolved of responsibility if recurring famines could be 'scientifically' attributed to 'natural' causes, as opposed to being consequences of political and economic policies. Also, earlier explorers were more open to interacting and learning from the natives they encountered, whilst later colonial administrators started dismissing indigenous knowledge and practices as inferior. They insisted on characterising the natives as lazy and in need of 'civilising', yet constructed spaces that physically separated Europeans from indigenous populations to avoid the 'degeneration' of white bodies in tropical environments. It is against this background that the atrocious conditions of indentured labour described by Alatas took place. Slavery might have officially been abolished in the British Empire in 1833, but conditions akin to slavery – and what can only be described as proto-apartheid – remained rampant.

While awareness about the climate crisis is rising exponentially in the Global North, many of the fixes being proposed amongst wealthy corporations and nations still follow the logic of colonial capitalism. Many of the solutions that seem attractive – such as electric cars, carbon capture and storage, and even tree-planting and reforestation – hinge upon political and economic decisions that will continue to impoverish the peoples that historically did very little to cause climate change and to exclude them in decision-making processes. Instead, the extractive industries – especially those focused on fossil fuels and mining – appear set to continue apace, in collusion with current and former imperial powers and their client states.

The climate crisis is political – it always has been. And it is still driven by political and economic decisions that determine the fate of bodies that matter and bodies that are considered disposable.

I was recently asked, at a panel discussion, if all this talk about the historic responsibility of the Global North and the legacies of colonialism in the climate emergency was counter-productive. Does it not create animosity and division, when what we actually need is a response that unites us all as one human family in the face of this global crisis?

I had a lot of sympathy for this question, and still do – it can be exhausting and a trifle annoying to keep harping on about highly charged concepts such as the Global North, Global South, colonialism, imperialism, capitalism, racism, and reparations. And so, I tried to be grown up. I tried my best to respond without resorting to abstract, potentially divisive terminology or invoking my own personal experiences of racial politics.

I told the story of Lloyd's, the insurance and reinsurance market based in London.

Owned by Edward Lloyd, this insurance market began in 1686 as a place where sailors and merchants could gather and talk about shipping news and business. This was in line with the growing concept and culture of 'free trade', including of goods such as tobacco and sugar and of enslaved labour. As slave voyages grew more frequent, the associated market for marine insurance became dominated by Lloyd's.

One clue about the relationship between insurance and slavery resides in a 1783 legal case, involving the slave ship Zong which – along with its cargo of enslaved people – was owned by a Liverpool-based consortium. On a journey from Ghana to Jamaica, the ship's freshwater supplies ran dangerously low. In response, the crew threw 130 enslaved Africans overboard. When the ship eventually docked, the owners filed an insurance claim for their loss. The case had to go to court because the insurance underwriter, Thomas Gilbert, refused to pay out. The court decided that the insurers were indeed not liable, and the focus throughout the case was solely on the insurance claim. Nobody was ever prosecuted for the mass murder.

No enslaved peoples were ever brought to work on plantations in Britain. Very few were brought in for domestic servitude. In effect, the insurance industry in this country enabled people, that the majority of

Britons had never met, to be kidnapped, enslaved, tortured, and murdered — and Britain prospered. After slavery was abolished, however, the 1837 Slave Compensation Act did make sure that reparations were paid — just not to enslaved peoples but to their enslavers for 'lost assets'.

In the aftermath of the Black Lives Matter protests of 2020, Lloyd's has apologised for its historic role in the slave trade and has pledged to support more initiatives around inclusion, diversity and social justice. It has also introduced an action plan to accelerate its response to the climate crisis. But it remains silent on the question of financial reparations for the victims of slavery and the people suffering injustice today. It has, however, promised to exit fossil-fuel insurance by 2030 — with the caveat that its clients and members simply cannot afford an immediate end to supporting the fossil fuel industry.

Currently, Lloyd's remains committed to underwriting the Carmichael coal mine in Queensland, Australia, spearheaded by the Adani Group — an Indian conglomerate — with the support of the federal Australian and Queensland state governments. If built, the mine would enable 500 more coal ships to cut through the Great Barrier Reef World Heritage Area every year for sixty years. This would most certainly destroy the ancestral lands, waters, and cultures of indigenous people without their consent, which is why the Wangan and Jagalingou Family Council have said no to the project five times. The mine would also increase atmospheric carbon pollution by 4.6 billion tonnes. Now, amid global backlash, more than seventy financial institutions, including eighteen insurers, have withdrawn from or agreed not to be involved in the mine.

Not Lloyd's.

Having said all of this, it would be a mistake to portray Lloyd's as an evil entity that is intentionally willing planetary destruction. It's not. Lloyd's does what it does because of the structure and foundations of the insurance industry — it's about security and the protection of money and property within the global financial system which currently exists and relies upon colonial relations that never really ended. Within this larger system, it is not only the imperialist status quo and business interests that deserve scrutiny. The political and financial elites that lead postcolonial nation-states — many of them autocratically or dictatorially — are part of the problem, too. This is why Malaysia, for example, can make sweet-sounding pledges to act on climate change, even as deforestation and human rights abuses against indigenous peoples continue at a frightening speed. Incredibly, even the Malaysian government admitted the timber industry's human rights violations against indigenous communities, including the sexual assault perpetrated by timber workers on Penan girls in Sarawak – yet barely anything has changed.

So, what about these actual living bodies on the frontlines of climate breakdown? Are they just too indolent and feeble-minded to save themselves? Or are they simply unlucky enough to be suffering the worst impacts of climate change whilst having done the least to cause it?

AUTISM, YUSUF AND I

Naomi Foyle

The discovery of autism spectrum condition (or 'disorder' as it is medically deemed) is commonly accredited to Austrian psychologists Hans Asperger and Leo Kanner, who both wrote seminal clinical papers about autism in the 1950s. In fact, the term was coined in the early twentieth century by Swiss psychiatrist Eugen Bleuler, who used it to describe traits of social withdrawal seen in schizophrenic patients, and the condition was first described a decade later by Russian child psychiatrist Grunya Sukhareva. Her interest sparked by a boy she diagnosed as possessing an 'autistic proclivity into himself', Sukhareva closely observed six similarly distinctive children at her Moscow clinic and, in a paper published in 1925, noted in their behaviour a set of traits that map closely onto the Diagnostic and Statistical Manual of Mental Disorders (DSM-5) definition of autism today.

Sukhareva herself termed the condition 'autistic (pathological avoidant) psychopathy', and like other early researchers, focuses on white boys. As the current spate of late diagnoses in women, including my own in Dec 2020, has highlighted, for various reasons autism can go unnoticed in girls and women. But though, in Britain, with the public disclosures of autistic celebrities including Chris Packham and Melanie Sykes, a watershed moment has been reached in the history of this hidden disability, many questions remain. It seems relevant to ask: first, if and how autism is a physical condition; second, how and when is autism a disability; and finally, how might people differently-bodied for reasons including sex, skin colour, gender reassignment and (other) disabilities, experience being autistic in significantly different ways?

The answers to these questions are complex, and while I cannot claim to speak definitively on any of them, or indeed for any autistic person apart from myself, they are important questions for everyone to consider. For if autism, as John Duffy and Rebecca Dorner have suggested (2011), is essentially a 'narrative condition', it is inextricable from the story of the human species. Over the past year, in coming to terms with my own diagnosis, I have read books by autistic authors including Joanne Limburg, Camilla Pang and Anand Prahlad, and articles on autist-run websites like NeuroClastic and Autism Collaboration. Along the way I have discovered autism, or autistic-like traits, hidden in plain view in history – in the life and work of Emily Dickinson, Arthur Rimbaud, Virginia Woolf and Nina Simone; in Indian meditation practices and the European witch trials; in the behavior of characters in myth and legend and scripture. As an autistic person, I have found wise and empowering insights in modern commentary on the Biblical and Qur'anic stories of Yosef/Joseph/Yusuf, reflections that I will weave into this discussion of autism and the body politic, using the various spellings of Yusuf's name to reflect the rich cultural legacy of this hurt, gifted dreamer and his multicoloured coat.

Autism and the Body

Whether or how autism is a physical condition is not a straightforward question. Everyone can agree that the condition is based in the brain – NeuroClastic, a platform for diverse autistic voices, defines autism as a 'neurovariant'. It has also been linked to some genetic mutations and genetic engineering experiments are currently being done with the goal of making autistic mice more sociable. But there is no blood test or scan for autism: even if present and detectable in human beings, biomarkers will vary widely within a hugely diverse community of an estimated 78 million people world-wide. As a dictum in the autism community has it: 'If you've met one autistic person, you've met one autistic person'. All of this makes the locus of autism difficult to precisely define. But autistic people are having a go, and their own definition lays stress on the social nature of what is fundamentally a constitutional condition to be accommodated and celebrated, not a pathological one to be 'cured'. In this evolving collaborative project, Neuroclastic has collectively drafted a definition of autism that begins:

> All autistic people experience the human social world significantly differently from typical individuals. The difference in autistic social cognition is best described in terms of a heightened level of conscious processing of raw infor-

mation signals from the environment, and an absence or a significantly reduced level of subconscious filtering of social information.

That is to say, autism is essentially a human condition in which the sensory and intellectual world is experienced intensely, but the raw data of the social world is not apprehended or navigated with ease.

That's a fairly abstract opening gambit: Advanced Autism, if you like. More commonly, autism is defined as a spectrum of commonly held characteristics and observable behaviours. In his fascinating study, *Was Yosef on the Spectrum* (2018), the allistic (non-autistic) author Samuel J. Levine, gives a brief list many readers I am sure will associate with the condition:

> social challenges, punctuated by an inability to read social cues, understand and anticipate the feelings and reactions of others, and navigate social settings; attachment to animals or to inanimate objects in place of interpersonal relationships; heightened intellectual capacity and creativity in narrow areas of interest; repetitive and inflexible behaviors; an obsessive and compulsive focus on a private way of perceiving the world; and a rigid and literal perspective on truth, ethics and morality that sees virtue in extreme terms, rather than allowing for nuance.

As list of autistic traits, this covers a fair amount of ground but is by no means exhaustive: one might add self-stimulation, perseverance, conscientiousness, clumsiness, cognitively a slower processing time, disregard for conventional standards of hygiene, emotional dysregulation, atypical speech, exceptional pattern recognition, executive dysfunction, hyperempathy, sensory sensitivities, synesthesia, and extreme honesty, some of which Yosef demonstrates too. Some people also think autists might have stronger psychic abilities; and as a Tarot Card reader myself, when starting to think about this essay, without yet having heard of Levine's book, I had an intuition about Joseph, a Biblical figure I loved as a child due to his multicoloured coat and powerful connection to the dream world. Could he be ... I wondered. So, I read the Yusuf surah in the Qur'an and the Book of Genesis, searching for clues. In Pickthall's translation of *The Meaning of the Glorious Qur'an*, I was struck by Yusuf's moral righteousness with his master's wife, whose advances he rejects, even at cost of prison; and by verse 90: 'he who wards off (evil) and endures (finds favour); for verily! Allah loses not the wages of the kindly.'

Although these sentiments are expressed throughout the Qur'an, they seemed particularly to apply to Yusuf and his traits of moral certainty and perseverance.

The longer Biblical story revealed many more autistic-like traits – as the Torah and Jewish commentaries did to Levine. A quick Google search revealed that I was not the first person to think that Joseph might have been autistic, but although denied the thrill of intellectual discovery, I was still elated: not only to have had an intuition confirmed by scripture and scholarship – a book I quickly ordered – but to have made another connection with the autistic child that I was, a small girl unknowingly seeking self-representation in the world around her. But while I greatly appreciated Levine's careful and empathic consideration of Yosef's story, I object to the somewhat negative slant he gives here to autistic traits.

Social skills and face-reading can be taught and learnt, so should a supposed 'inability' be better described as a 'difficulty' or a 'struggle'? When allowed to pursue our enthusiasms, autistic people can achieve great things: why should these areas of interest be deemed 'narrow' rather than 'deep', or 'passions', even? Allistic people too have strong ideas about how certain situations should be handled – take etiquette for example – so is a strong need for routine really pathological, or more of a personal, even sometimes cultural, preference? Does not Greta Thunberg demonstrate that black-and-white thinking on serious moral issues is often needed to drive significant political change? And where in this list is the concept of pleasure: the experience of 'autistic joy', the intense, almost giddy high that comes from being immersed in one's own private world.

Part of the problem here, I think, is an over-reliance on stereotypes: overt behaviours that get taken as fundamental signs of autism, when in fact the condition is far more subtle and variable. I would go so far as to say that the term 'spectrum', although helpful in some respects, is also slightly misleading. As I understand and experience it, autism presents in clusters of traits – social, sensory, emotional, physical, verbal, intellectual, moral – each of which represents its own compass of possibilities. The now debunked 'extreme male brain' theory of autism, for example, which supposedly explained autistic boys' obsession with trains and number plates, has been finally put to rest by the realisation that many autistic girls (and also some boys and non-binary people) instead tend to express intense passions for animals and literature. Socially, the common stereotype that autistic people cannot make eye contact is quite often simply untrue of individuals on the spectrum, or complicated by the stronger ability (or desire) of autistic girls and women to mask their condition by learning and following social rules. Lack of eye-contact, real or supposed, has also been linked to a conjectured lack of empathy, or 'theory of mind', in autists, but this dehumanising argument is being challenged by the increasing understanding that some autistic people may in fact experience hyperempathy, perhaps leading to a disinclination to look directly into another person's eyes. The stereotype that autistic people do not understand metaphor can be similarly dismantled. Some autistic people find figurative language difficult to decipher, but I have taught many autistic creative writing students and they have all been able to use and understand simile and metaphor. For myself, I have realised that I do, on a visceral level, sometimes take metaphors literally – for example I have always found the expressions 'gets under my skin' and 'can I pick your brains?' creepy: they make me feel invaded. But I do know what they mean!

Differences, then, exist in all the areas that autism manifests, and the notion of a simple neurological arc, of 'neurotypical red', say, shading into 'spectrum adjacent purple' and then 'autistic blue', is erroneous. We are all three-dimensional beings and, like Joseph's coat, multicoloured. If I think of autism as a spectrum, I visualise a large, complex Alexander Calder mobile, a rainbow-coloured variety of twirling discs suspended from its various elegantly curved arms. In a neurotypical person, the discs are heavy enough to withstand average changes in a room's air flow and the colours go with the furniture and walls; in an autistic person, the discs might spin wildly when someone sneezes, or clash against each other or the wallpaper; the wires get tangled more easily and, if not cared for properly, there is a danger that in the end someone will take the whole thing to a charity shop or dump it in the bin.

The autistic mobile may also seem out of balance in some crucial way: the co-existence of these clusters of traits can lead to seeming contradictions in a person's psychology. Levine points out that the first mention of Yosef in the Book of Genesis refers to him as a shepherd, while the term used in the Torah is a *ro'eh et-echav batzoan* – suggesting to Jewish

commentators that, although younger than his eleven half-brothers, Yosef
leads them in his skill with the sheep. In the same passage, though, and
often later on, Yosef is called a *na'ar* – a child – an odd word for a
seventeen-year-old, but one that reflects the teenager's emotional
impulsiveness and inability to judge the effects of his words and actions on
others. He insists on telling his brothers about his dream in which eleven
stars bow down to him – a dream they too can interpret! Later in jail,
rather than building trust with his fellow prisoners, he rudely demands
help from the Pharoah's wine butler; when the butler does later grant him
an audience with the Pharoah, he openly contradicts the ruler in front of
his advisers. Yet in other ways he is sophisticated: a skilled interpreter of
dreams and a capable administrator. The co-existence of such apparently
contradictory traits is familiar to many autistic people and their loved
ones, and finding a plausible explanation for Yosef's behaviour, and the
behaviour of others toward him, is the aim of Levine's study, which seeks
to 'achieve a coherent and cohesive reading of the story'.

Indeed, from Yosef's habits of playing with his hair and rocking on his
heels, to his presumptuous communication style, Levine makes a strong
case for his place on the spectrum. And despite his own conventional view
of autistic traits, Levine has great respect for Yosef's gifts, praising his
brilliance at dream interpretation and his fearless honesty with the
Pharoah, who had no need for yet another 'yes-man' and appreciated
hearing the truth about the potential calamity facing his nation. Overall,
Levine's study is a scholarly and empathic exegesis of the Torah, Midrash
and classical Jewish sources, rooted in a compassionate understanding of
autism. It also demonstrates the truth of Duffy and Dorner's contention
that autism is a 'narrative condition'. By this they mean that:

> diagnoses of autism are essentially storytelling in character, narratives that seek
> to explain contrasts between the normal and the abnormal, sameness and differ-
> ence, thesis and antithesis. By "narratives" we mean, quoting Walter Fisher,
> "symbolic actions ... that have sequence and meaning for those who live, create,
> or interpret them" (58). Human beings are by nature narrative creatures, *homo
> narrans*, Fisher observed, that intuitively respond to stories and storytelling. The
> narratives of autism offer a collection of languages, a set of tropes, metaphors,
> and other symbolic resources that provide "sequence and meaning" for those
> who would interpret the behaviours and ways of thinking labelled 'autistic'.

The concept is a rich one, encompassing both helpful and unhelpful narratives of autism. Sticking with diagnosis for a moment, as Duffy and Dorner suggest, the process is an intensive process of verbal analysis. For adults, this is a series of questionnaires followed by a two-to-three-hour interview, meaning that diagnosis is ultimately dependent on the story you tell about yourself. Although I have a one-page letter from the NHS to confirm my diagnosis, the official document is twenty-pages long, and consists in large part of my own qualitative answers to the questions put to me by the clinician, many of them corroborated by my late mother's notes on my behaviour in my baby book. And if I had any doubts at all about my diagnosis, they were quelled for good when I visited the three shelves full of my diaries, which I have religiously kept over the years. There are far too many to read properly unless I took a year's retreat in a cabin in the woods (tempting!), but I pulled some down at random and opened the pages. Time and again passages leapt out at me, screaming 'I'm autistic!' — often written during times in my life when I struggled to connect with others, these diaries, especially the early ones, are filled with painful misunderstandings, youthful arrogance, intellectual passion and moral fervour. It's as though during the long lonely 'feral years' my autistic self had only one place, the page, where she could take off her mask and truly be herself. I marvel at that now, and also at the fact that she knew she had to keep this record safe — for a time when I might recognise and love her for who she is: me.

To conclude this discussion of autism and the body with the body, I understand that my brain is autistic (that is, it is a complex organ of consciousness constituted in such a way as to filter and interact with the world in a manner that can be defined as autistic) and I can also recognise how autism expresses itself in my physical experience: my sensory sensitivities and, in my case, woeful lack of dance, sport and musical skills (which for other autists could be areas of expertise). But ultimately my diagnosis has deepened my respect for the mystery of human self-consciousness: the fascinating questions of how we know who we are; at what levels we come to understand ourselves, even unconsciously; and how we construct the stories of our lives. I am well aware that the prevailing narrative of autism is a 'sad' or pathological one. Duffy and Dorner decry what they describe as the mainstream clinical view of autists as 'evolutionary deviant … [and] tragic figures', who generate in allistic researchers 'a novelistic, poetically intensified account of sadness – a rhetoric of scientific sadness – in which autistic people are mourned even as they are apparently explained'. But as I will discuss next, although I have certainly found being a 'feral autist' a struggle, receiving my diagnosis at last has been a profoundly empowering experience.

Autism and Disability

As defined by the Equalities Act 2010, a person (P) is disabled if:

(a) P has a physical or mental impairment, and
(b) the impairment has a substantial and long-term adverse effect on P's ability to carry out normal day-to-day activities.

At first, I was hesitant to say I was disabled by my autism. Aware that autism is not an illness, but a way of being-in-the-world inhabited by a minority of human beings across history and cultures, I resented the term 'Disorder' in my diagnosis and choose to use 'Autism Spectrum Condition' instead. I saw many positive aspects of my personality reflected in the traits – a strong sense of justice, attention to detail, ability to focus, passion, conscientiousness – all of which have helped me build a moderately successful writing and teaching career, and an active social and political life. I did, though, recognise that I have certain sensory challenges, for example with noisy environments and bright lights, and it would be advantageous for me to be able to request my legal right to 'reasonable adjustments' at work to ensure that I had a quiet office and acceptable lighting. Initially, I thought that was probably the extent of my own impairment. But as time has gone on, and I've learned more about the condition, and reflected more deeply on how it has affected my life path, I have changed my ableist mindset.

For in fact, my whole life has been very difficult at times. As my mother's notes confirmed, I struggled to make friends as a child, and was severely disturbed each time we moved (to three different continents over the first seven years of my life). I wet the bed for years, was a sleepwalker, and suffered from night fears. I was fortunate in Saskatchewan, where my parents deliberately bought a house within walking distance of a small elementary school that hosted the four year-long 'AcTel' (Academically Talented) programme. Here, and in a small high school, my love of writing was nurtured by caring teachers and librarians. But as a child I only ever had one friend at a time, sometimes a girl who bullied me, and was so shy in high school my nickname was 'Mousey': it was only through joining the acting club – learning how to be someone else – that I gradually was able to join a peer group, making lifelong friends I remain grateful for today. Still, though, my self-esteem was precarious, and I was highly resistant to change: I tried to commit suicide three times as a teenager, all three times after a forced change – moving city, and breaking up with my first boyfriend. I came very close the last time, taking a bottle of pills and ending up in hospital for three days. Though it was I, and not my siblings, who had thrown me down there, like Yusuf, at the age of seventeen I had ended up at the bottom of a dark pit.

I have never since made another attempt on my life, but I have circled that pit again many times. I have spent much of my adult life in and out of therapy, in part to address a long-standing family estrangement rooted in part, as I now understand it, in my undiagnosed autism: my extreme sensitivity to abruptly changing family dynamics and utter inability to communicate how I was feeling in ways that my family could hear and understand. Like Yosef in the Midrashic texts, I demanded my family bow down to me and my emotions. Their responses varied over the years, but especially after I moved back to England, and communication faltered, it often felt to me that we all had averted our eyes or turned our backs on each other. I relate this now with no sense of blame or guilt. The situation was impossible: I was autistic, and not only did my parents not know it, there was no way they could have found out; even 'autism experts' had no idea at the time how autism manifested in girls.

My mother, who died when I was twenty-seven, was sympathetic to me during my troubled period, but reading Levine's interpretation of Yaakov's behaviour towards Yosef, and his compassionate insights into the challenge of parenting autistic children, I understand that the way she loved me was not exactly what I needed. In the Qur'an, Jacob, a prophet himself, is stern with Yusuf, being aware of God's plans for him; in the Judeo-Christian tradition, though, he is a softer figure, tempted to indulge his sensitive and talented child, but not, as Levine stresses, offering the

protection and structure Yusef needs. Indeed the gift of the multicoloured
coat – perhaps, Levine suggests, a symbol of Yosef's complex nature and
many talents – only serves to make his brothers more jealous of him. I
didn't feel like a 'favourite child' – though my siblings may remember
otherwise – but while my mother treated me to boozy 'literary lunches'
and money for travelling, she did not help me learn how to set personal
boundaries. Autistic teenage girls can have difficulties in this area and, left
to their own devices, often run wild when puberty hits, as I increasingly
did. My mother's approach to sex ed, though, was hands-off, leaving me
a note one day to direct me to a package of books and condoms she had
hidden in the sewing drawer in the basement. I know that this detached
approach was both generational and culturally common – I doubt her
parents had 'the talk' with her – but had my autism been understood, I am
sure my parents and school would have put better support in place for me
as an adolescent, helping me with the hard transition at the end of my first
major relationship.

As can happen, family ruptures took a long time to heal, not helped by
the fact that I had moved back to the UK. As I have written before for
Critical Muslim, having cancer in 2016 was one of the best things that ever
happened to me, because facing my mortality snapped me out of a chronic
depression, and restored my family relationships to a harmonious and
affectionate state. Yet still I wondered how the whole traumatic
estrangement had come to pass, and seeking answers to this question, along
with learning more about autism at staff training and online, ultimately put
me on the path to requesting an NHS assessment. Although perhaps I could
have found my way to an assessment ten or fifteen years ago, the way I look
at it now is that by some miracle I survived cancer and was able to reach,
at last, the milestone of my diagnosis. In another parallel with Yusuf, my
reunion with my father has been a source of great comfort to me.

I am also close to my aunt and cousins in the North of England. But my
father and siblings are all in Canada, I live alone in the South East, and
between the pandemic lockdowns and my diagnosis, I felt a sadly familiar
sense of anxiety return. As the world stood still, some people suffered
huge financial blows, or were locked down with domestic abusers; some
people worked themselves to exhaustion on the frontlines; some were
furloughed and baked bread; others, despite it all, managed to achieve

huge successes. Working round the clock to cope with the steep learning curve of 'blended learning' in Higher Education (HE), while also covering for sick colleagues at Waterloo Press, I found myself in the shallow end of the second category — nowhere near as stressed and necessary as a medical key worker, but still, drained by huge and unexpected demands. I re-entered therapy and began a gratitude journal and daily meditation. But as I also reflected on my diagnosis, I could not escape the conclusion that in most respects life for any autistic person in a neurotypical world is genuinely a struggle.

Only 22% of autistic people in Britain are in any kind of employment: a shocking figure that puts autistic people in the lowest employment bracket for all disabled people. For myself, though I often work six days a week, up to twelve hours a day, financially my life remains an uphill battle. Although I have a half-time teaching job, even with a recent promotion to a Readership, I don't earn enough from the university to live on. The fact that my wages have not kept pace with inflation is a sector-wide problem, and of course the housing crisis also affects my situation. But my inability to get a more financially solid teaching job is related to my condition. Like many autistic people, I am bad at interviews — too slow at processing the questions, too honest in my replies and not good at self-promotion — and apart from the Readership (which was a written application) all my attempts to get on a better footing in HE have failed. After my illness I received Personal Independent Payments (given by government to those suffering long term physical or mental health conditions) for two years, but those have long ended and now I juggle various underpaid editing positions to make ends meet; throughout the last two decades I have been dependent on practical support including a capped rent set by a generous landlord, and two substantial grants from the Royal Literary Fund. I am grateful for my beautiful flat, many publications and the respect of my colleagues and the university. I also recognise that precarity is an occupational hazard in HE and poets are unlikely to be raking it in! I have a strong work ethic, pick myself up after knock backs, and have experienced the occasional financial success — most recently an Arts Council grant for a theatre adaptation of my SF novels. But it's all rather hand-to-mouth. Considering I am white and middle-class and my parents met at Cambridge, economically I don't feel particularly 'high-functioning', as some people might want to call me.

Financially, life would be easier with a partner to help shoulder burdens, or jointly invest in luxuries like pets or a camper van. But I am chronically single – not particularly by choice, but because I have found long term relationships impossible to sustain. They all have foundered for different reasons, but looking back at them through the lens of my diagnosis, I can see that mostly I have ended relationships due to difficulties with communication and, sometimes, sensory sensitivities – suddenly 'going off' the person physically. Being single, and occasionally dating, is not a bad solution – I enjoy my own company and a little autistic joy goes a long way. But looking back to times when I was trying hard to make things work with someone who also was making an effort, I do wistfully feel that had I been diagnosed earlier, things could have been different, if not with that person then with someone else I might have met in the course of being openly and more happily autistic.

Returning to the legal definition of 'disabled' then, things that most people, I believe, would define as 'normal day-to-day activities' – maintaining a long-term relationship, acquiring a mortgage, holding down a full-time job, even car or pet ownership – have always seemed, for me, impossible to achieve. I have never wanted children, but perhaps if I had been able to create a nest with someone else, I might have. Instead, all my energy has gone into self-regulation. At my lowest ebbs, I have felt like a freak, or a little match girl, shivering out in the snow as families celebrate Christmas in their warm living rooms. Thanks to my passionate interests and political and spiritual beliefs, I have adapted to my circumstances – I enjoy, even crave, solitude, and know that anyone on this planet who owns a pair of shoes is a fortunate human being. But I also understand the principle that, when it comes to autism, early interventions lead to better outcomes, and it is poignant to reflect on what might have been. Still – better late than never. I would like to believe that, armed at last with this crucial self-knowledge, and the support of autism activists, happier endings are still possible for me.

Whatever happens, the important thing is that I now have a new focus and direction, and nuanced choices about how to tell the next chapter of my story. Re-reading Joseph's story, in the Qur'an as well as the Bible, has helped me see my autism in a different light. The Qur'anic surah differs in many respects from the Book of Genesis, being shorter and, as Muhammad Asad explains, less focused on the family drama than the role of Allah in determining human fate. This feels significant to me, for ultimately, I do see my life as an expression of a higher, universal power. Why am I here? Is it to conform to social norms and be successful in conventional arenas? Or is it to follow my passions – for poetry, science fiction, anti-racist activism, social justice – wherever they may lead? What might God's purpose have been in delivering my diagnosis so late in my life? Is it in fact late, or right on time, coming at a point that enables me to enter the conversation about autism with over fifty years of insight into just how hard it is being autistic in a world so completely not, physically, socially or morally, built by or for us that it renders us invisible even to ourselves?

For in the end, like the pioneering disability activists who have done so much to shape this conversation, I have come to see my own autism though the lens of the social model of disability, which holds that an impairment exists in relationship to social structures. In the medical, or individual, model of disability, impairments are seen as deficits – inherent lacks which medical research must 'fix' lest they lead to tragic states of being. To avoid these connotations, I used the term 'alt-bodied' in my science fiction to refer to physically disabled people and am happy to refer to myself now as 'alt-brained' or 'alt-minded'. But although other terms for 'disability' have been tried out in the 'real world', none have stuck. For as the social model of disability contends, people *can* be disabled – by the world around them. In this model, impairments in themselves are seen simply as differences, examples of human diversity – and in this model, also, these differences can involve personal and, in an inclusive world, social gains. They become disabilities only when the world does not recognise, accommodate or celebrate them.

Of course, there are degrees of disability. To succeed at last, Yosef needed the Pharoah to give him a job he was good at, a wife to manage his social life, and some decent clothes. I need reasonable adjustments at work to enable me to do my job well and put me on a level playing field with allistic candidates in job interviews, while joining a self-help group for autistic adults has helped me work through my feelings about my various relationships and improve, I think, my emotional communication skills.

Autistic people who also have verbal and/or intellectual disabilities might well require round-the-clock, lifelong care – though with the aid of assistive technology, some nonspeaking autistic people can communicate very effectively. These very real differences have given rise to an on-going controversy about language and terminology. Again the term 'spectrum' proves problematic because it is often used to imply a range of autistic behaviours or conditions from 'mild' to 'severe' or 'low-' to 'high-functioning' – terms I and many autistic people find offensive, suggesting as they do that autism can be an insignificant or 'minor' condition, or that any human being can be 'low functioning', like some kind of cheap or obsolete device.

I might be said to be 'mildly' autistic, or 'high functioning', because I am intelligent and live independently, but what was mild about cutting my wrists and getting my stomach pumped at the age of seventeen? What is 'high functioning' about being fifty-four and never having held a full-time job? And is there really a need to subcategorise autistic people? A 2021 landmark report, *The Lancet Commission on the future of care and clinical research in autism,* co-authored by researchers, self-advocates and parents of autistic children, has just introduced the term 'profound autism' to refer to autistic people with high care needs. This is not to everyone's liking, though – already the backlash has begun on social media, and I have to say I can see why. My late diagnosis has been a profound turning point for me, and indeed, being a constitutional condition, utterly inseparable from oneself, autism is an inherently profound condition. And while 'profound' is obviously a better word to use in relation to people than 'low-functioning' or 'severely autistic', is there a need for such a blanket term at all, given that it doesn't even describe autism, but refers rather to the presence of verbal or intellectual disability? The Commission says it is just an 'administrative term', to help clinicians identify and meet levels of support need, but such terms, like the deservedly much loathed 'BAME', do leach into common use. Couldn't clinics and councils use a term like Autistic+ to indicate a person with additional conditions and needs? Plus at least sounds positive.

The controversy, though, should not be allowed to overshadow the significant progress represented by the Lancet Commission, which has largely adopted the social model of disability, stating that: 'Although autism is a neurobiological condition, the clinical challenges it raises for society and for a very heterogeneous group of individuals are predominantly not ones that are likely to be solved by biomedical solutions for most people in the near future.' Despite the alarming implication that 'biomedical solutions' might be applied to 'most' autistic people in the mid- to distant future to solve the 'challenges' we raise for society, in the overall thrust of its report, the Commission clearly advocates for urgent reform of autism research. It recommends a 'stepped care' program of personalised therapeutic interventions, developed in concert with autistic people and their carers, taking into account their cultural and economic situations, and based on a vastly improved international evidence base on what works best, for whom. After decades in which, as Paul Doehring reports, autism research has overwhelmingly focused on basic science – 'the characteristics, associated features, general trajectories and possible causes of autism' – at the expense of applied research – studies that directly test 'assessment or intervention practices with clinical populations and studies addressing factors that might influence these practices, such as disparities in access to services' – the Commission marks a welcome call to action from the medical establishment. One can only hope it is heeded.

For while it is true that early diagnosis and effective interventions can lead to better outcomes for autistic people, ethically, what sort of interventions should these be? Giving children genetic replacement therapy to make them play nicely with others in the sand pit? If we've learned one thing from the twentieth century, surely it is that eugenics belongs in the garbage bin of history. As an autistic person, I don't want to be medically 'improved'. I want society to change, not only to make my life easier, but to benefit everyone. Morally acceptable, effective and autism-positive interventions, in which families, carers and employers learn how to communicate better with autistic people and put in place proper support structures for us, are commensurate with a broader and compassionate social justice programme, an intersectional one that ultimately will make life better for all.

Autism, Racism, Sexism, Transphobia

My final question on the theme of autism and the body concerns other bodily differences and how they affect the experience of being autistic. The answer is powerfully: such differences can make all the difference in the world. Autism is a human condition: the traits are human traits. But how your body is shaped or shaded – your sex, your gender, your skin colour, or (other) disabilities – can lead to a late diagnosis, or no diagnosis at all; while the history of autism research is steeped in discrimination against people – both autists and clinicians – on the basis of their particular identities. These are weighty topics, and I can only really signpost them here, but evidence from the autistic community, at least, suggests that this is an area that is thankfully coming into focus after long neglect.

In relation to the history of autism research, boys and white children have been significantly overrepresented in clinical studies, for long periods exclusively so. At the same time, clinicians of Jewish ethnicity have been sidelined: three pioneering researchers, Sukhareva, and the Austrian physician Georg Frankl and psychologist Anni Weiss, who studied in the thirties children who would now be considered autistic, were Jewish, and it has been conjected that Hans Asperger, who worked at a clinic in Vienna under the Nazi regime, ignored their work in his own clinical papers for that reason. The jury is still out on Asperger, though. Newly discovered archival evidence indicates he sent up to two dozen children to a eugenics camp where he would almost certainly have known they would be killed. Some argue that he was an unwilling collaborator, a man who never joined the Nazi Party and was just trying to save his own skin and, perhaps, as many children as he could. But though he did denounce the Nazis after the war, it is hard to ignore the evidence that in the face of their murder engines he chose a path of complicit passivity, and 'Asperger's Syndrome' is another term many autistic people now reject.

In his focus on boys, Asperger also contributed to the enduring stereotypes that have so hindered countless diagnoses and, with them, a fuller understanding of the condition that wound up bearing his name. As Joanne Limburg, in her trailblazing and far-ranging memoir *Letters to My Weird Sisters: On Autism and Feminism*, notes, it wasn't that there weren't girls in Asperger's clinic: he simply had no interest in them and attributed all their 'disruptive' behaviour to the onset of menstruation. I have already touched on gender differences in the presentation of autism, and should clarify here that, like, all gender differences these are relative and not essentialist – I have met adult women who interact with others in an abrupt, socially challenging manner, and men who are hyperempathic. It is also the case that many autistic people do not relate strongly to the whole concept of binary genders: for myself, I have always felt like a person first, woman next, and have welcomed the move toward a far wider choice of gender expression. This is a topic treated perspicaciously by allistic trans academic Jake Pyne in the article 'Autistic Disruptions, Trans Temporalities: A Narrative "Trap Door" in Time', which explores how the life writing of trans, autistic and trans-autistic people can create powerful narratives of escape from confining neurotypical norms.

But if a difference in 'types' of autism can be noticed across the sex and gender spectrum, to the extent that entire generations of women, both cis and trans, and many men and non-binary people, have been left undiagnosed, it is unclear how much these differences are driven by biological or social factors. Do autistic girls, being female, inherently want to have friends and be liked, and therefore – like me, with my theatre buddies – diligently set themselves the task of 'fitting in', while autistic boys, being male, simply don't care as much if they have pals? Or is it more the case that all girls feel such an incredible social pressure to be kind and cooperative, that even autistic girls feel the need to conform, while all boys are discouraged against expressing their feelings to others, on pains of being called a sissy, or worse? It's a valid question, I suppose, but given the impossibility of removing human beings from their social environment, is it answerable? A more useful question is: given that we know autistic girls can and often do adeptly mask their condition, and in a society where females are expected to be quiet, submissive and into animals and poetry, how might adults in positions of responsibility better identify and support potentially autistic girls or any child who does not present overtly as autistic?

Like girls and women, people of colour barely figure in the history of autism research and, for a range of reasons, all related to institutional racism, their route to diagnosis remains fraught with obstacles. Terra Vance, writing for NeuroClastic, summarises the picture:

Essentially, people of colour feel that they will not be received with kindness, empathy, and respect when seeking supports from education and healthcare systems that are not represented equally by professionals of colour. They don't trust authority figures to have their or their children's best interests at heart. They fear that their children will not be truly understood and seen by professionals.

They're not wrong, either. Studies demonstrate that for people of colour, doctors hesitate more to make an ASD diagnosis compared to white clients, fewer dollars are spent on services and supports in their communities, they are 5.1 times more frequently misdiagnosed with behaviour disorders, and they are diagnosed later in life.

As a result of this endemic mistrust, Black and Brown people may be more likely to take care of their autistic children at home, or seek help at their local church or mosque. These can, of course, be beneficial environments. American researcher Brinda Jegatheesan studied three South Asian Muslim families with autistic children over seventeen months and reported that the parents considered their children a gift from God, while the practice of daily prayer appeared to have supported the children's language acquisition skills. In the UK, thanks to the activism of Muslim mother Sara Mangara, the Finsbury Park Mosque offered its first 'Autism Hour' in 2016, where autistic people and their families could come and pray, a project that has led to the establishment of the growing AutismMosque movement, with its vision of 'Opening Doors and Opening Minds'. But these experiences are not universal. In fundamentalist religious institutions and cultures, of whatever ethnicity, invasive conversion-type therapies or even exorcisms, may be forced upon autistic children.

Stereotypes, too, can inhibit the diagnoses of autistic people of colour. Racialised expectations of Asian children as 'shy', 'well-behaved' (read: trying desperately to fit in) and 'good at maths' can obscure their autistic traits in the minds of teachers. Similarly, as Vance observes, because, outside Africa, Black people's routes to success have been highly channelled through music, sport or performance, 'the specialised talents and highly-crafted skills of Black and Brown autistics are regarded as *expected*, while the struggles associated with being autistic are ignored'. Reading Vance's article immediately made me wonder about Nina

Simone, whose mental health battles are well documented: she was diagnosed with bipolar condition, but was known to be outspoken, abrupt in her manner, and to possess a powerful sense of justice. Could she have been autistic? We will never know, but it seems a possibility at least. Conversely, some autistic traits can be judged harshly for racist reasons: Jake Pyne cites a 2020 interview with mixed-race autistic-trans man Reynard, in which 'Reynard's comportment [is] interpreted as "aggressive and loud" only in white spaces'. Working class autistic people of any background might also experience such opprobrium in middle class circles – or in school. School exclusion due to 'challenging behaviour' is thought to contribute to the disproportion of autistic people in prison, where – like Black people – they are statistically overrepresented.

In the UK's hostile environment, a prison record can have far-reaching consequences, in particular for Black people not born in Britain. In the UK in 2018 eighteen-year-old autist Osime Brown was charged with helping to steal a mobile phone, an alleged theft that had occurred two years previously. Despite testimony from the older boys who actually did steal the phone that he had tried to stop them, Osime was given a sentence of five years – in itself outrageous for the theft of a phone by a teenager, especially considering that Osime had been placed in foster care after his diagnosis, and his mother given no support to help keep him at home. In prison, he was punished for his autistic behaviours by long periods of solitary confinement, and regular chemical and mechanical constraints, to the point where he developed a heart condition. During an operation on his heart he was not given enough anaesthetic. But his torture did not end there. After his release, his family had to launch a major campaign, fortunately successful, to stop the Home Office deporting him to Jamaica, where he could not have survived on his own. Osime did not even realise the country of his birth lay across an ocean from his mother's house. He was, in fact, lucky. Tragically – the tragic nature of autism lying not in the condition itself, but how completely and fatally it can be misunderstood – as is the case with Black people, autistic people are extremely vulnerable to police violence.

Autistic people who exhibit behaviours like hand-flapping can attract negative attention from strangers; they are sensitive to lights and loud noises, and might not respond as demanded to the arrival of police officers and vehicles. If they are Black, this can lead to fatal consequences. In 2015, the fifteen-year-old autistic African-American boy Stephon [pronounced Ste-FON] Watts was shot to death by two police officers in his own home in Calamet City, near Chicago – while distressed and brandishing a butter knife. In Colorado in 2019, Elijah McClain, a young Black man buying soft drinks in the local shop and wearing a ski mask to protect his sensitive face against the cold, was reported in a phone call to police for looking 'sketchy'. Elijah, who did not have a diagnosis but identified himself during his arrest as 'an introvert', was unarmed and slender and offered his ID to the police. The three officers tackled him to the ground, put him in a chokehold and eventually subdued him with an injection of ketamine, a significant overdose for his weight. Elijah suffered a heart attack in the ambulance and died in hospital without regaining consciousness. Initially there was very little public reaction to his death, but local protests ignited in the wake of the murder of George Floyd. In September 2021 the police officers involved were charged with 32 counts of manslaughter and criminally negligent homicide, and in November 2021 the City of Aurora awarded his family 15 million dollars for the death of their gentle son, a massage therapist who liked nothing more than to play his violin in the animal shelter, to help calm the strays in their cages. As recorded by the police, these are Elijah's last words:

> I can't breathe. I have my ID right here. My name is Elijah McClain. That's my house. I was just going home. I'm an introvert. I'm just different. That's all. I'm so sorry. I have no gun. I don't do that stuff. I don't do any fighting. Why are you attacking me? I don't even kill flies! I don't eat meat! But I don't judge people, I don't judge people who do eat meat. Forgive me. All I was trying to do was become better. I will do it. I will do anything. Sacrifice my identity, I'll do it. You all are phenomenal. You are beautiful and I love you. Try to forgive me. I'm a mood Gemini. I'm sorry. I'm so sorry. Ow, that really hurt! You are all very strong. Teamwork makes the dream work. Oh, I'm sorry, I wasn't trying to do that. I just can't breathe correctly. (Wikipedia)

It is hard to keep writing after reading those words. If readers need to take a break, light a candle, open a window, rage, or say a prayer, I understand. The best way, I think, I can honour Elijah McClain's memory at this point is to return to Yosef. Levine points out how often Yosef invokes God in the face of his oppressors – a dangerous move, in fact, for it exposes him as a Hebrew, an outsider, a member of a persecuted minority in Egypt. Like Yosef – and unlike Hans Asperger or countless others – Elijah held spiritual beliefs so strong that they gave him the courage to speak his truth to power, no matter the consequences. I doubt that anything he could have said, or not said, would have saved his life, or that Elijah had any conscious control over how he addressed his abusers. What he said as they choked him was a pure expression of who he was at that moment in time. Mixed up in that spontaneous reaction to a terrifying assault is a plea for forgiveness from his alleged killers, almost unbearably painful to read. But, I believe, or want to, this is not a soul-destroying submission to white supremacy – rather it is delivered in the flow of self-assertion, a lucid testament to a young man's moral beliefs, worldview and capacity for love, that, in its generosity, humility and insistence on our essential goodness as human beings, elevates him so far above his attackers that, no matter how long they live or how high they might fly, they will never touch the hem of his coat.

Conclusion

The story of autism is rooted in long, hard and often invisible struggle, but I would like to conclude on a hopeful note. As I've discussed throughout this essay, some of the key traits of autism are honesty, sensitivity, a love of animals, and clear moral standards, all of which are desperately lacking in our current political sphere and public domain. Although statistics put autistic people in about 1-2% of the population, from the number of people who have told me since my diagnosis that they think they are on the spectrum, I believe the true figure is much higher. My feeling is that when autistic people are a) assessed and identified more accurately and b) empowered to fulfil their potential, society will change immensely for the better.

What was Yusuf's purpose, after all? Why did God make him the way that he was and put him through his ordeal of abandonment, slavery and imprisonment? It wasn't simply to succeed in the end and wear fine clothes, or even just to reunite his family. Yusuf, with his spiritual insights and organisational skills, was needed by the Pharaoh to help shepherd his society through seven years of famine. We are facing far longer than seven dark years ahead: our planet, which hosts the only biosphere we are aware of to date in the universe, is dying, its climactic death throes giving rise to multiple catastrophes, hitting us from all sides. We do, though, have about seven years to make a vital difference: as has never been more clear, we need to radically overhaul our global economy by 2030. Autistic people, and not just Greta Thunberg, have a crucial role to play in this process. Campaigns to ensure we and all other neurodivergent people are no longer hidden, our lives valued and our collective voice heard, are inherently campaigns that challenge dominant and ecocidal social values of competitiveness, aggression and cruelty. Like other progressive and inclusive social movements, the autism-positive movement promotes instead mutual aid, care and diversity – within which, as symbolised by Joseph's multicoloured cloak, lies the beauty, strength and wonder of life itself.

ENHANCEMENTS

Wendy L Schultz

Over the last decade or so, we have seen the tide of populism rising everywhere. Populism is defined as 'support for the concerns of ordinary people' or 'appealing to or being aimed at ordinary people'. This begs the question, what is ordinary? And who among us would want to be merely ordinary? Garrison Keillor's description of the 'ordinary' Minnesota town of Lake Woebegone comes to mind – 'Welcome to Lake Woebegone, where all the women are strong, all the men are good-looking, and all the children are above average.'

Keillor's Lake Woebegone is imaginary, and pokes wry fun at middle-class, 'ordinary' America. But is Lake Woebegone actually the future? What will average be anywhere in the world, in an era of human performance enhancement? When everyone is augmented, who is 'ordinary'? What will ordinary look like in postnormal times? The changes erupting around us will transform old notions about what we take for granted, create novel new forms of humanity, and new human tribes.

Human performance enhancement, or human augmentation, refers to the artificial enhancement of human abilities through chemical, technological, or biological means, or by application of mind-body practices such as yoga. The purpose of human enhancement is to improve faculties like mental performance, physical strength, speed, and stamina. Although performance enhancement is not a new phenomenon, advances in science and technology are promising to scale up its impact significantly in the future – and make it widely available for those unable to summon the discipline to achieve mastery in either ancient or modern mind-body practices.

So, what performance enhancement can we expect in the near future?

The obvious place to start is chemical enhancement. Drugs can improve people's current condition or boost human capabilities. An interesting development within this field is the emergence of cognitive drugs that promise to improve higher mental functions such as learning, concentration, and memory. The next category of emerging innovations is external technological enhancements. Of course, in one sense all technologies enhance human capabilities. Recent innovations, however, are directly affecting what human bodies and minds can do. Better powerpacks and control systems are improving the lightness and ease of use of *exoskeletons* designed to augment human muscles to restore movement or lift heavy weights. On the emerging edge of innovation are more novel technologies that might augment the mind or improve human design at the core by editing our DNA. These novel technologies include trans-cranial direct current stimulation, which uses electric currents to stimulate specific parts of the brain to improve attention spans and memory, and consequently, workers' productivity. Increasingly sophisticated brain-machine interfaces promise not only to boost brain power, but also to give people extra capabilities such as controlling objects with their thoughts.

A range of more speculative technologies is also emerging on the longer-term horizon. One such idea is an exocortex – an artificial external information processing system that would interact with and augment the biological brain. Taking this a step further, the concept of mind uploading moves human enhancement into the realm of science fiction. This technology suggests that human thoughts or emotions could be uploaded to non-biological substrates like computers, thus entirely merging man and machine.

In the field of nanotechnology and nanomedicine, the ability to manipulate human bodies at the nanoscale might give rise to a whole range of human enhancement possibilities such as modifying humans to amplify intelligence, to improve memory capacity, or to transmit and receive data directly to the brain. Nanotechnologies could also enhance the body's ability to repair itself, lowering the incidence of cardiovascular problems such as arterial plaque, clots, or aneurysms.

Artificially grown body parts – via biological manufacturing – are also likely to be widespread in the not-so-distant future, enabling humans to replace malfunctioning organs with new ones nurtured from their own stem cells – obviating the need for a demanding regimen of anti-rejection drugs. In the future, body parts could well be printed as well as grown; 3D printers have already been used to print jawbones, human cells, and blood vessels.

The opportunity to alter human genes artificially provided by genetic engineering is likely to create both opportunities for human enhancement as well as tough ethical dilemmas. In the future, it might be increasingly easy to manipulate people's genetic make-up to make sure they are fit for specific work by enhancing their ability to cope with stress or eliminating the gene(s) associated with impatience, frustration, or rage.

Our increased understanding of how our brains work, and the connections across thought, brain activity, and physiological response, gives us more and more information about how to be better operators of our own bodies. This increased understanding of mind-body practices also provides new insights into the effectiveness of both new and age-old mind-body practices and disciplines such as yoga.

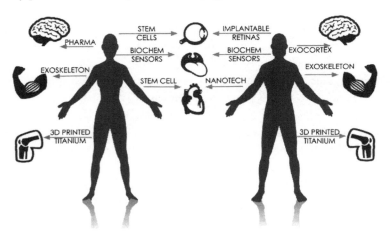

Let's take a more specific look at how these categories of enhancement might play out in day-to-day life, starting with our work and jobs, and expanding to leisure and spirituality.

Chemical Enhancement

Drugs have been used for human performance enhancement for a long time. Ritalin and Modafinil are two of the most popular drugs that boost human performance. Modafinil increases levels of wakefulness and alertness, and Ritalin improves concentration and learning power. A survey of 1,400 adults carried out by *Nature* found that one in five took Ritalin, Modafinil, or beta-blockers to stimulate focus, concentration, or memory. A later study in 2018 determined that over 20 percent of Americans had used prescription brain-boosting drugs in the past year; over 4 percent had used modafinil.

In the future, smart drugs could be used to control people's moods, treat severe mood swings, or provide humans with 'super memory'. Researchers from the University of Southern California report that pathological rage could be blocked in mice, suggesting a potential new treatment for severe aggression. Researchers at Baylor College of Medicine have discovered that mice learn better when the activity of PKR (a molecule normally elevated during viral infections) is inhibited in the brain. Their results show that if they inhibit PKR genetically, brain cell excitability increases, which results in enhanced learning and memory. Once you learn, it helps to remember. Scientists at the Weizmann Institute of Science in Israel prevented cognitive decline in rats with the help of the PKMzeta protein. The scientists discovered that loading the brains of rats with the protein strengthened their memories. The results of this study suggest possibilities for treating dementia.

Drugs are increasingly used to enhance various other body systems and functions. Take caffeine, for instance, which affects the nervous system and improves athletic performance. Almost three-quarters of the competitors at the Ironman Triathlon World Championships admit to having used caffeine to improve performance and 84 percent said that caffeine improved concentration. A chemical called AAQ that restores sight in mice could potentially be used to treat blindness in humans. Anabolic steroids are used to help athletes build up muscle mass.

Not all long-term implications of smart drugs and chemical enhancements have been studied carefully. The side effects of some drugs are not well understood. If smart drugs hide the risk of changing the pharmacology of the brain, or of creating dependency, backlash to widespread adoption might well arise.

Technological Human Enhancement

Novel neurotechnologies are in the early stages of translation from the laboratory to use in medical treatment or for non-medical applications.

Trans-cranial Direct Current Stimulation (tDCS) uses direct electrical currents to stimulate specific parts of the brain. tDCS is still an experimental form of brain stimulation, but potentially has several advantages over other techniques – it is cheap, non-invasive, painless, and safe. The Nuffield Council on Bioethics currently suggests that tDCS be used to treat Parkinson's disease, epilepsy, stroke, and severe obsessive-compulsive disorders. Reportedly, tDCS treatment could also help improve an individual's attention span, memory, movement, and coordination skills. Flow Neuroscience has developed a headset based on tDCS to treat depression and is seeking FDA approval. When commercially available, it will not require a prescription. Halo neuroscience has commercialised a variant of this idea with the Halo Sport. This device sends weak electrical pulses into the brain, priming neurons to enhance brain plasticity prior to physical training to increase its effectiveness.

Machines can not only help us improve our brains, they can also give us additional capabilities. Brain-computer interfaces (BCIs, also known as brain-machine interfaces, BMIs) are devices that read brainwaves and could let us control the machines around us just by thinking. They can be either external sensors worn as headgear, or internal implants.

An early experiment in BCIs, BrainGate, was a sensor implanted in the brain allowing paralysed patients to reach and grasp objects with the help of a robotic limb. The device uses mini electrodes implanted into the primary motor cortex. Signals routed through a tiny box in the scalp are connected by a wire to a small computer. The computer translates the brain activity signalling movement into digital algorithms, and then transmits those algorithms to the robot limb. The BrainGate BMI enabled fifty-eight-year-old Cathy Hutchinson, who was paralysed by a stroke, to grab objects with the help of a mind-controlled robotic arm.

More recent implantable BCIs include Synchron's Stentrode, designed to help patients control mobility-assistance devices with their brains. The Stentrode is a flexible device small enough to be inserted and implanted via the brain's blood vessels. Once in place, it can interpret electrical data emitted by neurons. It is currently undergoing clinical trials. Neuralink, owned by Elon Musk, has tested its device in a rhesus monkey, enabling it to play the computer game Pong with its mind. Advances in BCI ability to interpret neurosignals are accelerating because researchers are applying evolving AI pattern detection capabilities to improving BCI performance, and applying them to increasingly open-source, large-scale clinical datasets.

External brain-machine interfaces are commercially available now. They are both less expensive and less risky, but signal capture is less complete. Among the first such devices is the Emotiv EPOC, which is a multi-channelled wireless headset that detects the brain's electric signals regarding facial expressions, emotional states, or intent, and translates them into software instructions. A simpler example is the iBrain from Neurovigil. This light-weight BMI consists of a basic fabric headband that holds a tiny device containing a small electrode close to the skull. The iBrain reads single-channel brainwave activity and transmits it wirelessly back to a computer. As an example of a single-function BMI application, the Neurowear Mico headset reads brainwaves for the very specific application of letting your mood choose the next song you hear.

'Exocortex' refers to expanding the capabilities of the human brain by direct link-up to external memory and processing technologies. This could be any combination of artificial external information processing devices that augment a brain's biological cognitive processes. An individual's exocortex could consist of linked external memory modules, processors, IO devices and software systems that would interact with, and augment, a person's natural brain functions. Mobile phones and other essential electronic devices are sometimes described as proto-exocortices. Individuals with significant exocortices, classified as cyborgs or transhumans, are expected to emerge after 2030. Although the exocortex is not a popular concept among the general public, futurists and scientists believe that it is a tool that will help humans cope with ever-increasing information load and shortening attention spans.

Kernel is one company working to evolve technological capabilities in mind/body/machine interfaces (MBMIs). Kernel's team want to create a 'neuroprosthesis' that will help people to learn faster, remember more, and co-evolve with artificial intelligences. They are beginning with work on approaches to measure and stimulate the electrical impulses of masses of neurons.

Mind uploading, or non-biological personality storage, suggests that cognitive processing can be implemented on substrates other than our current neurons. This might be achieved by incrementally replacing neurons with synthetic neuron-equivalents. Thus, the 'software' of a person – the thoughts, emotions, or humour – could be uploaded to computers. Mind uploading could allow humans to inhabit computer networks and engage with computer programs as if they were artificial worlds. Advances in molecular manufacturing could, on the other hand, reverse the uploading process and print humans with flesh and bones but with minds enhanced from the virtual experience. The technology is still speculative, but adherents forecast that if mind uploading becomes possible, virtual experiences will be indistinguishable from physical experiences by 2050. Mind uploading also raises the prospect of digital immortality.

A number of technology devices promise to restore or augment natural sensory abilities. Subretinal implants inserted under the retina have allowed blind people to see shapes and objects. Researchers believe that this technology could change the lives of patients with retinitis pigmentosa, which affects nearly 200,000 people globally. Advanced nanomaterials – flexible carbon nanotubes and quantum dots – are helping accelerate creation of artificial retinas that could detect both patterns of incoming light and changes in light intensity. Potentially more effective solutions are evolving in bio-nano-materials research, adapting the photosynthetic membranes that convert light to chemical energy in plants, which also generates a small electrical charge. These already function at the nano-scale, would not corrode as metal sensors do, and could use the eye's lens itself to capture images, rather than bulky glasses.

Cochlear implants are small electronic devices that provide a sense of sound to deaf or nearly deaf individuals and can therefore restore or augment the sense of hearing. By the end of 2019, approximately 736,900 registered devices had been implanted worldwide. Traditional cochlear implants stimulate the remaining nerves in the cochlea with electrical charges; research suggests that stimulating nerves with infrared light could offer greater sound resolution.

Haptics technology gives people the sense of touch in computer generated environments or during telework and tele-operations – it allows people to experience touch over a distance. Innovations in 'contactless haptics' involve air jets or ultrasonic radiation to simulate touch and could also vary temperature and other sensations. Haptics could be designed to 'amplify' the sense of touch, allowing people to 'feel' micro- and nano-textures. Artificial noses, consisting of chemical sensors connected to computers, could potentially restore the sense of smell, or amplify the sense of smell by, in one example, connecting mass spectrometers into the brain-machine circuit.

Exoskeletons are external mechanical frames powered by small motors that attach directly to the human body. They are used both to rehabilitate and to augment human performance: they can help restore movement where limbs are damaged, or amplify workers' strength in moving heavy objects. The evolution of exoskeletons can be illustrated with two examples – General Electric's prototype from the 1960s, and the muscle suit developed recently by Hiroshi Kobayashi's team at the Tokyo University of Science.

General Electric's Hardiman was funded by the U.S. military and was designed to mimic users' natural movements, enabling them to lift heavy weights. The suit itself weighed 1,500 lbs. and included twenty-eight joints and two grasping arms connected by a complex hydraulic and electronic network. In contrast, the wearable robot developed more recently in Japan comes with PAMs – pneumatic artificial muscles. Affixed to the hips and shoulders, the lightweight exoskeleton enables users to carry items as heavy as 40 kilograms with little to no difficulty.

Exoskeletons are already becoming widespread. In 2012, thirty-two-year-old Claire Lomas demonstrated their application in sports – she completed a sixteen-day marathon wearing a 40-pound exoskeleton strapped to her lower body. Currently, wider adoption could be stifled by their high price – the suit worn by Lomas cost £43,000. But as prices drop and the technology becomes widespread, other potential problems could include exoskeleton-enhanced accidents, vandalism, or violence in the workplace – or exoskeleton-enhanced crime.

Nano, Bio and Genetic Enhancements

Nanomedicine is the medical application of nanotechnology. It has two goals: 1) to understand how the biological machinery inside living cells works at the nanoscale; 2) to re-engineer nanostructures and apply them to disease treatment. Nanotechnology may initially enable innovative medical treatments, such as remotely operated microsurgical procedures and cardiovascular repair from within arteries. Researchers have recently demonstrated a nanotech-based adaptive delivery carrier for biochemical therapies formed by small molecules which self-assemble under specific temperature or pH conditions. These could provide cell-specific, targeted treatments for specific diseases or conditions.

In the longer term it could also create a new range of human enhancement possibilities – modified physical appearance, extreme intelligence, and improved memory capacity. Current types of enhancements like plastic surgery or chemical enhancement might become obsolete if nanomedicine becomes widespread. For this to happen, issues related to toxicity and the environmental impact of nanoscale materials need to be better understood.

Recent medical advances suggest that we are already on the road to producing our own replacement biological body parts. In 2011, an artificial windpipe – the world's first synthetic organ – was successfully transplanted into a patient. Grown from inert scaffoldings coated in the patient's own stem cells, such synthetic body parts cannot be rejected and eliminate the need for a donor. Lab tests suggest that artificial organs could be grown within a week.

Experiments in labs all over the world have demonstrated the potential of using pluripotent stem cells to grow eyes, hearts, skin, bones, muscles, brains, and livers. Creating a biologically compatible 3D scaffold on which organs can grow is the tricky part. Recent experiments used 'a near-infrared laser to trigger chemical adhesion of protein messages to a scaffold made from biological polymers such as collagen'. This bio-based scaffold would support natural growth of replacement organs.

Scientists have printed both cells and blood vessels using 3D printers loaded with biomaterials. Printers build up tissue structures layer by layer with artificial cells using sugar as the building material. In an early example, surgeons 3D printed a replacement jawbone and implanted it as part of reconstructive surgery for a woman's face. More recently, bioengineers have printed complex vascular networks; the blood vessels, ventricles, and chambers of a heart; and an artificial bone matrix. Ongoing experiments are bioprinting skin, corneas, ovaries, kidneys, livers, and pancreas. The science is, in fact, advancing faster than the regulatory and ethical discussions needed to manage it.

Genetic engineering is the alteration of the genetic code by artificial means. Gene therapy allows for the replacement of damaged or non-functioning genes with healthy, active genes, with RNA interference selectively knocking out gene expression. A biotechnology discovered in 2012, called CRISPR-Cas9, can 'edit' gene sequences by snipping DNA strands. This already powerful gene editing tool was further improved in 2018, enhancing its accuracy and extending its reach across the genome. Genetic engineering has been used to allow infertile women to have children.

In the future, genetic engineering and gene therapy can also be used to treat genetic diseases.

It took thirteen years and $2.7 billion to edit the first human genome. By 2021, the cost had dropped to $750 and the time to a few days. The drop in price and the increased commercial availability of genome analysis has driven an explosion in human genetic data, with massive datasets available for comparative analysis and diagnostics – leading to more insights about what human health issues gene therapy might address.

As genetic therapies become increasingly cheap, effective, and accessible, more radical and controversial applications might emerge – changing people's physical appearance or improving mental faculties like memory and intelligence. Ethicist and philosopher Peter Singer believes that genetic engineering might enable us thoroughly to reshape the human species. At least one case of gene therapy has already involved editing the human germline of the patients – that is, the genetic code that is passed on from parents to children via ova and sperm. Many countries ban gene therapies that edit the germline, yet where one case exists, more will inevitably follow.

Even without germline editing, genetic engineering/gene therapy presents powerful possibilities for therapeutic intervention. A recent clinical trial deployed CRISPR-Cas9 gene editing therapy to treat a rare and fatal condition, transthyretin amyloidosis. Four weeks after a single treatment, the levels of bad protein causing the deadly condition plummeted over 80 percent. Gene therapy applications for the nervous system might soon become available. For example, an experimental gene therapy injected into the brains of patients with Parkinson's disease improved tremor, stiffness, and other movement symptoms. Gene therapy might in future treat congenital anosmia – the inability to smell. Researchers at the University of Michigan have used gene therapy to regrow cilia – the cell structures that are essential for olfactory function. The results of this study could lead to one of the first therapeutic options for congenital anosmia.

Stem cells have an enormous potential for the treatment and augmentation of various human senses and body functions. Stem cell treatment improves the vision of blind people significantly. Stem cell technology might also cure deafness. Scientists have recreated the sensitive 'hair cells' in the inner ear that enable hearing using stem cells. Researchers at the Cedars-Sinai Heart Institute also found that stem cell techniques can boost the production of existing adult heart cells (cardiomyocytes) and could improve the hearth's natural repair mechanism. Stem cell transplantation also holds promise for treatment of spinal cord injury treatment and for neuro-degenerative diseases such as Parkinson's, multiple sclerosis, and amyotrophic lateral sclerosis. But in future the possibilities may include improved healing, increasing lifespan, enhancing cognitive abilities – or simply adjusting the location and size of fat cells and re-growing hair.

Mind-Body Practices

Mind-body medicine focuses on the interconnection among the brain, the body, the mind, and behaviour. Mind-body practices work under the premise that the mind can affect various body functions and could therefore be used to improve health. The popularity of mind-body practices in the West is increasing. The University of Maryland suggests that mind-body programmes are now established in many schools in the U.S. and around the world.

Although mind-body practices are usually applied to treat illness, they could also be used to simply enhance the functions of the human body. Various practices reportedly improve brain cognition. One such is Neuro-Linguistic Programming (NLP), which aims to improve performance by understanding how individuals organise their thinking, feeling, language, or behaviour. NLP coaching is increasingly used for success in business in the fields of sales, marketing, management, and others.

Yoga is also known to have a positive effect on cognitive functions and memory by reducing the stress levels in the body. A study conducted at the

University College of Medical Sciences & Guru Teg Bahadur Hospital (Delhi, India) revealed that pranayama (breathing practices) and yoga-asana have a beneficial effect on improving cognitive brain functions in diabetics. The practice of yoga is also associated with numerous benefits ranging from strengthening the musculature and joints to improving the function of various organs such as the heart, kidneys, and the digestive system.

Relaxation is a technique in the mind-body field of practice that balances nervous system activity. Relaxation techniques reduce the stress response of the autonomic nervous system and could help people feel calmer and think with improved concentration.

Questions and Challenges

Developments in all these areas are converging rapidly and promise to shake up daily life, work, and leisure activities, reshape bodies and redefine what it means to be human. And many of these developments, which raise deep moral and ethical questions, are progressing without public debate or even awareness. It is also critical for communities and organisations both to understand that various human enhancement technologies might hit at roughly the same time, creating the potential for transformative turbulence in society, the economy, and governance. Equally critical is for everyone to remember that any innovation that arises will not long remain in the use for which it was originally designed. Inevitably, artists will make it a medium for new artworks; children will make it a game; youth will use it to rebel; and organised crime will use it to exploit human weakness. How will these varieties of human augmentation fare when filtered through those patterns of adoption?

Consider chemical enhancements. What if organisations actually incentivise the use of smart drugs to increase productivity? How might such a programme interact with long-term worker health, workplace safety, and employee insurance arrangements? Would firms that incentivise use of enhancement drugs be responsible for ongoing supply if employees become drug-dependent for life? What if those organisations were religious and spiritual centres, encouraging the use of novel pharmaceuticals in traditional spiritual applications to open the mind and spirit and the third eye?

Similar questions can be raised regarding technological human enhancements. Could regular tDCS sessions become the norm to ensure that human attention and memory are boosted at the start of each day? If tDCS use becomes widespread among adults at work, might this lead to schools offering it as an educational enhancement to students? What health staff would organisations require to perform, monitor, and regulate tDCS sessions? How might the long-term risks and impacts of use affect workplace insurance and employee health plans? We could face a future where the built environment responds to people's thoughts and feelings – how could this change personal and public communications? Could this revolutionise monitoring of public sentiment, workplace morale, and employee and customer satisfaction? Would a backlash over its intrusiveness generate new 'anti-thought monitoring' regulations? As information overload is expanding exponentially, people in the future might need exocortices to process huge data volumes to keep pace at work and in daily life. Will businesses provide exocortices for employees in the future? If they do, how might that amplify data security issues? What government regulations might be necessary to guarantee that using an exocortex would not interfere with a person's natural abilities to think?

If mind uploading becomes possible, it will further blur the boundaries between man and machine and run afoul of prevailing public values. How might such an exercise change someone's personality? Will the schools of the future need to familiarise students with the benefits and techniques of mind uploading?

Even deeper questions arise from the developments in nanotechnology, biological manufacturing, and genetic engineering. Will plastic surgery evolve into computer-controlled nanobiomanipulation? Will nanobio experts be doctors – or biosculpture artists? Both? Would such enhancements be lifestyle accessories, or ordinary benefits, like health insurance, or workplace perks, like access to the executive gym? Who will be the arbiters and influencers of nanobio health and cosmetic sculpture fashions? If biomanufacturing promises to keep us all healthy for longer, how will life trajectories change? Will the simple pattern of growing up, getting educated, getting work, and retiring fracture and become more complex? Might simple bio manufacturing equipment be standard for first-aid in all workplaces, leisure and sports centres, and public spaces? Will governments in the future incentivise certain patterns of genetic make-up in their citizens? How will this conflict with parental rights? If genetic manipulation of current and future (unborn) citizens becomes a common practice, what social havoc and social divides will arise between the genetically enhanced and non-enhanced populations? Will businesses in the future increasingly rely on gene therapy to ensure that their employees have necessary aptitudes for a specific job? Will genetic optimisation be the new have/have not gap?

When we extend our senses and ourselves out into the natural world, and into the digital metaverse, and are connected in augmented reality or the virtual reality of the metaverse 24/7, never offline, embedded in digital worlds as the digital is increasingly embedded in us, what will we consider commonplace? Boosting our brains? Recalibrating our minds? Offloading our memories? When we have refined our ability to copy, edit, and paste the grammar of our genome with elegant accuracy, what will we choose to do with the building blocks of nature, and of ourselves? Match pharmaceuticals to our personal biochemical profile to tailor drugs to our needs and moods? Redesign our looks, our cognitive functions, our innate capabilities, and what we once thought defined our humanity, to suit new climates, new ecosystems – or new fashions?

We need to give urgent attention to these, and other similar questions. The ordinary is set to change; and we need to think ahead about how the ordinary might be enhanced in a variety of ways: with cognition boosting drugs, brain-machine interfaces, and genetic therapies. We should all consider what the possibilities of human enhancement imply for societies in the coming decades.

Humans invented agriculture to mass produce food. We invented manufacturing to mass produce goods, and we invented digital infrastructure to mass produce information. We have now invented biodesign to mass produce novel life. We *are* the novel life we will mass produce in the future. As novelty in living systems generates both turbulence and adaptive emergence, our understanding of 'ordinary' humanity, and our inner selves, is set for some profound changes in postnormal times.

NORMAL INDIAN WIVES

Chandrika Parmar

With the worst of the pandemic year's lockdowns seemingly coming to an end in India, the first day of summer was a rather run of the mill typical day. The literal season's change emphasised the spirit of hope after the difficult first half of the year. But any high-minded idealistic dreams quickly dissipated with the discovery of the body of Vismaya. The twenty-two-year-old student, in her final year of study of Ayurvedic medicine and surgery — an alternative traditional medicine practiced in India — was found dead at her in-law's house in the small town of Kollam in the state of Kerala. Vismaya had committed suicide by hanging in the house owned by her husband of thirteen months, Kiran. Considering all social standards, Vismaya and Kiran's match was perfectly respectable. Kiran, an assistant motor vehicle inspector, had been reportedly unsatisfied by the dowry from Vismaya's family. He had supposedly expressed unhappiness with the new car gifted the couple by Vismaya's father, worth 11 lakh rupees. The car was accompanied by the additional gifts of 1.25 acres of land and 100 sovereigns of gold. The assistant motor vehicle inspector's expressions of disappointment were made evident by WhatsApp messages of photographed welts and open wounds on Vismaya's body that she sent to her cousin the day before her suicide. Kiran had been habitually harassing his wife for some time, arguing he 'deserved better'.

On the same day, on the other side of Kerala, the body of nineteen-year-old Suchitra was found hanging in her in-laws' house. For three months she had been married to an Army Jawan, junior infantryman soldier, who was often away from home. Alone, Suchitra was subject to the harassment of her in-laws over the modesty of her dowry. Still on this same solstice day, only a few miles away, at Venganoor in the Kerala State Capital of Thiruvanthapuram, only married for one year, the body of another recent wife, this time twenty-four-year-old Archana, was discovered. It is alleged that she self-immolated. Her parents told police that her husband, Suresh, had been quarrelling with her, demanding more money in the dowry from her family.

Just another day in Kerala.

In 2005, the Indian government passed legislation to combat domestic violence across the country called the Protection of Women Against Domestic Violence Act (PWDVA). Ten years later in 2015, the National Crimes Records Bureau (NCRB) revealed over a million cases had been filed pertaining to 'cruelty by husband' or in relation to 'dowry'. Similar cases registered under abetment of suicide have increased year on year. From 2005–2015, an average of twenty-two women per day died in dowry related disputes. In 2020 alone, approximately 7,000 women – nineteen per day – were killed over their dowry.

What allows for this silence? An acceptance of a split existence is forcibly endured where one believes themselves to live in a society of laws that protect people, yet everyday they are faced with violence. Twenty-four-year-old Anshu was two months into her marriage when the abuse began. Her husband would slap and kick her when differences arose. Anshu reached out to her mother-in-law confiding in her the abuse she suffered. The mother-in-law's response was 'all this is normal. Men in this family do this'. Anshu's family would not learn of the abuse until the severity reached the point where she suffered a fractured arm and serious head wounds. At this point she decided to leave the house. Safe perhaps, but still in 'a dilemma then, because filing a case meant that my marriage is going to break up and we were going to have a divorce'. Societally, still another dark fate.

The National Family Health Survey of India indicated that, from 2015-2018, almost one in three married women aged fifteen to forty-nine years old experienced spousal violence of either a physical, emotional, or sexual variety. Around four percent faced violence during pregnancy. Of the women who have admitted to having faced domestic violence, only 14 percent have sought help. A majority have neither sought help nor told anyone about the violence they have experienced. While the PWDVA has constituted a large step for awareness, it has done little in breaking the silence that allows this issue to persevere. The stigma around speaking out has endured.

The 2019–2020 National Family Health Survey of India demonstrates how dire the problem was prior to the Covid-19 pandemic. 70 percent of women who experienced spousal violence kept quiet and did not reach out to anyone. In Gujarat, only 15.4 percent of abused women reached out for help, but this did not include reaching out to figures of authority such as doctors, police, lawyers, or social services. As demonstrated in Anshu's case, social stigma emboldened fear of the consequences of speaking out in India. This kept women quiet, only confiding in close friends or family who often pressured them into the silence that has become dominant as the norm, veiling the truth of domestic violence. And this was the situation before the lockdown. The arrival of Covid-19 forced families into an indefinite and often quite dangerous confinement where victims would be locked in with their aggressors.

But social stigmas alone cannot explain the prevalence of such an injustice. In 2021, one abused wife spoke up, taking her case to the Chattisgarh High Court. She alleged that her husband had forced her to engage in sexual intercourse with him on several occasions. She noted in her allegations that he had, against her will, inserted his fingers and even a radish into her vagina. On 23 August, the high court discharged the husband, dismissing the rape charge. In the court's opinion, 'the sexual act between a husband and his legally wedded wife is not rape even if done by force or against her wish.'

Less than a month before the Chattisgarh High Court's ruling, the Sessions Court in Mumbai heard the plea of a woman who suffered paralysis after forced intercourse from her husband. In the Court's opinion 'the man's act of forcible intercourse could not be considered illegal since he was her husband.' The court added that it was 'unfortunate' that the young girl had suffered paralysis, but that the husband, and thereby his entire family, could not be held responsible.

Both the Chattisgarh and Mumbai courts cited the infamous Exception II of Section 375 of the Indian Penal Code. It states, 'that sexual intercourse by a man with his own wife, wife not being under eighteen years of age, is not rape'. Avantika Mehta, writing for *Newslaundry*, pointed out that the 'honourable courts' were not offering an opinion, but instead just reiterating what is the official legal position on forced intercourse between a husband and a wife. A condoning of rape culture that cannot be challenged or otherwise interpreted in the courts.

Following the infamous 2012 Delhi gang rape case that shook the nation, a committee was formed, chaired by former Chief Justice of India, Justice J.S. Verma. In 2013, the Justice Verma Committee recommended the removal of the marital rape immunity, arguing that 'a rape that actually occurs cannot legislatively be simply wished away'. The committee's advocacy was unsuccessful in persuading the government to change the law.

In 2016, debate erupted on the floor of the Rajya Sabha (The upper house of the Indian Parliament). Kanimozhi Karunanidhi, a Member of Parliament from the Dravida Munnetra Kazhagam political party, asked the ruling party if they had any plans to change Article 375. Haribhai Parthibhai Chaudhary, then Minister of State for Home Affairs responded with a defence of the 'sacred institution of marriage'. He also noted that it was not justified to criminalise marital rape in India. He argued that 'the concept of marital rape, as understood internationally, cannot be suitably applied in the Indian context due to various factors, including level of education, illiteracy, poverty, myriad social customs and values, religious beliefs, mindset of the society to treat marriage as a sacrament'. It was all rather normal.

Normal won the day in 2016 and has endured until today, allowing for stories like Sheela's to be ordinary. Sheela was married at eighteen. 'I was born and brought up in a conservative family. After my twelfth board exams, my father arranged a marriage with a man ten years my senior', she says. She became suicidal within the first month of her marriage as she suffered extreme domestic violence. She did not want to tell her family out of fear. Her husband would control everything in Sheela's life. He would decide when she should wake up, what she should eat; and even what she would wear. 'He snatched away my phone so that I could not inform anyone of my situation. He made me delete all my social media accounts. Whenever I did anything without his knowing he would beat me up.' It was not just the physical body that he broke, 'he corroded my self-esteem; he broke me emotionally to the core. I started having panic attacks. They would aggravate at night,' she recalls. In marriage, time fell away as Sheela was suspended in the darkness of abuse. She is still haunted by her experience, even after getting out of the situation. 'I was only eighteen when I got married. I am twenty-six now. The time I spent in that house haunted me for a long time. Many people think that a married woman cannot be raped, but I was raped by my husband.'

After hearing Sheela's story, the author and columnist Pooja Priyamvada tweeted: 'lots of things get normalised in a culture like ours that believes marital rapes don't happen, emotional abuse is not valid. Sheela's story is not just her story. Similar stories abound. It could be anyone. Maya, Sobha, Gita, Sita, Janet, Salma'. Sheela was fortunate for when her family learned of the reality of her marriage, they supported her and got her the help she needed. No one wants to talk about what is occurring in our homes or the violence that resides inside them. These are often chalked up as private matters. It is a disease that pervades all levels of society and has gained tremendous visibility, globally, as the hidden pandemic underlying the Covid-19 contagion we are still reeling from. While reports are bringing visibility to the issue of domestic abuse that ranges from Ireland to Turkey, all across Asia, and even throughout the Americas, a deeper discussion remains long overdue in India.

Women in India are conditioned, from a young age, to submit to unfair treatment, even violence, in our society. They grow up being told that they must 'adjust' in marriages. The impetus is forced upon them, the stability of a marriage is their responsibility. Marriage is for life, and it is what 'good girls' do. They keep marriage and family going. The idea of the 'patient, all suffering, sacrificing good wife' abounds. And if they cannot manage, then a different sort of hell awaits them.

The families of divorcees often refuse to accept their daughters back as if they are a commodity with a strict 'no-returns' policy. The societal and family pressure pushes many women to stay in broken and abusive marriages fearing the stigma of being a 'woman left by husband' and the financial pressures that follow. The mesh of Indian society is quick to question the integrity of a woman when something goes wrong, pressuring her to accommodate rather than offer her support for her fight against injustice. The default setting of the society is to find fault with the victim, empathy a rarity. Most families are more concerned about the social fallout of the potential separation than the survivor's need to be comforted. Men, the default bread winners, could not possibly be at fault. A debilitating shame still accompanies the 'divorcee', 'separated', 'left by', or 'has left her husband' tag. There is an acculturation process of not showing the husband in a bad light and putting up the show of a happy couple/family, regardless of the reality. Time is supposed to reform the husband. 'Give it time, things will improve' becomes the chorus the victim is forced to tow.

The complexity spirals out of control when children are added to the equation. Children are one of the most compelling reasons why many women continue to stay in abusive marriages. They suffer in silence as mothers. Or there are other sisters in the family who need to be married and there is a fear that families don't marry into families where a sister is a divorcee. Nandini, a balloon vendor, was struggling to live with her in-laws while she was continuously subjected to physical violence. She told of how her husband used to beat her when she was pregnant with their second child. Nandini says in Hindi: 'I just want to educate my sons now. My life is over now, but I want to educate my children and move out of this space then. I will do whatever it takes, the rest is up to the children.' When we look around us, there are several well educated, professional women who are in abusive marriages because of their children.

In my numerous interviews over the last couple of years, the themes ring loud and clear, declaring the normalisation of violent, coercive relationships. The justifications read like a script: financial security, not wanting to break up the family, a need to give children a complete home, and the key ingredient to encultured silence, 'I am not alone, this happens in all families'.

In 2012, feminist poet, author, and activist Meena Kandasamy took everyone by surprise with a shocking article in the magazine *Outlook*. The article was a very public statement on her own broken marriage. She recants her journey through self-loss and recovery as she deals with being 'married to a violent man who treats me with nothing but distrust and suspicion'. Against the societal backdrop of India, I have painted thus far, it is not hard to imagine that Kandasamy found herself on the receiving end of severe critique from all sides. Most revealing was the criticism levied against her for keeping quiet on her story for so long, something that was contrary to her role as an activist and feminist. She was branded a traitor to the feminist cause for having borne the violence of her husband. In the appearance of contradictions within her various selves, Kandasamy reveals a deeper nuance to the phenomenon of domestic violence in India.

Kandasamy's essay explores the various dimensions of physical and emotional control and violence. It illustrates how the victim becomes lost in the void of abuse through a gradual surrendering of personal and emotional spaces. She follows how the abuse becomes all pervasive with time and how the abused loses agency incrementally. In the early days of their marriage, love won out as her husband's words would smooth over his indiscretions. 'In this honeymoon period, every quarrel follows a predictable pattern: we make up, we make love, we move on. For the sake of survival, I surrender my space.' And as it continued, it progressed, bit by bit. After two months he cajoled her into parting with her passwords such as the one used for her emails. Then he took over her emails 'with the same liberty with which he used to select my clothes'. At first, she resisted his take over. 'Why do you need my password, I ask. You have mine, he says. But I did not ask you for it, I say. You don't love me enough, he says. Possess me so that I can possess you for possessing me: the thoughts of a possessed, possessive man who has made possession into his single obsession. There can be no secrets when love has become a cruel slave-era overseer.' His possession grew as he began responding to emails on her behalf. 'He proposes the idea of a common e-mail address one week; it is enforced the next. He makes personal boundaries disappear. I am isolated from all my friends and family. As an act of purification, 25,000 e-mail messages are erased on New Year's Eve. I become the woman with no history.'

She recollected how 'sex begins to replicate the model of a market economy: he demands, I supply'. She bleeds 'every single time', and he appears to find pleasure in that pain. The first time he hits her, she remembers hitting him back. So, he hits harder, and she quickly comes to realise she is no match for him physically. In the process she learns 'that anything can become an instrument of punishment: twisted computer power-cords, leather belts, his bare hands'. Then there are words to 'sharpen his strikes'. Words to make her feel like a 'fallen woman'. While he 'inhabits the moral high ground' the spaces that she inhabits are condemned. 'Literary festivals are brothels, women writers are whores, my poetry is pornography.'

One day, when she found herself unable to continue to bear him whipping her with a belt, 'I threaten him with police action. He retorts that no man in uniform will respect me after reading a line of my verse.' Battered and reeling from a recent outburst she considers that 'I have no friends in that small world – only his colleagues who think the world of him and his students who worship the earth on which he walks'. Spaces continue to evaporate before her eyes as she continues. 'Sex becomes submission, and in this role-play of being a wife, I remember nothing except the relief of being let go, being let off after being used up. In this marriage of martyrdom, kisses disappear.'

And all of it for naught as the pain is compounded when she discovers his deceit, his living a double life. He had previously been married before his marriage to her. And this was after a grand total of four months of marriage. Trapped in a suspended timeline, living and reliving the trauma, coping as best as she could to get from one normal day to the next. With little space remaining that she could call her own, she went to the police, bringing with her a nine-page complaint in which she detailed everything that had happened to her. The officer who received her said she was 'very kind' and, being handed the nine pages said, 'you have written a novel!'

Eventually, Kandasamy would write that novel – a 'representation of her story'. *When I Hit You: Or, A Portrait of the Writer As a Young Wife* was published in 2017. The story anonymised the narrator to universalise the experience. Kandasamy had learnt that 'being feminist, outspoken, successful and loud' was no protection against violence.

The book is a fictional account of an abusive marriage collapsing, portraying it as a mutual crumbling. The marriage leaves marks on the bodies of both the husband and the wife. There are several instances where the book dwells on how domestic violence marks the body: Thin red welts on her arms where her laptop cord has lashed her; scorched skin over his ankle after he holds a ladle over the stove and then presses it to his legs until she agrees to see a gynaecologist about starting a family; aching where the broom had pummelled her back. A burn – almost freckle like on his elbow where he holds a glowing match singeing himself until she gives in and deactivates her Facebook account; the slackening of her legs, how she learns to go limp when he takes her to bed to punish her, to tame her. The biographical nature of the story shines in a scene where the husband wipes the hard disk of the writer wife, erasing and belittling her work as her labour disappears. He asked, 'should I remind writer madam that she is also a wife?'

Kandasamy's work brilliantly illustrates the banality and brutality of domestic abuse, the devious politics that go into the husband-wife relationship, bereft of meaning to the point of being easily replaced with any of several labels that denote a relationship of dominance and submission. Control becomes the arc of marital violence. Control over a woman's body, woman's spaces, who they are friends with, whether they can be financially independent. Even thought processes are dominated, reason and logic play to the rules of the husband who holds all the power. And the emotional scars, although invisible to the naked eye, leave marks as deep and impactful as the physical ones which mar their bodies in stark visuals.

Real women bear the reality of what is brought into the light through Kandasamy's novel. You would not know it today, seeing Sushma with her two daughters, Pooja and Yamini, but Sushma has a very troubling past. When she was younger, she was drugged and forced to marry an alcoholic man named Prem. Her sudden and radical new life was filled with the routine of daily physical violence that accompanied the other emotional and sexual abuse dished out by Prem. She did everything she could to escape from running to the neighbour's house and hiding, to complying with any demands Prem presented. Even today, Sushma's body is permanently scarred with marks of her abuse. Her lower abdomen features a scar from when Prem struck her with broken glass. Her foot never healed properly after he struck her with a stick. She now has a permanent limp. Stones thrown at her as she ran from him have left their marks on her legs. Each attempt to escape that house – that prison of abuse – was conducted without money or anywhere to go for support. And most times he followed her, ensuring the cycle would repeat again and again.

Once escape became futile, her quest for a solution turned inward. She went out to ask other women how they lived with their husbands, how they went about making them happy. The only remaining modicum of control she retained gave her only the power to blame herself. She returned to these women she consulted, asking to borrow lipstick, lotion, or other make-up to make herself look pretty for Prem. She reasoned that maybe he used to hit her because she was not pretty enough, did not get ready, and was always working. Maybe because the colour of her skin was black. There was a sense that she felt that she even deserved to be abused. To her it could not be the complete fault of Prem, in fact, less and less his fault the more she reasoned. It was on her to make the adjustments necessary to get better. This feeds into a larger socialisation process that infects the way we bring up our girls. Essentially it is a peer pressure that demands that they need to look a certain way to be accepted by the society, and most importantly by their partners. And that they should look inside and question their own self before trying to pass the blame onto others, regardless of the circumstance. Failing to do so results in a feeling that they *deserve* the violence. Or maybe they did something or said something and thus, 'they asked for it'.

Aside from the disturbing imagery Kandasamy relays through the novel, flashes of her shared experience with countless other Indian women, her themes and reflections resonate deeper than the surface level brutality. She clarifies that it is not just the body that is violated and repossessed, but that this dominance carries forward into other spaces. And that there is no protection for domestic violence so willingly enabled and condoned by society. Privilege, be that financial or educational, in this instance, cannot serve as armour against domestic abuse.

Neither the genetic blessings of good looks nor all the money in India can stand against the endemic systems of domestic violence. Several high-profile cases have come to the fore, including: the former Miss India, who went on to be the 1999 Miss World, Yukta Mookhey; the well-known television actress Shweta Tiwari, who went through domestic violence in both her marriages; and the famed Bollywood actress Preity Zinta all faced the stigma of domestic violence throughout their lives. It took them years before they could work up the courage to acknowledge the violence in their lives before walking out on their abusive partners. After escaping their abusers, another cycle of abuse began in the hostility that accompanies those in India who stand up to domestic violence. Preity Zinta was trolled relentlessly, some referring to the whole thing as one big publicity stunt. Other trolls claimed she 'deserved it' for making bad movies. In an interview, Shweta Tiwari said 'people still criticise me for taking a step against domestic violence. But whatever I did, made my daughter intelligent and strong. I want to tell and demonstrate to my daughter I am always with you, but you need to fight your own battles'. She focusses in on the misconception behind staying quiet for the sake of the family or the children, when, in actuality, carrying on when faced with abuse teaches the wrong lesson to our children. She emphasises that in choosing to remain silent, we set the example for our children, who will learn to also stay silent. This norm must be broken by breaking silence today. Tiwari shines light on the cultural frameworks that govern our lives. In talking about domestic violence, even just once, you are already trespassing on the supposed taboo spaces. In opening the dialogue for a second time, it becomes easier for people to say: 'the girl must have some flaws, some intrinsic problems, that is why her second marriage also did not work out'.

Silence is programmed and incredibly difficult to override. Where Tarana Burke and the #MeToo movement have made tremendous strides in the US and elsewhere around the world, the problem is compounded by stubborn inflexibility that constitutes the foundations of the toxic normalcy of domestic violence in India. The domestic family is cast in a powerful metaphor that provokes societal outrage whenever it is critiqued. The family as a symbol of security, stability, solidarity, and even romance, is often defined in a stereotypical sense in terms of love, honour, sacrifice, and shame. It influences the politics of the everyday. Reinforced in tradition, custom, and laws, like Section 137.

The family as a hive of trauma is more fit for psychopathology than sociology, but it may more accurately describe the state of things. Violence is conventionally tied to public consciousness through large scale events or through the statistical mosaic of demographics. Unfortunately, this means that violence against the individual falls out, only appearing as an aside in headlines, as quickly forgotten as considered. Its habitualness is then not even acknowledged, and you can forget about it being chronicled. Particularly in India, but also in many other places, as the pandemic has brought to light, the whole concept of the family needs to be re-read. This revision must capture the origin of silences in order to bring them out into the open. We really need to interrogate the categories, micro cultures, and power dynamics within the family unit. Family as stability and safety remains, but it is corrupted through the pressures of a dominating patriarchal culture where the individual is nothing without a good name or an exemplar family, except for maybe in the case of possessing tremendous wealth. Family also is a unit of coercion, bound to the unwritten laws of shame and honour. Faced with such counter intuitive needs which appear contradictory and are most certainly unsustainable such as the sacrifice of one family member for the survival of the family reputation or the normalisation of violence within the home in order to promulgate the illusion of the classic happy family when, within the walls of a home, happiness is conspicuously absent.

Let us recall the normal in terms of an Indian household. One in three women suffers physical and sexual violence at home. That third of women are faced with shrinking personal and emotional spaces, the peer pressure to remain quiet cuts off most available help, and the only avenue left to many, the family, is dependent upon its honour and reputation over the wellbeing of its individual components. At least in this scenario, women may get the relief of their spouse going to work or the ability to go outside and breath, at least momentary, free air. But the Covid-induced nationwide lockdown, which began on 24 March 2020, cut off all that relief, and now the victims were confined to perpetual proximity with their abusers. A national disaster was on the horizon with millions of migrant workers racing, often for their lives, to get home while the other half of society found themselves in home – as a prison. Without the ability for many to work and the uncertainty of how much aid would be made available, tensions were at their highest and for many wives, their worst nightmare was now something they would not be able to wake up from in the foreseeable future.

During the first twenty-five days of the lockdown, the number of domestic violence cases reported had doubled. The National Commission for Women reported that there were 239 complaints registered between 23 March and 16 April 2020. This more than doubled the reports from the preceding twenty-five-day period. Women's organisations across the country also reported a surge in the number of distress calls being received during this phase. The self-quarantine was a less than apt term to describe the situation women facing domestic violence were in, they and their abusers socially distanced from others, but never far from each other. After the initial surge, the number of daily complaints shrunk as the lockdown dragged on. With restricted mobility and access to communication, it likely became increasingly difficult for those being abused to reach out for help. Government printed signs and viral social media graphics depicting the phrase 'Stay Home, Stay Safe' accompanied by a warm home and the national flag – *Tirangā* – were oblivious to the open mockery they posed to victims of domestic violence. While physical violence was more apparent, sexual violence during the pandemic amplified its depravity to include coercive sex, non-consensual sexual intercourse, and not using or not allowing the use of contraceptives. Help organisations not only struggled to provide case to case assistance, but also to answer increased number of calls for contraceptives and emergency contraception. The limitations on mobility were one thing, but as supply chains broke down, a despair settled in.

Shanti, a resident of Lucknow, told me: the 'government says that this lockdown is necessary. But it has become a problem for me. Earlier he would be out for his job. I only had to deal with him at night. Now he is at home. He wants sex at any time. His usage has increased. He monitors me and all my activities. If I reply to him, then he beats me up. I have no choice. Rather than dealing with this, I would prefer to die with Corona'. In Chennai, thirty-five-year-old Pushpa spoke of her experience in the days before 24 March 2020. 'My torture used to last for barely an hour.' During the lockdown, 'I am harassed 24/7 as my husband remains home and is denied alcohol'. Chennai and Bangalore police received numerous calls from wives of techies and businessmen too. However, the wives and partners were reluctant to give a written petition. Sometimes, women would call the control room but disconnect the line before giving details.

In 24 Parganas, West Bengal, a thirty-four-year-old woman called the city helpline facilitated by Swayan, an NGO working in the space, explaining how her husband, who had abandoned her eight years ago for another woman, suddenly returned during the lockdown. 'He is now sexually abusing me daily' she sobbed into the phone. Archana, a twenty-four-year-old from Delhi echoed an all too familiar sentiment amongst victims of domestic violence when she put a question to her neighbour, 'whom do I fight, the distant fear of the Coronavirus or immediate fear of my husband who slaps me just because the *dal* was not cooked properly today?'

So, what is this space called the home – the domestic? We use domestic space in opposition to the idea of the public space. The domestic is the source of the private, the intimate, the familial. The very ecology of the domestic blinds us to the intensity of the violence that occurs within that space. We ignore the repetitive events, the endlessness of harassments, the lethal tyranny of shrinking spaces - not just physical but where the body becomes the site for rituals of machismo, where mere adjectives like brutality are inadequate. An old saying states that every individual is a home with four rooms, a physical, a mental, an emotional, and a spiritual. But too many have had their happy homes repossessed or reduced to a single, empty room flat, lucky to even retain a dusty, confined closet.

Not just in India, but throughout the world systems and structures flourish that keep such practices hidden in the shadows. It is far too easy to encounter these narratives and ask 'why does she stay?' The main hurdle to understanding comes in the form of over generalisation. The 'typical domestic violence victim' does not exist, likewise there are no 'typical' domestic violence survivors. Moreover, our present world of extremes, devoid of compassion, thrusts agency upon victims in a vulgarity that mirrors the way in which that agency was diminished in the first place by their abusers. Empathy is far too often an overbearing undertaking. Many who read these recanted stories may have gone through such violence themselves or know closely one who has or even continues to go through it, if you are not of the fortunate to have never experienced such powerlessness. These impediments turn us into silent spectators and between the levels of blindness and silence, we abet, together, a reign of brutal tyranny. But, in conducting this investigation, it is my wish that this is not where the article ends, to be closed and for all of us to carry on with what business we have. A few features have stuck out in this study that might progress us towards provoking a long overdue social dialogue.

As we listen to the stories and engage with life experiences discussed above, three major factors stick out. First is the idea of the normal. The victim is forced to return to the idea of the socially defined normal. See herself as an accomplice of violence. Victimhood is perpetually stained by guilt enforced by social demands for normalcy. The 'new normal' phenomenon demonstrates this point on a larger scale, following a major disruption, we rush to get back to normal, but sometimes there is no going back to normal, do we appreciate this? What have we learned that we will take forward into a truly *new* normal? Second the factor of time. Violence in domestic spaces unravels like an endless serial. The same act is repeated regularly. The endlessness of marital rape brings with it an infinity of waiting. Time becomes eternal in domestic space. How do we differentiate the marks of age from the marks he leaves on us? There is little hope for relief or reform. Between the categories of perception and insanity of time lurks the third key factor: silence. The sheer silence that surrounds domestic violence. The conspiracy of indifference adds a veneer of monstrosity. The long eras of silence without protest or solace fashions domestic violence into a form of tyranny. And the silence of India is layered in a troublesome history needing to be unpacked concerning cast and class, gender, race, religion, and culture. Each time these topics are discussed, it is as if the issue of victimhood is rebooted, and too often left unaddressed at the deeper level. The victim is helpless because she is read as part of the problem. We need to deconstruct and reconstruct domestic space to capture the grammar of violence.

To set this discovery up we need to define and differentiate the contours of domestic space. This time, we begin with the body which defines the body politic of domesticity. The body becomes a site, an object of brutality. Although the diversities of violence visited upon the body require a catalogue of their own, in this exploration we can begin outlining new spaces that account for psychology so that an understanding or at least an appreciation of both the physical and mental can have their place. Trauma loses its potence as a catch-all for experiences beyond words. We can then see the minutiae of trauma beyond generalisation while also seeing the way in which it connects bodies. The repetitiveness of pain and the emptiness of silence, teased out, create psychic and symbolic wounds which are ignored in conventional social science. Memory, fear, stigma has little space in the legality of these discussions. A social space is created in which we find the victim and the modes of their repression. The asymmetry of woman and man as well as a host of other categories of identity can be given the systematic analysis they need. And then the connections between these spaces are lain bare and this is where the societal conversation really takes off.

The law and language we take for granted is ill-equipped to grapple with the concept of domestic violence. Law, intended to protect for the empowerment of freedom, is overbearing in its prohibitions to the point of enslaving its citizens. Language, intended to clarify our ideas, instead muddles our categories and colonises our thinking processes. Language grants power to laws, casting them as immovable constants encased in roles and statutes, naïve at the narrative level, but strong enough to put down reason and not get hung up with ethical contradiction.

Storytelling, I propose, or even as suggested by others, polylogue, can rescue domesticity. In telling our stories and the stories of others we exorcise and deconstruct our language from its misogynist tendency to fetishise the normal, further victimise and disable the victim, and aid in the dominance and proliferation of patriarchal spaces. A more sophisticated language born into the world can wash away the corruption that ossifies our laws. Accompanied with a hearing aid and an interpreter, laws can more humanely map the intensities of pain between screams and silence. We have a tremendous project before us in interrogating concepts and constructs alongside language and laws. We need to shape a newly understood conception of domesticity which will empower us to take on the issue of domestic violence and seek solutions beyond the silence and normalised trauma.

Let us talk about it. Let us break the silence.

SLAPSTICK TRAGEDY

James Brooks

The title glows in stylised fuchsia, purple, and white lettering on a black background. A synth melody enters over constantly shifting chords and a programmed hi-hat. The screen cuts to a blast of vibrant coastal light and the camera pans behind young, suntanned, sunburnt, mostly female, bodies – arms aloft in skimpy swimwear, dancing, jumping in slow motion – as the four-four beat rises up from underneath the music, prefiguring the 'drop'. The camera floats now among them, staying mostly at torso level, cutting off their heads. The first clear point of focus, as an ultra-processed vocal melody enters the soundtrack, is a bronzed midriff which the camera glides down to land on smoothly gyrating hips covered by yellow bikini bottoms. The camera points skyward for the second, panning across the elated face of a reveller as she shakes her head and holds the neon orange funnel and neon green tube of a beer bong up to the cloudless sky.

A weird vocal sample – 'You guys, oh my God!', sounding as if recorded on a cranky dictaphone – enters and then, there *is* the drop. A paralyzingly powerful bassline shudders to life, overwhelming the speakers. A man in baggy blue beach shorts, his face obscured by the beer can he drinks from, grabs his crotch. Bikini-clad buttocks are twerked in slo-mo and, in one of the few shots to outlast the two-second mark, beer pours over shimmying, enhanced breasts. There's a cut, but it's only to a close-up of the shimmying, enhanced breasts. Middle fingers are raised, tongues extended and a man mimes masturbation with an open beer bottle. You think this scene, such as it is, will end as the music relents and the camera floats around a group of women suggestively sucking red, white and blue ice lollies sat in a patch of beach grass, but no, there's more. A line of women lie face up on the sand, propped up on their elbows, drinking beer that pours on them from cans held at crotch-level by men standing over them, imitating urination. White teeth are bared in belligerent ecstasy. It ends in a smash cut to black as reverb from the stopped soundtrack drifts spectrally out into the darkness.

This scene opens Harmony Korine's 2012 *Spring Breakers*. Korine is a singular figure in independent cinema. Despite now approaching his fiftieth birthday, he is still referred to as an *enfant terrible*, which stems, at least partially, from the visceral nature of his best work (the other part doubtless comes from the ramshackle public persona he cultivated in his early career). The sequences in his films are rarely as bombastic and in-your-face as the *Spring Breakers* opening but otherwise, in its intense physicality and withholding of moral judgement, that scene is consistent with much of the rest of his output. Any other director may have laced the sequence with a sense of moral corruption or, more likely, let the plot unfold to make such orgiastic thrill-seeking seem morally suspect in retrospect. Not Korine – he is happy to shoot a scene of (literally) naked hedonism and let it stand as exactly that. His four most effective feature-length films are all driven by a concern for the material world – with human bodies the most frequent point of focus – apparently unencumbered by any desire to make it conform to our psychological, narrative, moral, or other metaphysical expectations. Such a 'blank' approach is prevalent in avant-garde filmmaking, and ubiquitous in the kinds of films shown as installations in galleries, but rarely practiced with such dedication in general-release features. Accordingly, his films have been derided as pretentious and self-indulgent. But their startling originality has also been praised, perhaps most effusively by the late Roger Ebert when he wrote that Korine 'belongs on the list with Godard, Cassavetes, Herzog, Warhol, Tarkovsky, Brakhage and others who smash conventional movies and reassemble the pieces'.

I'm not sure that Korine does belong in such rarefied company. Even so, like those directors and unlike most of his well-known art-house contemporaries, Korine is able to extract the raw material of existence buried under a cacophony of societal and cultural narratives. He achieves this via an idiosyncratic filmmaking style that combines elements of improvisation, cinéma verité, and, in his early films at least, an almost total disregard for plot. That Korine got his break as a scriptwriter – for Larry Clark's game-changing and controversial 1995 movie *Kids* – is ironic, because his films often pay scant attention to the original screenplay. With the exception of one exchange between the lead characters, his second feature, *Julien Donkey-Boy*, dispensed with one entirely. Korine is instead reliably open to anything that occurs or is present on location (he doesn't use sets) which may include interactions with local residents or passers-by. If something or someone appeals to his greedy eye there's a good chance it'll end up in the final cut. He always wants to shoot 'the real world', even if he dresses it in fictional garb.

Korine, then, is a materialist working in a medium dominated by idealists. I mean this in the philosophical sense, where 'idealists' are not people who follow lofty ideals or high moral principles (surely no-one could reasonably accuse Hollywood filmmakers, at least, of that). I'm talking about filmmakers for whom the physical matter in their films is subservient to the plot, to character development or overarching meaning: its ideas, in other words. The predominance of such idealism in cinema is why bodies seem strangely immaterial to most films, no matter the genre. In most modern movies, bodies are endlessly pliant vessels in service of characters' motivations, rather than the essential physical matter underlying and limiting all human experience – a development which has only accelerated with the introduction of computer-based post-production techniques. Accordingly, modern movie characters are rarely properly grounded in any specific, contingent corporeality. In simplified terms, they don't have to look a certain way. This, in turn, means that their appearance is determined by external factors, of which the principle one will be whatever is deemed to be 'attractive' in the dominant culture, therefore ensuring saleability in the mass market. That is why there are perfectly proportioned gym-honed young adults cavorting onscreen at your local multiplex right now.

Spring Breakers was Korine's first film to cast bona fide film stars and not hide their looks under make-up and/or drastic wardrobe choices. And even in that film, the experiences of his four lead characters – three of which were played by former Disney starlets – were contingent upon their lissom, post-pubescent bodies. Before *Spring Breakers*, the conventional film-star physique was rarely in evidence in Korine's films; he was after more interesting bodies. As Korine disclosed to *Vertigo Magazine* shortly after the release of his first feature-length film, 1997's *Gummo*,

I cast purely visually, I never make people audition or read or do any of that stuff. I know that if someone looks a certain way I want to photograph them. That's all that really matters to me. I just want to photograph different types of people, different faces.

Both in form and content, *Gummo* can be understood as the blueprint for Korine's subsequent films. It tracks a loosely intersecting band of characters living on the poverty-stricken fringes of the tornado-blasted backwater of Xenia, Ohio. The town's disintegration is presented in bodily terms by the opening voiceover:

A few years ago, a tornado hit this place. It killed the people, left and right. Dogs died. Cats died. Houses were split open and you could see necklaces hanging from branches of trees. People's legs and neck bones were sticking out. Oliver found a leg on his roof. A lot of people's fathers died and were killed by the great tornado. I saw a girl fly through the sky and I looked up her skirt. Her skull was smashed.

The first diegetic words spoken onscreen come from scraggly teenager Tummler (Nick Sutton). In the middle of a make-out session in the front seat of a wrecked car, he pulls back and tells his partner (Lara Tosh) blankly, 'You have a lump in your titty.' We only see this girl once again, in a hospital bed surrounded by relatives with helium balloons printed with well-wishing messages floating pathetically in the air. She delivers her lines straight to camera, a tight close-up on her face:

The doctor said they're gonna have to take off one of my boobies and I know what happens when they do that. Boys'll stop looking at me and once, when I finally meet a guy that likes me, and he sees my scar, he'll just stop talking to me for no reason. Boys are like that.

Gummo is a film concerned with how people's lives are circumscribed by the physical, including by their bodies. It is also a film that makes physical absence palpable. Both Tummler and Solomon (Jacob Reynolds), his friend who accompanies him for most of the movie, have had a parent die. This is never belaboured but just referenced in two scenes, one with each of them and their surviving parent. The scene in which scrawny Solomon performs exercises in front of a dance-studio-style mirror in his dilapidated basement while his mother tap-dances in his father's old shoes is both absurd and poetic, and conjures a sense of a showbusiness act carrying on with ever shabbier performances long after its main star, and the audience, has left.

The film's overall structure can feel as if it too has been ripped apart by a tornado, with its logical sequence blown free of its foundations, transported aerially, mixed up and then deposited in disorientating new arrangements. There are unexplained nightmarish anomalies sometimes featuring never-seen again characters, which seem almost to have been sucked in from other nearby films. These include: an unidentified girl narrating a tale of sexual abuse over shots of herself (or maybe someone else?) playing alone by a large muddy puddle at the back of a house; home-video-style footage of redneck teens airing their hatred of black people and discussing their time in jail; and an even shakier, grainier sequence, soundtracked by death metal, of a Satanic ritual. More than anything else there is the sense of a smooth narrative replaced by discontinuous segments in which characters perform 'routines', be it Solomon doing his exercises in the basement, a boy wearing novelty rabbit-ears hapharzardly playing a squeezebox in a toilet stall or a young woman with learning difficulties running back and forth between a tree and a wall.

In its disjointed way of proceeding via set routines, in its raw physicality, its attention to oddball characters and so much more, *Gummo* strongly recalls the Hollywood slapstick comedies of eighty years before. This is surely no accident; Korine has spoken of his love of vaudeville and in particular Buster Keaton in several interviews. Yet Korine displays none of Keaton's meticulousness in either cinematic design or execution. Instead, Korine's work, and in particular *Gummo*, presents more as an update of the hastily assembled and anarchic Keystone Studios comedies which launched the film careers of such silent-screen luminaries as Mabel Normand, Roscoe "Fatty" Arbuckle, and Charlie Chaplin. If it is correct that Korine's brand of disjointed, often improvised, and physically-focused filmmaking has appeared, so to speak, twice, we should remember to add, the first time as farce, the second as tragedy.

If so, then the personal tragedies lived by Korine's characters are indicative of a wider one – America's. As with *Gummo*, the Keystone comedies were shot on location by legendary studio head Mack Sennett. As the academic and writer Alan Bilton notes in his excellent collection of essays, *Silent Film Comedy and American Culture*, their energetic, outlandish stars rubbed up 'against a bracingly mundane reality, dusty roads, dilapidated shacks, fenced off factories, the rather rundown sobriety of early twentieth-century Los Angeles'.

More than eighty years' later, the backdrop to *Gummo* is markedly similar but the film's feel is entirely different. The Keystone comedies were produced at the dawn of modern consumer capitalism for a working and lower-middle class audience new to the idea of 'leisure time'. They carry in their scratched frames the ebullience and optimism of a society in the ascendant. *Gummo*, on the other hand, is clearly a film made on the way down. While there are moments of joy, its poverty-blighted characters mostly perform their desperate routines as if trapped, with no hope of escape or better days to come.

Perhaps *Gummo*'s most emblematic scene in this respect takes place in a kitchen where a group of the characters, the men mostly stripped to the waist, have gathered to drink and talk. After a few awkward attempts at conversation and arm-wrestling contests that leave the losers disgruntled, the scene cuts to a man wrestling a chair with some aplomb – scrabbling around on the floor, emulating the moves he'd make if the chair were somehow alive and fighting back. The others urge him on. 'Don't let him git on ya, man! Get him over! Get him over!' Up to this point the scene is a retread of the kind of slapstick routine where an inanimate object is accorded sentience on equal footing with humanity; perhaps the most accomplished example is an 'argument' between Chaplin, Normand, and a boxer's training dummy in the Keystone short *Mabel's Married Life*. But then a larger man steps in, picks up the chair, kicks the seat out and the mood shifts to something more sinister and revealing of the pent-up aggression inherent in a life lived within the constricting boundaries of extreme poverty. The exhortations from the audience likewise darken in flavour: 'Fuck him up! Come on! He ain't got no damn business fucking with you like that! Dig his fucking grave, man!' The chair ends up flattened, and with its splayed legs resembles nothing so much as roadkill, uncannily acquiring the characteristics of having once been a living thing, a body.

Korine's next feature-film project would once again push vaudevillian comedy into more disquieting territory, but also add wildly daring elements of performance art and the kind of self-destructive pranksterism later popularised by the TV show *Jackass*. For *Fight Harm*, Korine headed out into the streets, tailed at a surreptitious distance by a film crew, and picked fights with strangers. Korine does not have the physique of a streetfighter; the whole point was that he would lose, badly. There were rules, as he explained to the *New York Press* in 1999,

> I couldn't throw the first punch and the person I was confronting had to be bigger than me. Because that's where the humour comes in. It wouldn't be funny if I was fighting someone my size. They had to be bigger than me, and no matter how bad I was getting beat up – unless I was gonna die, that was the rule, unless I was like passed out and they were still killing me – they [the camera crew] couldn't break it up.

What was Korine hoping to achieve in this near-suicide mission? He is quoted in the *Venice Film Festival Review* relating that he 'wanted to push humour to extreme limits to demonstrate that there's a tragic component in everything.' Elsewhere, he described his imagined final product as looking 'like a cross between Buster Keaton and a snuff film'.

Fight Harm was never finished. After somewhere between six to nine fights, hobbled by mounting hospital bills and two broken ankles (snapped during the same fight), Korine was left with only 'fifteen minutes of pure, hardcore bone-breaking', he told the *New York Press*. He was left rueing his lack of planning: 'What I didn't really think about was how short hardcore fights last.'

Had *Fight Harm* ever made it onto the big screen, or even onto smaller ones, it would have been likely been dismissed outside a few high-culture publications as unworthy of analysis, a forbiddingly nihilistic subcultural product like a death-metal album. That would have been unfair. Once again Korine was deploying his peculiar physically-focused filmmaking techniques to probe fundamental psychological and cultural questions: what makes us laugh? why? where does comedy end and something crueller begin? For sure, if he had completed the film, he might not have achieved the artistic aims he was originally reaching for. But like all his work there would have been insights from his trademark blurring of categories – between comedy and tragedy, intellectual high concept and brutal physical execution, and, as the Australian art critic Wes Hill noted in his evaluation of Korine's similarly extreme fourth film *Trash Humpers*, 'between failure and transcendence'.

Korine's next completed feature turned out to be 1999's *Julien Donkey-Boy*, a claustrophobic domestic drama. The film centres on Julien (Ewen Bremner), a man with schizophrenia, and his dysfunctional family, dominated by his overbearing father (Werner Herzog, the influential film director namechecked by Roger Ebert in the quote above). Shot on digital video but transferred first to 16mm and then 35mm film for a grainy, low-resolution aesthetic, the film looks superficially nothing like *Gummo,* for which cinematography was handled with painterly sensitivity by Jean-Yves Escoffier. Otherwise, *Julien Donkey-Boy* represents a transposition of the approach pioneered in *Gummo* – where, following the lead of slapstick comedy, so much of the acting is done by the body – to a family drama and character study.

Like *Gummo*, *Julien Donkey-Boy* proceeds by way of physical routines, only this time with any humour drained or blackened. Indeed, the most memorable routines are performed as made-to-fail tests set for Julien's brother Chris (Evan Neumann) by his bullying father. Again, much attention is paid to how, in their limitations, our bodies undercut and mock our metaphysical self-conceptions. One of the cruellest (but also funniest) scenes depicts Chris, who dreams of becoming a wrestler and a 'winner', being hosed down with cold water by his father. After repeated injunctions, delivered in Herzog's thick German accent, to 'be a man and quit that moody brooding', Chris cannot obey the command to stop shivering. He is castigated, 'A winner doesn't shiver!'

Paradoxically, while the able-bodied characters in *Julien Donkey-Boy* are frequently pushed up against and discomfited by their bodily limitations, the disabled characters overwhelmingly transcend them. We meet the family's armless neighbour (Alvin Law) who, after wowing Julien's father with a card trick performed with his feet, tells him about 'positive thinking. I know it sounds like crap but it works for me.' The father's response is to reject this. 'You're a cheater', he tells the man. We also meet visitors to the centre for blind people where Julien works who include a talented rapper (Victor Varnado) and a bubbly young girl (Chrissy Kobylak) who relates that she would never have conceived of herself as blind had others not foist that label upon her: 'I used to think that I could see a lot, but I found out that I couldn't see very much, that my vision was almost slim to none.' It is all reminiscent of photographer Diane Arbus's famous quote about her marginalised and frequently bodily diverse subjects, to whom society applied the tag 'freaks' − 'Most people go through life dreading they'll have a traumatic experience. Freaks were born with their trauma. They've already passed their test in life. They're aristocrats.'

Julien Donkey-Boy's greatest triumph, however, is in its treatment of Julien himself. Korine does not entirely eschew the illusion of 'getting into the character's head' via expressionistic techniques, but nonetheless mostly films Julien observationally. The result is a character study that is more behavioural than psychological, with Bremner's fully committed performance given the space needed for full impact. Nonetheless, *Julien Donkey-Boy* also exposes one of Korine's shortcomings as a filmmaker when, in its final ten minutes, he forces a melodramatic denouement on a film that has no need of one. It's as if towards the film's end, Korine loses his nerve in delivering another jumbled ethnography and makes a late doomed stab at closing a non-existent narrative arc.

After *Julien Donkey-Boy*, Korine descended into drug addiction and depression, re-emerging around 2003 to document his friend David Blaine's stunt where he lived in a Perspex box hung above the River Thames in London for forty-four days. Rather than return to the grimy low-budget filmmaking that made his name, Korine's next full-length feature, which hit cinemas five years later, was the $8.2 million *Mister Lonely*, featuring Diego Luna and Samantha Morton, both indie-film hot properties, in lead roles.

In its first twenty-five minutes, *Mister Lonely* promises a profound, elegant and wildly eccentric meditation on the mythical power of fame. We follow a Paris-based Michael Jackson impersonator (Luna) busking in full Dangerous-era outfit in the Jardin des Tuileries and talking to his agent (Leos Carax, another unconventional film director) who specialises in lookalikes. He is on a sad quest to achieve transcendence by inhabiting the body of another. This is made explicit in his opening monologue whispered over images of nuns performing a river baptism on an infant.

I have never felt comfortable the way I am. All I want is to be better than myself, to become less ordinary and to find some purpose in this world. It is easier to see things in others, to see things you admire and then try and become that. To own a different face, to dance a different dance, and sing a different song. It is out there waiting for us, inviting us to change. It is time to become who we are not. To change our face and become who we want to be. I think the world is a better place that way.

The film even starts probing the question of whether our emulation of the famous – the dematerialised gods of secular culture, their iconic images everywhere – is a subconscious attempt to join them in the symbolic world and attain immortality. In one tragic and unsettling scene, the impersonator entertains the dementia-afflicted inhabitants of a care home. In between dance moves, he tells them,

You know something? If you want, you can live forever. Don't think because you're old you have to die. Who says that? That's not true! We can live forever, yeah! Let's be children forever! Let's be the age we wanna be!

A separate storyline involving – wait for it – missionary nuns who discover they can jump out of planes at altitude and survive unscathed, builds obliquely on this theme. In these segments, Werner Herzog does another powerful turn for Korine as a German priest. But the film never delivers on its immense initial promise. The Michael Jackson impersonator joins other celebrity lookalikes on a commune in the Scottish Highlands, which makes for sumptuous and surreal visuals, and not much more. The sections with Herzog and the skydiving nuns are more enjoyable but still not compelling. Towards the end, Korine once again contrives a sudden melodramatic denouement, this time even more jarring than *Julien Donkey Boy*'s.

Mister Lonely has all the hallmarks of a film made by a once promising filmmaker unable either to recapture his early, punky vitality or develop a fulfilling mature style. It seemed likely that he would be destined for a career directing more conventional films, mostly using the scripts of others, with diminishingly frequent flashes of brilliance. Instead, Korine made a pair of films that return to the bracingly materialist orientation of his early work – where existence is grounded in bodily reality – but where his characters' surrender to their bodily desires pushes them (both the characters and the films) into the realms of fantasy. In this way both films are dissections of the

American Dream, itself built on the endless stoking of material desires and in which, to borrow from Marx, 'all that is solid melts into air'.

Korine titled his fourth film *Trash Humpers* so that all who paid the price of admission would know what to expect. 'I didn't want to fool anyone,' he told the audience at the 2009 Toronto Film Festival premiere. Sure enough, before the film's first minute is over, we have watched three people, fully clothed and wearing grotesque latex masks, arduously rubbing and pumping their groins against the trash. The first addresses herself to a five-foot-high rectangular plastic bin, then two nearly identical men get to work on a pile of bulging black PVC sacks dumped outside a house. Over the following seventy-seven minutes we will follow them around the kind of blasted suburban landscape we visited in *Gummo* (both films were shot in Korine's hometown of Nashville, Tennessee) as they variously smash old electrical equipment, get drunk and pass out under bridges, and sing demented nursery rhymes in screeching, affectedly redneck voices. We will also join the humpers in the homes of people barely less grotesque than them as they laugh maniacally at homophobic non-jokes or set childishly cruel tasks for their hosts. The whole deranged carnival is shot on VHS tape by one of the humpers, Hervé (Korine himself), whose lunatic commentary soundtracks much of the film. Hervé occasionally appears in front of camera, participating in the madness.

It's all fun and games until someone gets hurt, as the saying goes, and of course someone does. In what is the single most disturbing shot in Korine's filmography, after an apparently unrelated scene, the camera is trained on the naked, faintly grey body of a man lying prone in some grass a few feet away, his feet toward us. We can only assume he's dead. We slowly circle him and behind the camera Hervé starts singing a demonic nursery rhyme in his creaky, lilting voice: 'Three little devils jumped over the wall, lopped off your head and killed you all.' At this point we realise we can't actually see the head. The body's left leg is hitched up and as we continue to move slowly around it, we see the scrotum hanging pitifully between the thighs. The shot lasts only twenty seconds but feels much, much longer. More powerfully than any other shot featuring a pretend corpse I have ever seen in a film, this segment presents the body as a paltry *thing*, a simple lump of matter. In their dehumanising plastic masks, copulating with inanimate objects as if with equals, the trash humpers' activities during the film's prior thirty minutes have already stealthily fed us this idea, which perhaps makes it all the more effective when eventually delivered point blank.

Yet for all its grounding in the material and the corporeal, *Trash Humpers* is a profoundly dreamlike film (nightmarish, if you prefer). This is in part thanks to the action unfolding in the ghostly mist of VHS film stock. But mostly it is because, like in dreams, we are witnessing the free play of the subconscious. In this, *Trash Humpers* follows Mack Sennett's Keystone films, particularly the earliest ones, where, to quote Bilton again,

> if one wants to grab a woman one grabs her; if you desire to indiscriminately smash up somebody's car, home or hat, there's nothing to stop you [...] In Freudian terms, Sennett's films represent an aggressive de-sublimation, a throwing off of all the repressive restraints of civilised behaviour.

Korine's trash humpers have de-sublimated and de-socialised to an even greater degree. Extending the Freudian analysis, we could say that the humpers act as if they were no more than embodied ids, following the pull of their untrained libidos wherever it leads them. They have regressed back through the Freudian developmental stages, through which the child learns to satisfy its pleasure-seeking libidinal drives in socially acceptable ways, to their nascent state of 'polymorphous perversity' – total libidinal incontinence. Indeed, there can be few actions more indicative of anarchic polymorphous perversity at play than self-gratification with discarded inanimate objects.

And so, in a way that Freud would have thought impossible, the trash humpers are free to act out their basest desires heedless of societal constraints. They are aware of this. Or at least Hervé is. Driving at night through the residential suburbs, he delivers the film's only coherent monologue.

> I can smell the pain of all these people living here. I can smell how these people are trapped in their lives, their day-to-day lives. [...] All these people going to work, going to pray on Sundays, playing with their children. Why would anyone choose to live that way? That's a stupid way to live. [...] See, what people don't understand is that we choose to live like free, free, free people. You know, we choose to live like people should live.

He is wearing a sweater bearing the confederate flag when he says this – the preeminent emblem of America's untrammelled id – and you half expect him to say: 'It's the American Dream y'all.' He doesn't, but identically motivated characters in Korine's next film will.

From a film-industry perspective, there might be no two films helmed by the same director less alike than *Trash Humpers* and its 2012 follow-up *Spring Breakers*. The first is a defiantly unsaleable blast of art horror, the latter a brazenly commercial exploitation thriller with former Disney starlets in the lead roles. Yet the two films are in fact companion pieces and their set-ups neatly align. *Trash Humpers*'s quartet of miscreants maps comfortably onto *Spring Breakers*'s more photogenic foursome, right down to the presence of 'evil twins' – a pair of characters who look almost identical – within each group. As we have seen, their opening sequences also match up, with both giving ticketholders an immediate taste of what they were promised on the cinema-marquee title-board. One slight point of difference, however, is that we enter *Trash Humpers* with all four characters fully formed, whereas one, maybe two, of the *Spring Breakers* quartet still have some character development to do.

The one who has the furthest to travel to become the kind of wanton hedonist that the film's title denotes is Faith (Selena Gomez), who we meet lost in thought in a college Bible group. We imagine her contemplating the moral dimensions of joining the annual festival of beachside revelry soon to start. The 'maybe' is her friend Cotty (Rachel Korine) while the 'evil twins' – who we first see writing obscene notes to each other at the back of a lecture theatre – are Brit (Ashley Benson) and Candy (Vanessa Hudgens), both clearly impatient for the end-of-term blow-out to get underway. Of course, this being a Harmony Korine film, 'evil twins' is misleading as any moral judgement is scrupulously avoided. And once again, the humanly physical is foregrounded. As in *Gummo* and *Julien Donkey-Boy*, the lead characters spend much of their time in a state of partial undress. Only this time that trope is a commercially advantageous one, as it involves four beautiful young women clad in flimsy bikinis.

The group's initial problem is financial; they don't have enough money to join their classmates living it up down in St Petersburg, Florida. It becomes ethical when Brit and Candy hit on the idea of stealing a car and holding up a fast-food joint with fake guns. Before the heist gets underway,

Candy psyches up her two co-conspirators (Faith is excluded) with the injunction to 'pretend like it's a video game', one of several phrases to be replayed in incantatory voiceovers later in the film. 'Pretending like it's a video game' is the condition of entry for joining the uninhibited exertions that ensue. In a psychological sense, it is an order both to depersonalise – disconnect the inner self from one's body and its actions – and derealise – treat the outside world as if unreal. This is the same schema that played out in *Trash Humpers* with its presentation of the body as a paltry physical object and simultaneous prioritisation of libidinal fantasy over any sense of social reality (Freud would say the pleasure principle over the reality principle).

The heist, which is successful, portends that the quartet's spring break will be about more than letting off steam with a little drunken debauchery, and so it goes. After a drug bust at a party, the group fall in with a dealer, gun-toting criminal and rapper going by the name of Alien (James Franco). Faith gets the jitters and exits early, but the three others stay on and join his crew.

Korine depicts the team's acts of violent gangsterism identically to the beachside saturnalia of the opening scene, and the trio take to both with equal alacrity. Here we are back in the realm of polymorphous perversity, of seeking libidinal satisfaction via any and all routes, of limitless self-gratification. The accumulation and display of material wealth, violence inflicted in the urge to dominate, unimpeded sexual indulgence – it all blurs into one big mass of bodily pleasures. 'Seeing all this money makes my pussy wet!' exclaims Candy after the fast-food heist, and Brit replies: 'It makes my tits look bigger!' Meanwhile, Alien and his rival and former mentor Archie (Gucci Mane, a well-known rapper) concur with Hervé's implicit definition of the American Dream as being more to do with following one's unrestrained libidinal urges than owning a house and providing for one's family. 'It's the American Dream, y'all,' Alien will say showing off his stockpiles of weapons, drugs and cash to his new recruits. Druglord Archie speaks similar words while being sexually serviced by one of his entourage.

Spring Breakers adds elements of sexual and racial politics to *Trash Humpers*'s analysis of American culture. Alien bails the four women out of jail after the drugs bust because they appeal to him as accoutrements. Soon after, there is a scene on a boardwalk as the sun sets where he admires his newly acquired wares. In this world of universal objectification, the women are thus both objects of desire and, when acting on their own libidinal urges, objects that desire. But that's only the white women. The black women in *Spring Breakers* are in Archie's entourage or work at his strip club. They are depicted as mute objects for display or sexual gratification, little better than chattel. Korine might claim he was commenting on cultural misogynoir rather than reinforcing it with such casting choices; I find that reading difficult to accept.

White fetishisation of black bodies and an imagined version of black experience come to emerge as dominant themes in *Spring Breakers*'s final reel and are essential to its remarkable climax. As Richard Brody observed in *The New Yorker*, the film swallows whole the mass media's 'stereotypical and reductive view of Black life as one of drug dealing and gang violence'. It thereby posits black individuals – or rather black men – as the top cadre of players in this particular version of the great American video game and thus worthy of emulation. This analysis underpins a vital strand in the plot because Archie, the local kingpin, is black, while Alien, his challenger, is white (and wears cornrows).

The film's climax comes when Alien, Brit and Candy attempt to raid Archie's island compound. As they land the motorboat and step onto the boardwalk the tone shifts to one of derealised reverie. Diffuse synths float over the soundtrack and the world moves once again in slow motion. We have entered, we know it, the dream, the video game. At this point Korine performs a bold creative trick and bathes the scene in ultraviolet light. The colour wash, as Brody ably describes,

> turns their bathing suits fluorescent, makes their masks glow blue, and—most remarkably—greatly darkens their skin, in a cinematographic version of black-face, with light bulbs (or digital effects) taking the place of minstrels' cork.

In the very final shot, the image on screen is flipped upside down so that the world turns on its head. As Brit and Candy run off down the boardwalk, their newly black bodies disappear out of the top of the screen. The meaning is clear, and, given the actual state of American racial politics, highly perverse; in this fantastical vision of American capitalism, Brit and Candy have just levelled up.

With this shot, Korine, too, seems to move from one world to the next: from a world in which the physical and the corporeal is paramount, to that where objects and bodies are mere cyphers, symbols representing ideas. He shifts from materialism to idealism and in so doing loses his creative spark. This would at least seem to be consistent with any reasonable evaluation of *Spring Breakers*'s follow-up, 2019's tedious supposed comedy, *The Beach Bum*. That film follows blissed-out stoner poet Moondog (Matthew McConnaughey) on a shambling quest to fulfil a condition in his late wife's will and thus inherit her fortune. Anyone expecting Korine to revisit his restrained, surreally poignant treatment of grief and physical absence in *Gummo* will be sorely disappointed. Instead, what we get is a scene near the end in which Moondog and his friend Rie (Snoop Dogg), who was also his wife's lover, reminiscing over how good she used to look performing sex acts on them.

Korine's vision here is finally overcome by the pathologies of the society he once documented: namely, bodily objectification and retreat into libidinal fantasy. But it is more telling to observe what he, following the lead of the brutalising culture he lives in, now leaves out: empathy, compassion, love. And that, at the societal level at least, is the real tragedy.

A WOMAN IN GOD'S LAND

Themrise Khan

'When you see the spectacle religion puts on here you don't want to be a believer', writes Guy Delise, in his graphic novel *Jerusalem. Chronicles from the Holy City*. That is how I felt after performing the *Umrah* two years ago (pre-Covid), a mini pilgrimage to Makkah and Medina that can be performed throughout the year, to pay respects at Islam's holiest site, the *Ka'bah*.

Like many organised world religions, Islam remains caught in a conundrum of extreme interpretations, by both Muslims and non-Muslims, men and women (but mostly men). This latter gendered aspect is perhaps the most controversial element within Islam and its believers.

In Pakistan, my country of birth, Islam is heavily patriarchal in its interpretation and women have been its main casualties. From family planning and reproductive health, to child marriages and forced conversions, to inheritance and dress codes, everything is controlled by a sense of religious purpose. But Pakistan, like many other Muslim nations, is also undergoing a tug-of-war between invading modernity and religiously inspired tradition. As more women graduate from university, fewer enter the workforce. As more women attempt economic independence, even more succumb to domestic violence as a form of male subjugation. As more women ask for their rights as equal citizens, more turn to preaching a narrow version of Islam. As more women attempt to follow feminist principles of equality and inclusion, the more their lives are threatened for it by religious zealots. While there is no rule that states tradition and modernity cannot go together, this dichotomy is creating a stark division between how Muslim women want to see their religion themselves (or don't) and how they are being coerced into doing so by a patriarchal society at large.

My umrah sojourn was clearly defined by this division. What should have been the most spiritual journey of a Muslim's life - with the potential to turn even a sceptic into a believer – ended up instead, being a journey of excess, both material and spiritual, spurred by both patriarchal dominance and female circumspection.

To be clear, this was not a journey by choice, but by obligation.

I had been trying to organise the hajj pilgrimage for my family for as long as I could remember – my mother and two aunts, three 80 years-plus, feisty, independent, but devoutly religious women whose life-long wish was to see the Ka'bah. But patriarchy had stood in the way in the guise of a *mahram* or a male companion required for the pilgrimage, a compulsory requirement for women under a certain age. And not just any male. It had to be one with whom the women in question could not have an illegal sexual relationship with, that is, either a husband, brother or father. Choices that were limited in our family.

But when Saudi Arabia initiated a spate of travel policy changes for female pilgrims above a certain age, a window of opportunity emerged. It was now or never. Despite not needing a male companion any longer, I never-the-less requested my mother's male cousin to accompany us, purely for logistical reasons – looking after three health-compromised elderly women was not something I could manage alone in a strange land. The irony was that he could have taken us on this journey years ago had it not been how Wahhabi Islam defined companionship.

Ultimately, as opportunities aligned and aeroplane tickets and hotels were booked, and visas secured, the stage was finally set for our first journey to a land indelibly embedded in the mind of every Muslim.

I was the child of an educated and 'liberal' family in Pakistan. My mother and aunts, a family of refugees after the partition of the Indian sub-continent in 1947, were highly educated and bold for their time. Bolstered by my late grandmother, the family matriarch, they paved the way for my own independence. From the way they dressed, to investing in higher education, to earning their own income. But it was Islam that formed the foundation of their belief system, particularly in their later years.

Ever since I was a child, they instilled in me the need for Islam to be an unquestioning part of my life. And for a long time, it was. I prayed, fasted, abstained, and believed – unquestioningly. But my doubts began to surface as Pakistan witnessed a religious revival of sorts in the mid 2000s, particularly after the Lal Masjid incident in Islamabad in 2007, a religious uprising led by a controversial Islamic cleric and his followers which ultimately led to a bloody showdown with law-enforcement and forever blurred the lines between religion and State in Pakistan.

Around the same time, as I became both financially and socially independent, more and more Pakistani women began taking to the hijab and the niqab in an attempt to allow religion to dictate their lives. The more I felt the pull of freedom from social and religious norms, the more society around me began to morph conservatively. The contradictions were too obvious to ignore. How could a woman be an astrophysicist, yet refuse to show her face to anyone other than her husband or father? How could a woman silently stand by and claim that her husband has the right to three more marriages but she herself does not have the right to ask for a divorce? How could a woman believe that she was ordained by God to be hidden away at home, when Aisha, the wife of Prophet Mohammad, was the most brazen and public of female Islamic leaders?

Harder to reconcile was the fact that Islam's holiest site lay within a country which continuously indulges in human rights abuses, particularly against women. And this was just the beginning of the many dichotomies the umrah posed for me.

As a woman, the biggest challenge was the hijab, which I have always vociferously opposed and earlier referred to as a chokehold for women, both figuratively and literally. Feminist writers like the late Nawal El-Saadawi have described it as 'a tool of oppression of women'. But wearing one for the first time in my life when we went to purchase the garb for the journey, made me think it was far more than that. It was the loss of my identity as a woman and as a human being. And it provided me with a taste of what was to come on our journey.

The overwhelming feeling of suffocation I experienced as I tried on the *ahram,* the required dress code for umrah, at one of the 'exclusive' boutiques that now litter the country, made me feel as if I was going fully armoured into a battle. A battle against religious ideology and an armour that is one of the largest emerging markets in the world worth billions of dollars. Rhinestone encrusted sleeves, silk, satin, chiffon, take your pick. Looking at myself in the mirror in the head-to-toe garment which includes a full-length full-sleeved coat, a 'cap' to cover one's hair and the headscarf, I couldn't recognise myself.

Not only did this put the validity of the definition of modesty into doubt, but also exposed the approach taken by religious leaders in the Muslim world – that the hijab is one of the greatest signs of a woman's piety. But according to some scholars of Islamic History, the discourse on the hijab and the niqab is fundamentally modern and has no equivalent in traditional discourse. A point more Muslims need to be made aware of.

Instead, the hijab has come to dominate modern-day Islam, if there even is such a thing. Pakistani scholar Afiya Zia, in her book *Faith and Feminism in Pakistan: Religious Agency or Secular Autonomy*, claims that the resurgence of the hijab, home-based female preachers and the growth of female religiously inclined political leaders in Pakistan, is the result of many years of faith-based empowerment. Religious political groups have been positioning the hijab as an active symbol of resistance against the threat of Western values, that have only added to this growing 'trend' of female modesty. Modesty that requires three layers of clothing.

But despite my personal reservations, I was genuinely open-minded towards performing the umrah and welcomed experiencing the spiritual peace that everyone attributed to being under the shadow of the *Ka'bah*. And to spend time with the three most important people in my life on the most important journey of theirs.

And so, as we began our journey to Saudi Arabia, my main concern was, how am I going to help my family dress every day?

Our first port of call was Medina – the city of the Prophet. The imposing green dome of the *Masjid-e-Nabawi* caps the Medina skyline among the desert dunes and scattered disarray of four and five-star hotels. Cranes dot the skyline, reflecting the sun's radiating heat, as even more hotels are under construction to appease Islam's teeming hoards.

I felt slightly at ease on our first stop of the pilgrimage, seeing both men and albeit, *niqab*-clad women dotting the streets and markets, filing in and out of the Mosque gates unfettered. The *souks* outside were full of shoppers, the hotels lively. But in a moment of jarring incredulity, there, in full view outside one of the entrances to the second most sacred mosque in the Muslim world, was one of the most revered international clothing brands, H&M. Right next to a takeout Starbucks and Boots chemist. It was a baffling way to begin a revered religious pilgrimage and would have been the perfect blend of tradition and modernity, had it not been so blatant in its extreme depiction of the two. Particularly as the H&M openly displayed flimsy sleeveless tops and dresses being lapped up by women whose eyes I couldn't even see, let alone the rest of them.

As I browsed through the racks sipping my Starbucks latte, having just prayed in the *Masjid-e-Nabawi* right outside, I couldn't help but think my doubts made some sense.

Medina was a classic illustration of the dichotomy of race and class. Affluent Arab and Middle Eastern women wore silk and beaded *ahrams*, carried branded handbags and wore designer sunglasses. Sudanese and Somali women set up obstructive makeshift camps all over the mosque courtyards to feed their wailing children. Indonesian and Malaysian women ignored everyone else and pushed people vigorously with their weaponised elbows. Pakistani women threw garbage outside the garbage cans even when they were empty. For someone who staunchly defends human rights and opposes classism and racism, I was probably one of the most racist and classist among the hoards as I desperately tried to navigate three aged women through the throngs of indifferent female bodies.

But nowhere more jarring were women's offences against each other, than when I attempted unsuccessfully – twice – to take my family to view the *Roza-e-Rasul*, the Prophet's grave, entombed under the spectacular green dome of the *Masjid-e-Nabawi*. Men could view this sacred site anytime from their section. Women were restricted to only twice a day.

A narrow hallway through the centre of the women's side of the cavernous mosque, led to the small enclosure which could only accommodate a couple of hundred at a time. Thousands of women awaited to enter. Refusing to back down, they continuously pushed ahead an area at least a quarter of a mile towards the enclosures entrance, despite being instructed not to by the niqab-clad Saudi ushers. Most of them literally hanging from pillars, shouting in Arabic for women to just stop moving. But no one was listening. And it wasn't just a mass of women pasted together like super-glue. It was a bone-breaking crush which drew the air out of our lungs.

A lack of orderly management to control crowd flow aside, this was not reverence or worship. As I desperately pleaded to a woman who I recognised as a Pakistani, 'please, please turn back, don't push ahead any further'. She replied with the most innocent of expressions, 'but why?', as she continued to push us towards the sea of unquestionable reverence.

We were all in tears by the time I managed to extricate my shell-shocked mother and aunts towards the exit, without accomplishing our goal. Never had we been so happy to be alive.

'It's the perfect relaxing holiday destination. Who needs to go anywhere else?', regaled our male cousin smilingly, as he sat with four *ahram*-clad women outside the mosque on foldable chairs, eating ice cream later that evening. I could think of quite a few, I thought silently.

Still, the expectation of finally seeing the *Ka'bah* in the Sacred Mosque was palpable. As we left Medina on the final leg of our journey, we were required to stop at the *miqat*, the point from where pilgrims, perform their final ablutions and proceed to Makkah. Ushered towards the women's area, a mass of screeching, heaving women jostled for space among toilet stalls, changing stalls and ablution stations. One look at the chaos and we opted to forgo the experience having already 'cleansed' ourselves before leaving Medina.

Patience grew thin as we hit evening traffic entering Makkah. With all roads leading to the mosque blocked for the evening prayers, it took us almost two hours to reach the hotel, at the foot of the *Masjid-al-Haram* no less. Desperate to begin what they had waited for all their lives for, my family could no longer contain their excitement as the imposing mosque complex, gleaming in floodlights appeared before us. One of the most beautiful pieces of Muslim architecture I have yet seen, it glistened like a fairy-tale in the dark of night.

Armed with three women on wheelchairs, we eventually made our way through the hotel shopping complex and out onto the open compound of the mosque – immediately between a KFC and a McDonalds. Capitalism refused to give it a rest. Our first view of the House of God was from above, on the roof of the mosque under a starless sky and beneath looming clocktower hotels, shopping malls, and a mass of super-cranes. But there it stood beneath us. The cuboid monolith, surrounded by a sea of circulating worshippers chanting in reverence – the *Ka'bah*.

I have to admit, it was fairly overpowering, even for me. More so, as I saw tears welling up in my mother's eyes, a recent cancer survivor, as she finally laid eyes on the one thing that defined her existence. I began to feel glad I came. But as we began the seven required circumambulations, or *ta'waf*, around the *Ka'bah*, a different picture began to emerge. Couples sat together taking selfies against the backdrop. A woman was face-timing her mother. Workers were collecting and stacking chairs in a corner. Children were running and playing as their parents watched. Several men were sprawled out asleep on the floor. It all seemed — so normal.

In between the pain of the hard, uneven floor beneath my bare feet, the attempt to focus on prayer, keeping track of the location of three elderly women on wheelchairs and how many rotations we had completed, I couldn't help but notice how earthly everyone was behaving. It was distracting and yet fascinating at the same time. As the rituals finally came to an exhausting end, it was close to midnight. And on that note, we turned towards the camera for a family selfie against the gleaming backdrop of God's home.

'The Kaaba', wrote Lady Evelyn Cobbold in 1934, 'has never been supposed to possess divine attributes nor is any prayer addressed to it; even the idolatrous Arabs before the days of the Prophet never worshipped the Kaaba, but the idols they placed in it. The "Tawaf" is a symbol, to use the words of the poet, of a lover making a circuit round the house of his beloved, completely surrendering himself and sacrificing all his interests for the sake of the Beloved'. Lady Cobbold , or Zaianab as she was known after her conversion to Islam, was the first Western woman to be allowed to perform the hajj. She described a time when the hajj was both a rite of passage for Muslims, as well as a rite of maturity for the world around them. As we spent our remaining days in the environs of the *Ka'bah* itself, the change in this form of thought, less than a mere hundred years ago, was more than apparent.

As mounds of worshippers circled the *Ka'bah*, moved to touch, kiss, and worship it, the experience was coupled with memorialising it on their phones, as I myself was selfishly lured towards briefly doing. But I drew the line at facetiming it to family at home, in real time. Many did not. But it wasn't this spectacle of religion that confused me as much as it was the people who swore by that religion. Women yelled into their mobile phones mere feet away from the *Ka'bah*. Groups of pilgrims pushed violently to get close to the revered *hajr-e-aswad* (we never could) and wailing men and women refused to move away from the walls of the *Ka'bah*.

As more and more questions entered my head at every step of the journey, the more deafening was the silence that greeted them. The utter reverence and submission that the pilgrimage required, meant that I could not even question, let alone ask for answers. Even my family, who were often disgruntled at the state of affairs around them, were content to bask in prayer under the protection of Allah, rather than wonder if things could have been different.

It was an isolating feeling as I too wanted to bask under the same protection, but too many questions overpowered my reverent submission. Was this the 'progressive Islam' that Pakistani-American theologist and scholar, Riffat Hassan first spoke of in the 1990s? Build seven-star hotels and shopping malls that can satiate the appetite of women, but don't let them dress the way they want, lest they tarnish anyone's piety? Allow women to avail of technology, but don't allow them to marry of their own free will? Police women, but let men go free?

Speaking of policing women, the female *shurtas* or guards responsible for the women's section in the mosque, reminded me of Harry Potter's terrifying dementors. Tip to toe in black niqab; no defining anatomical features visible, not even their eyes or finger tips. They floated eerily amongst the female worshippers, occasionally bursting into high-pitched shrieks as they spotted a straggler. Their pudgy, black-gloved fingers would suddenly emerge in front of my face as I would walk through the Haram and attack the loose strands of hair that dared to peek out from under my hijab. Random female worshippers would come up to me and attempt to forcibly pull my *ahram* over a sliver of an ankle showing or tuck their fingers to pull down my sleeve beyond my wrists. Meanwhile the male *ahram* requires men to expose their bodies.

Egyptian-American writer Mona Altahawy wrote about her sexual abuse at the hands of male worshippers during hajj in her 2015 book, *Headscarves and Hymens*. But this was a form of sexual abuse not many women speak of. For some reason, I felt more violated than if a man groped me. I could blame a man for being a sick misogynist. But what could I blame women for? Being too conservative?

As I failingly tried to find some differentiation between the scores of women clothed tip to toe in the sprawling compound of the *Haram*, I couldn't help but think that surely, other women also saw the contradictions through their overpowering niqabs?

As a researcher and women's rights advocate, who falls under the traditional definition of a feminist, I found it difficult to reconcile Islam with feminism. Despite Islamic feminism actually being, in fact, a thing, or what Fatima Seerat has termed a convergence of Islam and feminism. Several scholarly works have been produced on the subject, which frame Islam as an empowering tool for women. For instance, the late Pakistani-American scholar Saba Mahmood, in her seminal publication, *Politics of Piety: The Islamic Revival and the Feminist Subject*, views Egypt's women's mosque movement as a form of women taking over public spaces traditionally designated for men. Even if it perpetuated the traditional discourse of women's subjugation and subordination to God.

But embracing Islam as a form of religious empowerment is not empowerment if you consider women to be inferior to men. This is not a resistance against the unequal treatment of women, as feminism typically is, which is why scholars such as Asma Barlas and Amina Wadud have objected to their gendered interpretations of the status of women in Islam as 'Islamic feminism'. They see feminism being a Western construct that does not accurately reflect the role of women in other non-Western contexts. It ignores the historical and political role of women in Islam's history, as scholar Fatima Mernissi has avidly documented. A true convergence of Islam and feminism would be for women to believe in Islam as a liberating ideology that does not judge women according to male eyes.

But it is only male eyes that consistently judge women. In Islam or otherwise. As when our male companion noticed a slight gap between my ankle-length socks and my *ahram* and remarked, 'is that how you are going out?' no matter that he never batted an eyelid when I wore Western garb back in Pakistan. What would transforming myself into a faceless entity in Makkah or Medina achieve in terms of my journey into the heart of Islam for a few days, if I practised the complete opposite away from it? Why could I not believe in God or religion here, the same way I believed in it anywhere else? Surely, this was the one location where I could shed all my inhibitions and just be myself. Surely that is what oneness with God truly signifies?

But the dementor *shurtas*, or my family would not let me. I was forced to comply with a set of rules that I had no control over. The more awe-inspiring I found the *Ka'bah*, every time I laid eyes on it, the more suffocated I felt, both literally and figuratively at how Islam had been re-defined for women and women alone.

As we finally returned to Pakistan after our week-long pilgrimage, so overwhelmed were my family with the experience, they now want to go again. Little did we know how the world would change so drastically only a year later.

As I write this post Covid-19, our journey now seems in the infinite past. As images of an empty Haram were splashed across the media, many in Pakistan could not believe that the *Khana-e-Ka'bah* had not proven invincible to the virus. As Saudi Arabia shut down Makkah and Medina and then itself, followers of Islam in Pakistan seemed oblivious of the message, as thousands of (male) worshippers thronged neighbourhood mosques for prayers, risking the lives of millions.

But these images also showed a different side of Islam. In pandemic self-isolation, the *Ka'bah* was indeed a sight of peaceful reverence. Socially distanced from the ennui filled ruckus of consumer capitalism and selfish modernity. Stunning and ethereal in the deafening silence that reverberated from the images, it stood towering and powerful in the gleaming but empty marble courtyard. This was the Islam I wished I could have been a part of. This was the silence I yearned for. This was how I wanted my oneness with Allah. This was what a woman should, and now demonstrably could, be. Free in God's Land.

THE HUNTER INSIDE

Aamer Hussein

Monday. The phone begins to ring in my pocket as soon as I disembark in Karachi. It's an occupational hazard here – people want to know where you are, how far you've got, how long it will take you to find them. I wonder how long I can ignore it, until I reach the baggage retrieval hall. As usual the suitcases are coming in. I pick up mine without a thought. I tell Kashiff, who's here to receive me and texts me that he isn't allowed into the waiting area of the building, to meet me outside. Hobbling along on my swollen ankle with a case that's heavier than it should be, I step out into the October afternoon light; it's hot, but not unbearable. No sign of Kashiff, who keeps sending photographs of where he is. I can't see him. Finally, I understand that he's beyond the precincts of the building and drag my case to where he's waiting to greet me with two hugs. He manages to negotiate a fair price with a cab driver, as his Uber app isn't working. In thirty minutes – one of Karachi's advantages is that you can get to the heart of the city from the airport in so short a time, even with the afternoon traffic – we pass the familiar landmarks of my formative years, Frere Hall's gardens and steeples and the now derelict Metropole, and at 3pm I check into the Gymkhana, where I'm staying. We order cups of tea in my familiar rectangular white room with a Van Gogh repro on the wall. I know that the following days are going to be crowded with what Kashiff calls my surprise guests.

The journey from Islamabad was short and easy. But I'd slept only about three hours: after a very long walk in the city's Jasmine Gardens and then a search for supper at one of its numerous 'markaz' areas, under gathering thunder clouds and flashes of lightning, the evening before my departure, I'd sat up almost all night because of a storm, and given shelter from the rain until nearly dawn to the companions who'd taken me around. They were both on motorbikes and couldn't ride home in hard rain on hilly paths.

I am expecting just one visitor at 5pm, my friend Shama who wants to greet me after my thirteen months away from the city, and to run through the passages she's going to read at the launch of my new book on Wednesday. But my friend and editor, Shahbano texts to tell me she's approaching my club and will drop by to welcome me. I now have two guests to tea. Shahbano orders fries, which we eat while the two of them, who hadn't expected to be here at the same time, discuss the excerpts to be read, while I listen in placid exhaustion.

At some point I'm back in my room and hungry. I order a meal of rice and two curries, chicken and prawns, from Room Service. After we've eaten, Kashiff reminds me to open my suitcase to give him a gift I've brought him from London. I unzip the case. Instead of my clothes and books I see a folded traditional cloth bedizened with mirrors, a woman's yellow dress with a pattern of appliqued red flowers, and recoil – this isn't mine, I exclaim, and dash to the telephone before Kashiff has time to take in what's happened. Reception tells me that I can only call PIA from the downstairs desk; I can't make external calls from my room. I rush downstairs.

It's a losing battle. No response from anywhere. Tomorrow's the Prophet's birthday and everything's going to be shut. The worst of it all is, I've got my whole week's stock of Enzalutamide, my lifesaver, in the case; only one morning's supply in my hand baggage. It's a ritual I'm so used to it's become invisible; four pills at the same time every morning after my first few cups of tea. (I'm also used to the side effects: insomnia, mood swings, memory gaps.) Missing one day is permissible. Miss two and the doctors say I'm in danger. My painkillers are missing too.

But in the morning, after multiple calls, Kashiff manages to find someone in the airport who tells us to rush over there with the case. Kashiff has never seen me so fraught before. I have almost nothing in my hand luggage and though the bathroom is well-equipped with toiletries I'm tired of the sticky clothes I've been wearing for the last twenty-four hours. I need a change of underpants.

Kashiff has known me for nearly four years, since we first met over cups of tea and cigarettes after a talk I gave at the Lok Virsa in Islamabad. He'd come across me through the occasional columns I write for *DAWN*. He'd taken a postgraduate degree in Islamabad and was leaving for his native Larkana the next day. We planned to meet again in Karachi, in summer. He was a very talented singer and gifted videographer. He had a long stint working in an archive in Karachi, where he also took music lessons. I met him once for tea, and once for supper, on my next trip when I was there to complete work on a new book; he attended a talk I gave at a bookshop. But when I returned a couple of months later to launch the book he was nowhere to be found. Later he wrote that he'd decided to go back to his lands in Larkana and become a gentleman farmer there. By the time he got back in touch I'd broken my leg in two places. But just two months after I was allowed to walk, unaided, I made it back to Pakistan four times in as many months; on the second of those visits, I'd already been diagnosed with cancer. Kashiff came to Karachi, travelling overnight on two of those trips, to spend an afternoon with me on one occasion and two on another. On the third of my visits, I'd lost my sister to a savage attack from the same hidden hunter that lives within me; and I'd been told that I was at Stage 4. But I decided to go ahead with a masterclass, and the Karachi launch of my first Urdu book. Kashiff was unable to leave his lands to come over to the city.

But we met again in Karachi when I flew back, via Islamabad and Lahore, in September that year as soon as I was given leave to fly after the various lockdowns. We'd been corresponding throughout the pandemic after my mother died in April, and my disease had metastasised; my treatment underwent several transformations. At times I'd despair of it all, and of ever seeing anyone in Pakistan again. I was in double isolation; like my artist friend Rabbya in Lahore, with whom I'd spent my last hours in Pakistan before lockdown was announced a few weeks later, Kashiff had been a constantly encouraging presence during those days when all communication was virtual. I can't remember how long exactly I was 'shielding' during those months. News from my tests was more and more dispiriting as cancer spread to my bones.

Then there was the reassuring news that I'd responded well to the wonder drug and only needed to attend hospital after three months. And on that trip to Karachi, which was also in semi-lockdown, I saw Kashiff, and Shahbano and some other friends, nearly every day.

(There's an unspoken conspiracy among them all that they won't talk about death, and when I address it, they insist I'll be around for many more years, though the oncologists predict a maximum of four. Excessive attention is paid, instead, to my bad leg. The hunter inside remains in hiding. But though they avoided the subject my friends were aware that this might be my last trip to Karachi.)

A few days before flying to Karachi I'd taken a cab from Islamabad to Lahore on a fine September afternoon, past fields of fruit-bearing trees. As evening fell, Rabbya was waiting under the mulberry tree outside her house to go to dinner at the house of a writer friend after a reviving brew of tea. The next day she'd master planned a drive in the heat of a late Lahore morning to the tombs of Nur Jehan and Jehangir. I have idyllic photographs of the day, taken by both her and me, in the monuments and in their gardens. At the airport the next evening, when I asked her if she thought I'd ever make it back to Lahore, she replied: You've hopped across a continent and up and down staircases with your conditions, you'll be here again. In time to see the mulberry tree outside my window laden with white fruit. So, I'm like the proverbial bad penny, I said. With renewed lockdowns in both our countries I never made it back for the mulberry season.

Rabbya was right. Now, after thirteen months, there's another book and another return. Today, though, I'm unable to reach anyone in Karachi to help me out, as phone lines across the city are shutting down. All communication lines from the Gymkhana are dead. We walk out in the midday sun, dragging the errant suitcase; Kashiff negotiates a fare with a taxi driver. We're almost at the airport's gates when Kashiff receives a call: No point in coming today. No one's working. But we're nearly here, Kashiff says. I lose hope. He politely insists that the guards call the airport official, whose name he's copied down, to attend to us. The official emerges at the arrival gate. There's a long conversation in Sindhi about my suitcase; they've managed to locate it because of all the tags I've retrieved from various places. It's gone to the town of Badin. Kashiff explains, again in Sindhi, that I have life-saving medicines in there and it's imperative I get them back that day. I move away to smoke a cigarette since I don't speak a word of Sindhi and can't really join them. Two guards are immediately beside me to offer me a light. The officials, after another long call in Sindhi, grudgingly give Kashiff the number of the passenger who's carried away my case. One of them tells me that PIA will now absolve themselves of the issue; the exchange of cases is the problem of us foolish travellers who made the mistake and any claims must be settled between ourselves.

Kashiff manages to make contact with the people in Badin who have my case, on the way back to the club. In his calm but persistent Sindhi conversation I hear the words cancer, medication, and worried. They promise, he tells me, that they'll get the suitcase to me before nightfall. They must be needing their own stuff, too. When we get back, we discover that all communication lines have been cut; any chance of help even from the friends who were waiting to visit is out, unless they just show up. It doesn't occur to me to call from Kashiff's number, and I realise he has limited data. Anyway, I have no real idea how they can help, unless they drive me all the way to Badin on a national holiday to pick up the truant case. In my dogged Londoner's way, I'd tried to handle it all myself but now, after the several calls I made from reception before their lines went down, Kashiff took over, and I am aware that I don't know how to manage the system in the city of my birth.

By evening, after several more calls, Kashiff's calm optimism is giving way to frustrated crankiness. I know these people, he says, they're lying, they'll never bring the case tonight, they obviously don't care enough about their own lost luggage: and the last time I told them you needed your pills, they said, Well God keep him safe, which was a way of dismissing your disease as your own business.

Night has fallen; I suggest we go out for a walk on the deserted street, to set aside the day's worries, and wait to see what tomorrow will bring. I'm strangely reminded of my shielding months at the thought of being shut away in my room at night with no clothes and limited contact. We cross a deserted square to the petrol station to the only shop that's open, buy two packs of local Marlboros, and walk back, laughing in dismissal of the errant suitcase, to the Gymkhana under a waxing red moon. In three days, I've been promised a ride on a boat, to see the full red moon rise over the sea.

II

Wednesday. I receive a text from Kashiff telling me the case is on its way. It's morning; I have my launch this afternoon and, recognising the pressures the city of my birth is placing on me, I know I'll have to be at the Arts Council long before my talk begins.

Today the influx of morning visitors, which I often find hard to manage, is welcome. My friend Nasir, who works nearby, is the first: I've known him six years, in which time he's published two collections of poems, and got married, too. He tells me that if he'd known in time, he could have had the suitcase picked up, or delivered. He wants to take me out on the passenger seat of his motorbike for brunch, but I'm still waiting for Kashiff. I'll take you to Urdu Bazaar tomorrow, he says. Then another writer friend arrives, Wasio whom I've known for as long; we've adopted each other as brothers. We've shared news of marriages, births, sickness, deaths, and books over these years, face to face, on the phone, on messenger. He whizzes me off in his car and insists on buying me new clothes, at a fancy boutique in a mall by the sea, for the launch of my book in the evening. We lunch.

On our way back to the club, I receive a text from Kashiff: my case is going to be dropped off at a junction not far away from where he's staying with his family, in the distant suburb of Malir. He'll collect it. He sends a photograph of the case, strapped to the top of a van. It's already 3pm. I know it won't be here before I leave for my talk at 4.30pm. I quickly shower and change before Shahbano comes to pick me up. But I've forgotten to buy new underwear.

Shahbano wants to take me somewhere nice for dinner after the launch, but I know I'll be too anxious to eat until the case arrives. Finally, it does. Without Kashiff. Reception sends it up, an hour or so after I reach my room. I think I've missed two days of medication; it's too late to take my pills now. What the hell. Perhaps the lost suitcase, travelling back to Karachi on top of a van, is going to be another recurrent motif in my dreams: the sheet of misplaced pills, as it's never been before, a reminder of a flame within that still wants time to flicker before it blows out.

The first response I get from a friend who's seen pictures of my talk on Instagram is:

Your clothes are ill-fitting.
Oh yeah, well.

I wonder where Kashiff is.

My friend Taha comes to keep me company while I unpack and unwind after my public appearance. Though we speak often, I haven't seen him face to face since before the lockdown. Kashiff texts just after he leaves, to tell me his best friend's father died; he's on his way back to his village. He sent the case with a cousin and wants to know if everything's in it. Yes, I got the pills, I say. Nothing else really matters. I don't hear from him again during the five remaining days of my stay in Pakistan, nor when I'm back in London. Perhaps the effort of reclaiming my case was too much for him.

III

I dreamed last night that I was about to die in the arms of a woman who may have been my mother. My eyes were closed; I knew that if I managed to count down to zero, I'd be gone. But when I passed the number one, I rose to my feet, lurched to the kitchen, and poured myself a glass of water. I was alive. I realised I was awake: I'd actually walked to the kitchen. It was 5am. Usually dreams of this sort leave me paralysed and sweating in my bed, afraid of the darkness and the day to come. Now all I had to contend with were the last two dark hours before daylight. Then I'd rise and begin, as I often do, to read or write.

I've had strange dreams since I came back from Karachi. One, I think, is recurrent: I'm running through a white underground tunnel. I know it's Karachi. In another, a friend who I have been cautioning from speeding on his motorbike is lying, bandaged from head to foot in surgical white, on a hospital bed. Each time I've woken up with a milder form of the high anxiety which caused me insomnia last winter; they called it suicidal ideation. It led my oncologist to assign me a counsellor, on Zoom, to discuss the connection between the disease and unresolved issues of grief and mourning. Over and again, in the dark months and until spring and lockdown's precarious end, I had to tell her: I had cancer before my sister died. I had a full diagnosis of an incurable form of it before my mother died. So, aren't these dreams a reaction to a year of lockdown, and don't they reach back, perhaps, to older losses, betrayals, conflicts?

Several months before the hunter within me was detected, I had a freak fall while opening the backdoor of my building; my leg cramped, gave way under me, and I slipped on a rain-drenched slope. I fell, if I remember face downward, on the pavement, somehow managing to break both fibula and tibia. Five weeks on my back, ankle full of metal, hobbling to the lavatory on a walker. Five weeks or more with a surgical boot, still not allowed to place any weight on the damaged ankle. Then, finally, a combination of boot and crutch; I started teaching again that way. Then, one day in July, I was free to walk unaided. I know that my freakish accident was the result of unexpressed emotional trauma. I'd been feeling that I was 'heading for a fall', and the feeling proved to be quite literal. It was my body, not my mind, that couldn't withstand the weight – deaths of friends, as well as loss and betrayal – that I'd carried for months. Just three months after my dismissal from the orthopaedic clinic, I visited my GP to tell him my leg hadn't healed. He insisted on giving me a battery of tests and suspected prostate cancer right away.

In the months that followed I was accused at different times by family and friends of bravery, courage, fortitude, fear, and anger. My first reaction to the diagnosis was that I didn't want to fight the disease. All I'd known was that, after hours suffocating in noisy machines with a body full of chemicals, I couldn't bear the indignity of any form of radiotherapy and chemotherapy. But friends and family forced me to change my decision. Then, partly because of the danger of travelling daily to the hospital during the pandemic, I was placed on the pills that I lost in the suitcase. They've been successful for longer than expected but every visit to – or call from – the oncologist is an experience of Damocles' sword.

I can't remember now whether it was one of the many oncologists I've seen since my diagnosis or my counsellor that said I should learn to live with cancer, not die of it. I feel that if my body was whole that might be easier. I hobble on with my metal ankle. I've treated myself carelessly and casually, pandemic permitting, disease and bad leg ignored whenever possible, as if each day is my last. As I reached the end of my talking therapy, my counsellor asked: Aren't you aware that you've published two books and several other texts during this period of grief, travelled to Pakistan in semi-lockdown, taught on Zoom, and given a dozen talks as well? Are you aware that you have friends in more than one country and how much they love and cherish you?

I'm glad I've told her all that. I don't like to enumerate my public activities to myself, am often dismissive of them to others. Though I never take love for granted, it often isn't enough. But complaining to a loved one that I feel neglected seems like a kind of suicide. Complacency would make me lazy. I want to go beyond these hazards. I will occasionally push my body to its ultimate resources: that crazy drive keeps me going. But sometimes I'm so tired that I just want to sleep forever. So, whose is the voice of denial that speaks to my counsellor, and makes her think I underestimate myself? Where is the voice of self-affirmation? Who enters my dreams at night, makes me wake up sweating? Is it the hidden hunter of disease or an older, crueller twin that lives within me? And which twin is the friend? And who is the adversary?

But this body is the only home I have; I have to learn to tame the twins, if indeed they're twins, and accept the doubled hunter, that unwelcome guest who lives inside me.

ARTS AND LETTERS

ALLAH, ASÈ AND AFROS

Adama Juldeh Munu

Photo courtesy of Nailah Lymus

Black hair is a language with many dialects. It is diverse in texture, curl patterns and styling, and speaks of ethnic markers, social standing, histories, joys, and complexities. But it is also a language that can be misunderstood and misinterpreted. Sometimes we, who own it, struggle to understand it. Some of us are tongue-tied as we placate a gaze not of our own choosing, in a system not of our own making.

But today, Black women are discovering ways of speaking their 'hair truths', by going natural, learning how to properly maintain chemically straightened hair, going for the 'big chop', trying out locs and plant-based extensions. Veiled Black Muslim women who have curlier hair patterns (see chart below) arguably hold unique perspectives into the relationship between the feminine, spirituality, and hair. One of these relates to the current natural hair movement, which like the Black Is Beautiful movement of the 1960s and 1970s, encourages women of African descent to celebrate the 'natural characteristics' of their hair.

Chart courtesy of Melanininterest.com

The 2010s spawned the rise of the YouTube influencer and subsequently hair tutorials and natural hair diaries, which heavily influenced my decision to go natural in 2013. But I also felt Black Muslim women were being left out of the conversation. So, over five years ago, I penned a piece in the *Huffington Post* called, 'Are Black Muslim Women Part Of The Natural Hair Conversation?' It was picked as one of the platform's top ten blogs in 2016.

While the hijab is no longer unheard of in the fashion industry – thanks to Black Muslim models and designers like Halima Aden, Ayana Ife, and Nailah Lymus – discussions around hair involving Black Muslim women are slow in taking off. And this is not without precedent.

Hair narratives for Black Muslim women reflect the struggle to be considered 'normal' in the communities that Black Muslims generally intersect. For instance, it could be argued that the wearing of the hijab may create the impression that 'Black hair struggles and joys' are not applicable to Black Muslim women. An example of this is the tussle that Black women have had in places of work, where their hair and traditional styles are in some instances seen as unprofessional. If a Black Muslim woman wears the hijab, that struggle is automatically replaced with the struggle for hijab to be accepted. On the other hand, discussions on hijab and hair within the wider Muslim community tend to leave out the distinct experiences of Black Muslim women.

Despite these difficulties, Black Muslim women are developing their own 'hair hermeneutics'. This is happening at a time that historian and anti-racist activist, Ibram X. Kendi describes as the 'Black Cultural Renaissance', where Black people are 'shedding what and who do not serve us'. The manifestations of this include better representations of Black people across the arts, culture, politics, and music, and greater efforts at self-determination. We see a greater presence of Black film biopics (*Selma, Harriet Tubman*), documentaries and series (*13th, Small Axe*), Black award shows (*Black Girls Rock, the MOBO awards*), the creation of Black economic strategies such as the 'Black Pound', diaspora initiatives such as Ghana's 2019 Year of Return initiative and the first African Union-CARICOM summit in Autumn 2021. Then there are recent music albums that amplify Black empowerment such as Kendrick Lamar's 'To Pimp a Butterfly', Beyoncé's 'Black is King', and Nas's 'King's Disease II.'

Besides the 2019 Oscar-winning animated film 'Hair Love', by athlete-turned filmmaker Matthew A. Cherry and other similar films and shows, nowhere has the subject of Black hair been more prominently approached than through song in recent times. India Arie's 2006 neo-soul classic 'I Am Not My Hair' and Solange Knowles's 2016 beauty anthem 'Don't Touch My Hair' pretty much mean what they say. These two songs also reflect different hair dialects that I believe exemplify Black Muslim women's narratives, and which incorporate their cultural and spiritual ties, that is to say: 'I am more than my hair, but my hair matters to me.'

I propose that 'Can't Touch My Hair' might be another suitable mantra for Black Muslim women, when one considers how the veil and the hijab relate to hair in Islam.

Dalilah Baruti's *How to Look After Your Natural Hair in Hijab* explores 'healthy' hair and the spiritual root of Black hair language for Muslim women. Not all cover their hair, but for those who do, the hijab is in conformity with Islam's sacred scriptures. As the Qur'an says:

> And say to the believing women that they should lower their gaze and guard their modesty; that they should not display their beauty and ornaments except what must ordinarily appear thereof; that they should draw their veils over their bosoms…And O you Believers, turn you all together towards Allah, that you may attain Bliss (24:31).

Baruti does not suggest verses like this specifically refer to Black hair, but she does draw upon the honour that Allah in the Qur'an confers upon the diverse phenotypic traits inherent in all of humankind: 'We have indeed created mankind in the best of moulds' (95:4). The celebration of the distinctive qualities and traits within the human race are also supported by: 'O mankind, indeed We (Allah) have created you from male and female and made you peoples and tribes that you may know one another' (49:13). The Prophet Muhammad is quoted as saying, 'Whoever has hair, should honour it' (*Sunan Abi Dawud*, Hadith 4163).

Black Muslim women have to take into account hairstyles that fit their Islamic lifestyle, which distinguishes them from both non-Black Muslim women and Black non-Muslim women. For instance, while protective styles such as wigs, weaves and extensions (both natural and synthetic) are primarily (but not solely) worn by some Black women, Black Muslim women's access to these are subject to debate among some scholars of Islamic jurisprudence. As Cambridge Special Livingstone PhD scholar, Michael Mumisa explains to me, jurists or *fuqaha* from some schools of thought are opposed to hair extensions of all types because of their reading of a hadith from the Prophet Muhmmad, that prohibits the use of human hair. On the other hand, jurists from the Hanafi school of thought allow the use of synthetic hair extensions. Muslim hair blogger, RaySunshine tells me that some non-Black scholars are becoming more expedient on matters relating to Black hairstyles. She mentions Assim Al-Hakeem, who in 2019, slightly changed his cautious *fatwa* on the permissibility of locs. They are associated with followers of Rastafari which forbids the cutting of hair. But locs are also worn by other Black women and men as a protective style, therefore Islamic rulings on such matters overridingly affect Black Muslims.

The hijab is often regarded as more than just a 'headscarf' by Muslim scholars, and yet the relationship between Black Muslim women and 'head coverings' is part of a wider story of what covering means for different women of the African diaspora. Among some ethnic groups, the headwrap is considered an extension of the hair and can appear as a short, patterned turban that covers the ears or a long flowing scarf that extends all the way to a woman's back. In *Veiled Self, Transparent Meanings: Tuareg headdress as a social expression,* Susan Rasmussen shows veils and scarfs can have distinct social and cultural meanings among Muslim groups in African contexts. In the case of the Tuareg ethnic group, the veil can be used for ornamental and flirtatious purposes for both men and women. And it is considered a sign of elegance which is why young women may take up the veil before menstruation or marriage.

Along the Gulf of Guinea, head wrappings tend to have a more ceremonial purpose rather than a diurnal one. This is particularly inextricably linked to the Black immigrant experience in the West where headwraps are, generally, worn during special occasions. For instance, among Nigerian Yoruba people and ethnic groups in Sierra Leone, *gele*s or *enkeychas* are worn during weddings, Eid, baby naming ceremonies known as *Aqiqahs*, and baptism. In Ghana, *dukus* are worn on religious days by Muslims, Seventh-Day Adventists, or Sunday church-going Christians.

'Mother of the South African nation' and former apartheid activist Winnie Madikizela-Mandela is credited for reviving the *doek,* which was imposed on Black women to 'control' their exoticism from white men in South Africa, according to Professor Hlonipha Mokoena of the Wits Institute for Social and Economic Research. She famously wore one to court to protest her husband, Nelson Mandela, being put on trial for leaving the country without a valid passport in 1962. She continued to wear the doek, inspiring others to embrace their cultural heritage. When she died, #AllBlackWithADoek trended on Twitter, showing South African women donning it in her honour. Likewise, a number of high profile continental African women have been pictured in headscarves, such as Tanzania's first female president Samia Suluhu Hassan, former Liberian president Ellen Johnson-Sirleaf , former Malawian president Joyce Banda and former African Union head Nkosazana Dlamini-Zuma.

Photo taken from director Nijla Mu'min's film '*Jinn*' (2018)

In the larger Black Atlantic diaspora, head coverings came to represent European colonial domination over enslaved populations. When enslaved Africans stepped off the slave ship in the New World, hairstyles and coverings that represented their various ethnicities, lineages, languages, religion and marital status were shaved or stripped off, thereby symbolising the cultural and physical uprooting that was intrinsic to the chattel slave experience. *Essence*'s 2020 'Respect Our Roots' article details the psychological and mental trauma that enslaved African women would have experienced, and how hair came to reflect their struggle for survival:

Before the captured boarded the slave ships, traffickers shaved the heads of the women in a brutal attempt to strip them of their humanity and culture. Perhaps colonisers recognised the significance of the elaborate strands. In any case, they sought to take away the women's lifeline to their homeland. As the women endured the rigors of slavery in America, braids became more functional.... [So] braiding becomes a practical thing... [Hairstyles needed to] last an entire week.

The overarching degradation of enslaved peoples was codified in a series of laws that set the stage for the appalling race relations that are central to the story of the United States.

During the eighteenth century, enslaved Africans in South Carolina were required by the 1735 Negro Act to cover their hair in head rags to accommodate the harsh demands of field work.

And in New Orleans, the 1786 Tignon laws required free Creole women to wear a *tignon* or scarf to signify they were members of the slave class, irrespective of whether they were actually free or not.

Imani Bashir, a Black American Muslim and travel writer based in Mexico, says that there has always been a distinctive relationship between head covering, Blackness, and faith in the US. 'I honestly believe hijab has an ancestral component that a lot of people don't know and don't realise. As somebody who comes from multi-generations of Black Muslims in the US, there is a history of Black Muslims who kept their *deen* (religion) by covering themselves, covering their hair, fasting during the month of Ramadan and during slavery. There's just a lot of intermingling of what it is to be Black, what it is to be Muslim, and what it is to be a woman.'

'The radical history of the headwrap', on the website Timeline, details how the Black Power movement and subsequently, conscious hip-hop artists like Queen Latifah during the 1980s and 1990s, would take back ownership and make the head wrap a powerful symbol of autonomy, with a nod to African heritage and Black pride. But in the United States, that sense of pride began much earlier in the twentieth century with the onset of the Nation of Islam (NOI). The movement played a vital role in rearticulating the feminine, spiritualism, and veiling that propelled the image of its female followers as a core representation of the movement's ideals and purpose. Women of the NOI are renowned for their distinctive form of hijab that comprises long white or other coloured gowns, and a head covering that may show the neck and flows behind the head, as opposed to the front of the neck and bosom, normally worn by Muslim women in mainstream Islam.

In *Women of the Nation: Between Black Protest and Sunni Islam*, former NOI member Shirley Morton says that the movement empowered her to embrace her 'natural beauty.' 'I am happy and proud to be Black... I know that I am the mother of civilisation. I wear the clothes of civilised people. My dresses are far below my knees and I love it... The honourable Elijah Muhammad teaches us that we Black women are the most beautiful of all women.'

Kayla Renée Wheeler, an Assistant Professor of Gender and Diversity at Xavier University in Cincinnati, Ohio, argues that Black Muslim fashion started in the United States in the 1930s. It was intrinsic to challenging both white supremacist beauty standards and Arab-centrism, and helped propel the creation of an Afro-Islamic diaspora fashion industry.

Writing for *BlackAmericanMuslim.com*, Wheeler says that she intends to explore how the NOI and Imam W. Deen Mohammed (the son of former NOI leader, Elijah Muhammad) encouraged fashion shows, textile classes, and opportunities for women to monetise their talents in design to promote Black self-determination.

Women of the Nation of Islam, courtesy of brendasbeignets.tumblr.com

Black Muslim women's participation in the natural hair movement can also be an interpreted as a form of resistance against capitalism's demonisation of the Black body and Black cultures. Eurocentric ideas of capitalism have a pernicious history, with exploitation at its apex.

As Hortense Spillers explains in *Mama's Baby, Papa's Maybe: An American Grammar Book*, the Black woman's body has provided, and continues to provide a parallel to the construction of white European and American women's bodies. That is to say every component of the Black woman's body is othered to accentuate not only the idea of a 'default' or superior femininity, but its own alleged inferiority.

In other words, beauty standards within the dominant white paradigm downgrade those who do not physically match or sustain the myth of 'Eurocentric beauty' as the standard.

The 'Black Is Beautiful' movement, propelled by the Black Panthers, was a powerful attempt to challenge and subvert the notion of 'Eurocentric beauty.' It popularised the Afro, worn by the likes of activist and academic Angela Davis, musician Nina Simone, and The Jackson Five. The current natural hair movement is inspired by such earlier efforts; and stands against rampant capitalism which has racketeered Black bodies and culture, and continues to do so to this very day.

Misguided ideals around Black beauty also extend to how Black women should best treat their hair. Nigerian-Irish academic and broadcaster, Emma Dabiri, suggests in *Don't Touch My Hair* that colonialism has played a role in creating the perception that dealing with one's natural hair as a Black woman is arduous and time-consuming. Speaking about braiding she says, 'I'm reluctant to describe this process as time-consuming because I'm keen to disrupt our deeply ingrained (yet recent and culturally specific) myth of time as a commodity...It is a process that brings people together and facilitates intergenerational bonding and knowledge transmission.'

It is a sentiment that twenty-nine-year-old Rwandan who works for Accenture, Nabiirah Kaseruuzi, shares:

It's a matter of self-love to have the patience to do your hair when you come out of the shower even though you know it will be covered. There's always a temptation to be negligent about maintaining your hair when you first start wearing hijab, and I was no exception. The question I had to ask myself is when I maintain and style my hair, is it for me, or the approval of others? I was taught the importance of self-care from a young age, so learning to groom my hair regularly, regardless of whether people see it or not, became a priority. Doing this brings me joy and makes me feel even more gratified to be a hijab-wearing woman.

Imani explained to me that she did not always veil, but that she appreciates how finding the time for hair has little correlation with the decision to cover. 'I love getting my hair done when I have the opportunity to do so, and I think more so me being a mum and not necessarily having time to do it is as a result of that and not necessarily because I wear hijab. Now granted, I do make sure that I go at least once every two months and I get my hair blown out by my Dominican aunties.'

However, when thirty-year-old Khadijah Antron who is Afro-Latina, first converted to Islam and decided to wear hijab, she found it challenging readjusting her hair care regimen – especially while living in Turkey, a Muslim majority country with a small Black population. 'I didn't have to cover my hair [before],' she recalls. 'Covering it causes it to dry [out] because Turkey doesn't have certain under-scarves. The ones they do sell are expensive and there isn't much in regards to hijab products that cater to natural hair and Black women. But I do all this for Allah and hopefully, the [wider] Muslim community considers [catering to] natural hair women.'

While countries like the United Kingdom and the United States are increasingly receptive to the appearance of Black women's natural hair, and styles such as braids, Afro puffs, and locs, some Black women complain about the lack of appropriate hairstylists and products in the areas they live and work, otherwise known as 'Black Hair Deserts.' In an article in *Allure*, sociologist Shatima Jones says that demographics, class, property costs, and gentrification all play a role in making Black Hair Deserts, which are 'a function of suburbs.' 'Who gets to live in the suburbs? Who gets to own a home? That's definitely a class dynamic, which [in] the United States, is closely tied to race', she says. In Khadijah's case, the gap between race and accessibility widens further in Muslim majority countries such as Turkey, where Black immigrants make up a smaller proportion of the populations than in Western European countries. But Black Muslim women are at a greater disadvantage in such cases.

Somalian-Australian academic Najat Abdi says:

As a Black Muslim woman raised in the Western world, we often come into contact with other brothers and sisters who are also of immigrant backgrounds, but may not necessarily understand the process of styling and maintaining Black hair. There are many salons that offer chemical straightening and other procedures aimed at vanishing the tightly wound coils of 4B or 4C hair, but rarely a salon where Muslim stylists have knowledge of Black hair care.

To address these issues, Black millennials are establishing online companies and smaller businesses that cater to Black women and their hair in western European countries.

In Britain, for example, companies like Afrocenchix are leading the way in providing suitable natural hair care products for Black women that are not easily found in mainstream cosmetic and beauty stores. In Brazil, Beleza Natural is one of the most important hair franchises catering to women of African descent. Social media too plays a crucial role for the black hair care community and its customers, and conversations are being had amongst Black Muslim women who are carving their own spaces online to navigate their 'coils, kinks, and hijab pins.' One of these is the Instagram platform 4C Hijabi (@4c_hijabi) that educates Black Muslim women on the science of hair growth and how best to take care of 'hijab hair'. These include tutorials on hijab-friendly styles, and a hijab edition of product reviews and podcasts. Its founder, RaySunshine, is a British-Nigerian living in Liverpool who started the platform in 2018.

RaySunshine explains that she simply wanted healthier hair but found it difficult to find resources which catered to Black Muslim women who wear the hijab. So 4C Hijabi was born. 'I have nothing against relaxing hair safely or straight hair, but I just find it odd so many of us don't know how to care for our natural hair. How can I say that I cannot take care of the hair that Allah has given me? I really wanted to understand the science behind it and when I found my natural foundation was solid, I started thinking I am a Muslim, I can't be doing frohawks under my hijab!'

But the issue of styling is not the only concern for Black Muslim women who cover their hair. There are other problems too.

As Tennessee-based, Khadijah Abdul-Haqq, author of *Nani's Hijab*, explains in a tweet: most fabrics 'snatches [sic] our hair' and 'then there is a whole thing with oil stains on your scarves. Not to mention braids and what styles to wear at *that* time of the month. Black Muslim women hair drama never ends.' 'That time of the month' is a reference to menstruation, whereby Muslim women are exempt from praying, fasting, and having sexual relations with their spouses. The latter has implications for Muslim women generally as a special bath is performed afterwards – and this includes wetting the hair. This means that Black Muslim women may feel more conscious about what kinds of hair styling they utilise outside menstruation. Generally Black women have Type 3 and Type 4 hair curls that tend to be drier, curlier, and do not retain moisture easily, which means Black Muslim women have to pay particular attention to the types of fabric that constitute their head coverings. Most Black hair care websites such as *Naturallycurly.com* advise minimal exposure of the hair to cotton and the use of satin or silk on the head while asleep.

Black Muslim women, like other Muslim women who wear head coverings, often hear questions about their hair and hijab. 'Do you wear that

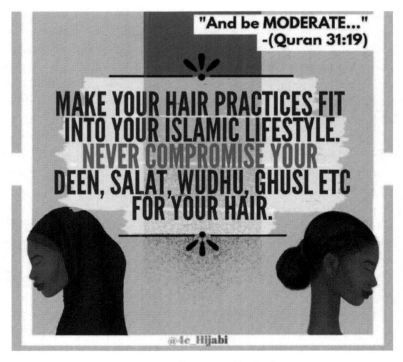

Courtesy of Instagram/4c_hijabi

Courtesy of Instagram/4c_hijabi

in the shower?' 'Do you ever take that off? 'Do you even have to take care of your hair under there? But Black Muslim women also hear a question that their Arab and Asian counterparts do not: 'How long is your hair?'

Personally, I remember younger Muslim girls at a mosque in South London asking their Black friends about the length of their hair and the latter's uncomfortable facial expressions.

While Black hair grows at the same rate as other human hair types, the idea that longer 'flowy' hair is desirable, is a function of Eurocentric beauty standards. Black Muslim women generally sit between this and the anti-Blackness and texturism from some Asian and Arab communities over what is considered 'good hair.' 'I remember taking off my hijab at my friend's engagement party of mainly Pakistani women, many of whom

were wondering what's underneath my hijab – me being a Black Muslim
woman. When I did, someone told me to simply put it back on', says
RaySunshine. But texturism and colourism can manifest itself for some
Black Muslim women in other ways too. As Najat explains:

> As a *Muslimah* of East African descent (specifically Somali), I come from a
> region of the continent where women exhibit wide variations of hair textures.
> My late father had very curly, coiled hair, while my mother has straight hair.
> Growing up amongst our communities here in Australia, one does see texturism being played out. There was always this quest to obtain silky, straight hair.

> Living in Australia and the constant representation of white women with
> straight hair being the so-called 'ideal', it had social, economic and romantic
> implications for Black women. As a teenager, I witnessed a pattern where sisters with Eurocentric features were given opportunities to progress. Despite
> the privacy the hijab provided, it was a common assumption that if a Black
> sister had lighter skin, and a narrow nose, then she had to have long, straight
> hair. Colourism and texturism were very much interconnected.

Such issues highlight the complexities Black Muslim women face
regarding their hair; and how they are navigating these in keeping with
their faith. It is not particularly easy when colonial legacies, as well as
Islamophobic rhetoric mean Black Muslim women's femininity is always a
target. But beauty and Islam are not anathemas. In fact, hair care is
praiseworthy and is considered an act of worship that is rewardable. And
while Black Muslim women share hair narratives with other Black women,
it is exciting to see how they are also forging a whole new discourse by and
for themselves.

CALL ME YUNUS

Mevlut Ceylan

Once there was and once there wasn't, when the flea was a porter and the camel a barber, when I was rocking my father's cradle, 'tingir mingir'.

It was the twelfth century and the Seljuks battled their way through Central Asia, withstanding the dangers that came upon their path towards Anatolia. The Mongols were everyone's nightmare as the Turkish *beyliks* fought to protect their provinces. Finally, in 1071, the Seljuqs defeated the Byzantines in the battle of Manzikart, providing a secure settlement for the *beyliks*.

We had many intellectuals that shaped the way of the Ottoman understanding. Great thinkers and writers like Ahmad Yesevi, Haci Bektashi Veli, Mevlana Rumi, Sari Saltuk and my sheikh Tapduk Emre, the master of Turkish poets. He is buried in a tomb in Emre village, Kula, Turkey. His tomb is visited by thousands of visitors each year.

Some may claim that I was born in the year 1238, some may argue otherwise. While my tomb is yet to be found, it is true that I had been around at the beginning of the thirteenth century. My poems are the lasting evidence.

Islamic tradition dictates my life. I found peace through Islam, as well as the ability to question what is and what is not. Is this reality? What is real and what isn't? Am I Yunus? Yunus Emre? Or is Yunus me? Are we all Yunus, like the prophet Yunus, making us feel the need to repent and be in constant repentance — *towbah*?

Submission: an integral part of what it is being a Muslim.

God permeates the whole wide World,
Yet His truth is revealed to none.
You better seek Him in yourself,
You and He aren't apart — you're one.

Come, let us all be friends for once,
Let us make life easy on us,
Let us be lover and loved ones,
The earth shall be left to one.

The reason for studying is to know one's self
If you do not know yourself
What good is this studying

Since Mevlana Hudavendger looked at us
His majestic glance is the mirror of our heart

The person who calls himself
A Muslim should know requirements of it
He should follow the order of God and pray five times daily

Haci Bektashi Veli was my guide and he advised me to follow the way of
Tapduk Emre and so I joined Tapduk Emre's *dergah*, a word of many
meanings: portal, place, threshold that gives dignity, order, stature.
If I don't say that O love,
The pain of love strangles me.'
If you want to clean the dust of the hearts
Tell that word, what is the essence of the word.

It is Your love that has taken me from me
What I need is you, You
I have been burning day and night
What I need is You, You

The dervish chest must be cut
His tearful eyes ready to weep;
He must be as docile as sheep.
You cannot become a dervish.

If anger exists, if it's true,
Muhammad would have felt it too;

So long as you have wrath in you,
You cannot become a dervish

I spent thirty years at Sheikh Tapduk's dergah, but felt like I had gained nothing. Instead, I felt disingenuous and felt like I had lost my connection with God. I believed it was time to leave, before I fell deeper into the pit of doom. I set off on a journey, hoping to find answers for my disorientation and despair. On my journey, I crossed paths with several dervishes that were also travelling. We enjoyed each other's company and decided to continue our journey together.

When night fell, one of the dervishes raised his hands to the sky and prayed to the Lord. Lo and behold! As soon as he completed his prayer a magnificent feast lay before us. The very next evening, the same thing happened after the second dervish opened his hands in prayer.
On the third night, it was my turn. I could not bring myself to tell the dervishes that I had fled my *dergah* in shame. And so, I raised my hands and prayed: 'Whoever these two asked, I also ask through that person'. I willed for my prayer to be accepted in order to save face. Alas! To my amazement an even bigger feast was spread before us. Before I could process how this had happened, my companions expressed their amazement and begged me to tell them who I asked through. I insisted they first tell me who they asked through, to which they replied,
'We were asking through the dervish, Yunus Emre, the one who worked at the great Tapduk Emre's *dergah* for 30 years'.

O God, if you would ever question me,
This world, be my outright answer to Thee:

True, I sinned- brutalised my own being,
But what have I done against you, my King?

Did your dominion become any less?
Did I usurp any of your prowess?
You built me a bridge to cross, thin as hair;
Out of your traps I'm to choose my own snare.

You can see everything, you know me – fine;
Then, why must you weigh all these deeds of mine?
Do you still seek revenge though you killed me,
Since I rotted, the darkest soil filled me.

No harm ever came from Yunus to you
Open, secret – all things are in your view.

Ego can get the better of man. I have learned this by seeing many people
fall into the trap of narcissism.

Don't boast of reading, mastering science
Or of all your prayers and obeisance.
If you don't identify Man as God,
All your learning is of no use at all.

The true meaning of the four holy books
Is found in the alphabet's first letter.
You talk about that first letter, preacher;
What is the meaning of that – Could you tell?

It has been said that I had three thousand poems and collected them in a
Divan. Through them, I share my soul. I belong to this World. I deal with
the pain and happiness of this material World:
I am not here on earth for strife,
Love is the home of the loved one;
I came here to build a true heart.

And yet, I remind myself that life is short. At the end of our lives, we will
sit in front of the Judge and be called to account for our deeds:
We have no knowledge of whose turn has come:
Dashing through men's lives as His own orchard,
He damns and strips anyone He chooses.

It is hard to find any references to my time period within my poems, but
what can be found are references to never-ending social problems which

have endured long past my time. The problems in my poems are universal
and timeless:
Masses become righteous if you become righteous,
One cannot find righteousness if you are crooked.

Oh dervish Yunus,
Don't tell this word
In a bent and devious way
A Molla Kasım comes and questions

Yunus to Mevlana: "You have written too much. If I were you I would say:
'I wrapped myself with flesh and bone
I've appeared as Yunus…'

Call me Yunus, the wandering dervish, one who seeks knowledge and
wisdom. That is the way of the Sufi, mystic Yunus, the student of Tapduk
Emre.
I am Yunus, the wandering dervish.
You are Yunus.
We are Yunus.

PAINTING POEMS

Nadeem Baghdadi

Everything

I am reading a book
I am reading in the sun.
I feel the sun on my skin
I feel the cover of the book in my hands
A gentle breeze passes by
The leaves rustle and I turn the page
The page is smooth to touch and rough also

I look at the ink that make up the words
The ink in the words is black
Intensely black
Then suddenly, unexpectedly a green bottle fly lands on the page
It is walking, taking quick steps, slight steps on the page
As if inspecting the words
These black words on this white page.
I sit motionless, watching the fly
I feel somehow privileged simply to watch
The green of its body,
And what a green it is!
The green is a green that is polished to perfection
It starts to rub its hind legs
Entwining them, smoothly, effortlessly
Now disentangling them
Now it starts to caress its eyes with its front legs.
And what eyes it has!
Intricate and vast.
Now its hind legs go over its wings
And what wings it has!
Delicate, light, transparent
And now it stands still.
I watched this spectacle unfold before me
I watched as a guest, an onlooker
To hell with this book that I read
No sentences, no words can compare to this fly
The majesty that stands still on this page
This fly is here, now
It is real, living
It has colour and vigour
This here, this aliveness, is what I have been searching for in books
I now realise that I have been searching for everything
And now it is here.
Everything is here, now.

I want to stand here for a while

I want to stand here for a while
I am not thinking of anything in particular
I am not doing anything in particular
I just want to stand here for a while

I can feel my breath
It enters and leaves me
Enters and leaves me
Enters and leaves me
As I stand here for a while.
I feel also my fingertips
They are cold
And occasionally they touch the rim of my coat
I see also, things, as they pass me by
A bird flying
A cloud floating
A leaf falling
All these things happen as I stand here for a while
But I am not thinking of anything in particular
Neither am I reflecting on things
I am thinking, nothing
As I stand here for a while

It's okay take your time

I don't need to be anywhere at the moment
I'm not busy
I'm not running late for any meetings or appointments
And I'm not at all in a rush

I'm not, as you say, pushed for time
I'm not double booked or double anything
So, it's okay, take your time
I don't need to be anywhere apart from where I am now
That is
On this park bench
Finishing off this apple
Avoiding the seeds and the plastic bits in the middle,
There is no bin
So, I hold the remains of it in my right hand
And I remember, I too have been late on many occasions
I too have missed out on things
Missed the boat so to speak
Golden opportunities, once in a lifetime chances, openings, breaks
Too Late, too old, too today and too tomorrow.
So it's okay, take your time.
And I realise you could also be late
To meet me and to see me
And I realise you may have missed the bus, the train, the plane, that lift
I realise you may be stuck in traffic and its rush hour and it's all a little
impossible
So, it's okay, be an hour late, 2 hours, 3, 4
Postpone meeting me, take a rain cheque, delay it for next time, the time
after
Next week, next month, next year, it's all fine.
But you'll find me where you left me, sat here on this park bench, holding
the remains of the apple now in my left hand.
So please take your time I'm in no rush.

Something is missing

Although I have everything
There is something missing
Although I have my health, my wealth, my family and friends
Yet there is something missing
Although I have a good job, a good wife, a nice house, a nice car
Still there is something missing
Although all my faculties are in working order, I can think for myself, go
for walks on my own daydream, sleep, eat
Yet there is something missing
I'm not behind on repayments or loans or credit cards
I don't owe money to anyone, no one owes me anything
I'm not depressed, sad or down on my luck
And It's not happiness because I see that now and again.
And It's not love, I feel that now and again.
And It's not wealth, I have enough of that now and again.
So, what is it that's missing?
I can't seem to put my finger on it
It is in the way in which a chance touch of a strangers hand brushes mine
The thing that is missing in me, is in there somewhere.
It is in the way I can feel cold water going through my body when I am
thirsty
The thing that is missing in me, is in there somewhere.
It is in the way in which I can feel the warm sun on my face after a long
cold winter
The thing that is missing in me, is in there somewhere.
And it is in the way the sunlight enters my room and casts its patch of
sunlight onto the carpet and I can see the dust particles floating inside it
The thing that is missing in me, is in there somewhere.
You may understand or you may not
But the thing that is missing are all in there somewhere.

@artist_nadeemb

TWO POEMS

Muhammed Bello

A Boy Has No Face

You had a crisis with your body last night
it seemed as though your body was going to fail you
a battle between your body & soul
your body needed the soul out
your soul gave a fiery battle—

you were simply there observing
it was beyond you
you simply lay there & moaned
not in pleasure but in torment
you needed the torment to end abruptly—

you murmured *God*
you called *mommy*
it was still just you
eyes turning
legs trembling—

you watched your body
& soul's intercourse
it was simply you
in a total loss of your body —

you watched them as they turned
tossed & kissed one another

you were simply there powerless
& watched your soul battle for its place in your body
it was a crisis—

you still wanted to call *God* & *mommy*
this time your tongue failed you—

you gnashed your teeth
the words burned in your throat
they inched to be spoken
you couldn't simply say them till you dropped
an unknown object—that was what you were
an object with neither a body nor soul—

you woke up the following day
with a smile on your face
"i made it," you said
it was only a crisis
a dream that has no importance.

Of Wanders & Wonders

This night, like every other night
accompanies a memory
the one he needs to be appreciative for
yet find its way to swallow him in its murkiness—

the one he was rarely enough
the one which makes the boy long for the last second—

the one that makes the boy ask for what he has done again
as you approach him with dark eyes—

dark like a pot that's kissed the stove,
you make him eat from the
dark like the goat you say is superior to him—

listen,
each breath is a challenge for him
i bet you didn't see it
how the boy waits for the awful stuff to happen—

like God hangs tight for the servant he adores
how the boy turns into a robot customized to just say *i'm sorry*—

as though he had a choice
it was the boy's passcode
before the boy got past & at last, escape
& the boy's caterpillar morphed into a butterfly.

MORTAL DANCE

Halimah Adisa

When You Realise You Are Mortal

You were searching through the rays of the moon
that transcended from the sky.

A moment of time with the seven levels of living
had you open up to a conversation,

and when at first you realized that you are mortal, you hid into a distance
of voidness suspended by

the clouds, chimneys, and falls.
You fall into tales: love that leads and that destroys.

And as of everything is of God, he gives to humans except space. So you
hid under the serenity of

anxiety. But how do you evolve eagerness?
You dance to its rhythm with a set beat of the

aftermath of hard work. You glow at the rising and setting of the sun.

You accept hatred from the horizon from which it has risen. And when
your mind finds you at peace with

how mortal you are, the yearning to understand that which is beyond
will grow; and at that, the fear of death will no longer linger.

Watch Me Do My Dance

You may put me down in the books of fate,
intertwined with history. You may pray me out of my dirt or you may
dwell me in in darkness shielding from the voice of my silent noise,
but mum like a grave, I'll keep still.

You may shroud me in tales that never existed. Make me up as one of the
villains. You may await my calls for help and fire me up with guilt. You
may torture me with your fictional soldiers,
but mum like a grave, I'll keep still.

Do you want to see me dance, swing my waist and call it home while I
await your faithful cries?

Do you want to see me grow, make a pot of roses and name me beauty
while I await your cherished tears?

Do you want to see me cry? Take the ocean out of my name while I await
your scented smile wishing that I scream help. But mum like a grave, I'll
keep still.

REVIEWS

BONDING IN ABRAHAMIC FAITHS

Giles Goddard

There seems to be a darkness at the heart of interfaith relations. It is not clear whether the darkness is a response to geopolitical factors – not only the significance of oil for the global economy but also the outworking of post-colonial politics in the post-imperial nation states – or a result of the growing influence of conservative interpretations of faith traditions. Or whether one is a cause of the other. It is difficult, if not impossible, to disentangle the political from the religious but, against a background of resurgent authoritarianism around the world, one question becomes more and more urgent: how can the Abrahamic faiths come together to make the world a better place? Or is the limiting of conflict the best that we can hope for?

It seems as if the early years of the twenty first century have continued and exacerbated one of the overarching narratives of the twentieth century: increase in inter-religious strife, particularly between the Abrahamic faiths, and decrease in trust and cooperation. There are many examples from which to choose. Trump's proscribing of travel from nine Muslim countries. Boko Haram (meaning 'Western Education is a Sin' in Hausa) destabilising an already fragile truce in northern Nigeria. Pressure on ancient Christian communities in Palestine/Israel and Syria to the point where they are unlikely to survive. 9/11, 7/7 and the Charlie Hebdo murders. The marginalisation of Christian minorities in Egypt, Pakistan, Indonesia and Malaysia.

During the twentieth century, the story is also one of violence, strife and murder. The Holocaust, pre-eminent among atrocities. The imperialist consequences of the collapse of the Ottoman Empire, American support for the Shah of Iran and the consequent hostility between Iran and the USA. The unholy alliance between the Saudi Arabian royal family and the Wahhabi religious establishment, exporting a particularly intolerant brand of Islam around the world. The sudden eruption of interreligious warfare in the Balkans. The rise of the religious right in America, doubling down on the uniqueness of Christianity and entering into alliance with conservative Zionists in order that millenarian prophecies may be fulfilled and conditions created for the return of the Messiah.

Craig Considine, *People of the Book: Prophet Muhammad's Encounters with Christians*, Hurst, London, 2021

Dan Cohn-Sherbrook, George D. Chryssides and Usama Hasan, *People of the Book*, Jessica Kingsley Publishers, London 2019.

Hugh Goddard, *A History of Christian-Muslim Relations*, Edinburgh University Press, 2020

The Church of England, *Living in Love and Faith: Christian Teaching and Learning about Identity, Sexuality, Relationships and Marriage*, Church House Publishing, London, 2020.

Beyond the Abrahamic faiths the situation seems as hopeless. Narendra Modi is actively pursuing Hindu nationalist policies which actively disadvantage one third of Indians who are part of other faith traditions. The Buddhist leaders in Myanmar are targeting the Muslim and Hindu Rohingya. And so it continues.

Perhaps the notion that these faith traditions can ever cooperate is a fantasy. History seems to indicate that the default position is one of strife. European history has been characterised by anti-Semitism. The treatment of Jews in England in the mediaeval centuries is a sad history of exploitation and extortion. Abraham of Bristol had one of his teeth extracted per day until he was willing to disgorge his portion of a tax slapped on Jews in 1210. Edward I expelled all the Jews in England in 1290 and there is little evidence of Jewish presence in England after that until 1655. The creation of Jewish ghettos in European cities was ubiquitous, and the dominance of some Jewish families in banking and finance was partly the result of policies which excluded them from other professions. Relations between Muslims and Jews were on the surface more positive, but the extent to which tolerance from the larger, Muslim populations in the Abbasid, Umayyad or Ottoman Empires was granted towards the smaller Jewish populations varied greatly from region to region or indeed from town to town.

Apart from diplomatic contacts – Elizabeth retained good links with the Ottoman and Persian empires – there was little interaction between the Muslim Arab empires and Europe, and less understanding. Christianity's dominance in Europe lacked even the formal toleration legally enshrined in the Ottoman empire, where Christians and Jews were identified as *dhimmi* and permitted upon payment of a tax to continue the observance of their faith. The establishment of European empires around the globe rarely if ever granted anything approaching equal status to non-Christians.

So it is possible that the current poor state of relations between the Abrahamic traditions is simply the outworking of a history of mistrust, in which case perhaps even the hope for better cooperation is likely to remain only an aspiration.

But is such a council of despair justified? Or is it possible to find, in the source materials for all three faith traditions and in the history, slivers of hope for a better way forward? The scriptures of Judaism, Christianity and Islam are by no means monolithically exclusionist. The Hebrew Scriptures certainly tell the foundational story of the Jewish people, the escape from slavery in Egypt and the occupation of the land which is theirs by God's divine covenant: but within the scriptures are writings which deliberately subvert this narrative of dominance. The Book of Ruth tells a story of integration; Ruth the Moabite travels with her mother-in-law into Israel and ends up marrying Boaz, a Jew. It is very possible that the book of Ruth was included in the Hebrew scriptures as a correction to the command in the book of Ezra that the Jews should 'put away their foreign wives', and she is named in the genealogy of Jesus in the Gospel of Matthew. The later prophecies in Isaiah are deliberately and clearly universalist:

> Arise, shine; for your light has come, and the glory of the Lord has risen upon you. For darkness shall cover the earth, and thick darkness the peoples, but the Lord will arise upon you, and his glory will appear over you. Nations shall come to your light, and kings to the brightness of your dawn. (Isaiah 60.1-3)

Christianity further widens the narrative. Salvation is by the grace of God alone, and the grace of God is the manifestation of the love which God has for all creation. So, according to the letter of St Paul to the Galatians,

> There is no longer Jew or Greek, there is no longer slave or free, there is no longer male or female, for all of you are one in Christ Jesus. (Galatians 3.28).

Jesus drew Jew and Gentile to himself, engaging closely with a Samaritan woman at the well, to the astonishment of his disciples (John 4) and a Syro-Phoenician woman whose daughter he, after some persuasion, healed (Mark 7). And an early disagreement between St Peter and St Paul about the extent to which ritual Jewish law should be followed was resolved by agreeing distinct spheres of operation and mutual obligations.

Two recent books, both excellent in their own ways, furnish us with the history of Christian-Muslim relationship. While Hugh Goddard's *A History of Christian-Muslim Relations* is a wide-ranging work, Craig Considine provides an in-depth consideration of the Prophet Muhammad's encounters with Christians in *People of the Book*.

There is strong evidence from within and beyond the Qur'an of close interaction between Christian, Jew and Muslim; and, as a result, the Qur'an does not speak with a single voice about the People of the Book (*ahl al-kitāb*). Christian and Jew are undoubtedly portrayed as falling short of the acknowledgement of the unity of God, *tawhid,* but the extent to which they fall short and how much they should be seen as allies and how much as enemies varies.

> Among the People of the Book there are some who believe in God and what was sent down to you and what was sent down to them, humbling themselves before God and not selling the verses of God cheaply: their reward is with their God, who is swift to reckon. (3: 199)

The Constitution of Medina, dating from around 627, recognises the reality of religious diversity – 'to the Jews their religion, and to the Muslims their religion'. It is mainly in the later revelations, perhaps a result of increased conflict between the Prophet's community and those around him, that the fearsomely quotable astringency emerges:

God cast terror into their hearts so that you slew some of them and took captive others. He made you masters of their land, their houses and their goods and yet another land on which you had never set foot before. (33: 26-7)

Perhaps something to juxtapose with parts of the Hebrew scriptures:

So, the people shouted, and the trumpets were blown. As soon as the people heard the sound of the trumpets, they raised a great shout, and the wall fell down flat; so the people charged straight ahead into the city [Jericho] and captured it. Then they devoted to destruction by the edge of the sword all in the city, both men and women, young and old, oxen, sheep, and donkeys. Joshua 6.20-21

There are several instances where contact between Muhammad and the early Muslims and Christians is recorded. One of the most significant is the encounter with the Negus of Axum (Abyssinia), to whom Muhammad has sent some of his followers to seek refuge from the Meccans, who were persecuting the nascent community around him. The Negus is said, at the end of a long debate, to have picked up a stick and declared that the difference between what he believes about Jesus and what the Muslims believe is no greater than the length of the stick: and he refuses to give the Muslims up to the Meccans. While the Qur'an is absolutely clear that there is no sense in which Jesus can be understood as anything other than a prophet, and that the concept of the Trinity is a distortion of the unity of God, it is also on many occasions respectful of Christians and Jews, with the exception of those who attack or seek to undermine the followers of the prophet Muhammed.

There is strong evidence that later in Muhammed's life, once Islam had become established as a powerful force in the area, the Prophet pursued positive relations with local Christians – often offering an antidote to the strife and tensions which had abounded previously. Considine examines in detail the account of his relations with the Christians of Najran in *People of the Book*. A delegation of 120 Christians met with the prophet and his followers in al-Masjid al-Nabawi, the Mosque of the Prophet, over three days in March 630. Out of the meeting, which covered such topics as the nature and significance of Jesus Christ and more practical aspects of mutual support, came the Covenant of Muhammed with the Christians of Najran in which, among much else, the prophet agrees:

> My horsemen, my foot-soldiers, my armies, my resources and my Muslim
> partisans will protect the Christians as far away as they may be located

And

> The Christians must host for three days and three nights any Muslims who halt
> among them, with their animals. They must offer them … the same food with
> which they live themselves, without, however, being obliged to endure other
> annoying or onerous burdens.

Considine observes that 'Muhammed's encounter with the Christians of
Najran is more than a mere example of religious tolerance … It follows
more closely with the theory of religious pluralism as developed by Diana
L. Eck', the noted American scholar of religious studies and author *of India:
A Sacred Geography*. This theory has four elements: (1) the recognition of
diversity within traditions, to be nourished because it leads to *'asabiyya* (Ibn
Khaldun's notion of social solidarity), (2) respect as a fundamental feature
of human interaction, (3) a culture of encounter across traditions, and (4)
regular dialogue to bridge the gap in cultural and religious illiteracy.

There was a significant level of religious pluralism and creative
interaction between Jew, Christian and Muslim from the ninth to
thirteenth centuries. The actions of the Crusaders are of course not
forgotten – the sacking of Jerusalem and the slaughtering of men, women
and children until the streets ran, by repute, knee-high in blood (although
massacres of the inhabitants of conquered cities was by no means unique
to Crusaders – and there were responses, at times equally ferocious, from
Muslim commanders). But in the same period, many of the great works of
Greek philosophy were translated into Arabic by Christian monks in
Muslim cities. Even before the formalisation of Christian and Jewish rights
and responsibilities under the Ottoman empire, the Umayyad and Abbasid
dynasties permitted open observance of non-Muslim faiths so long as the
correct taxes were paid. And the examples of *convivencia* – in Granada, in
Sicily under King Roger II – reflect a willingness to cooperate which goes
well beyond differences in faithful practice and religious belief. There is
much evidence of artistic and cultural cross fertilisation: the Dome of the
Rock seems to have been designed partly as a response to the design of
Christian basilicas in the Levant, and the cultural lives in the great cities
such as Thessalonika, Istanbul or Alexandria were richly interactive.

Moving to the more recent past, there have been significant developments in interfaith relations in the last fifty years. These were led, among Christians, by the Vatican and the World Council of Churches. As part of the Second Vatican Council, the encyclical *Nostra Aetate* was published in October 1965. This document was mainly intended to re-set Catholic relations with Judaism, after the horrors of the Holocaust which, although not directly attributable to Christianity, certainly grew out of the long history of anti-Semitism within the churches in Europe. For the first time the Church absolved the Jewish people of the guilt of killing Jesus Christ:

> The Church, in fact, believes that Christ, who 'is our peace', embraces Jews and Gentiles with one and the same love and it also believes that He made the two one (see Eph 2:14). She rejoices that the union of these two 'in one body' (Eph 2:16) proclaims the whole world's reconciliation in Christ. Even though the greater part of the Jewish people has remained separated from Christ, it would be an injustice to call this people accursed, since they are greatly beloved for the sake of the Fathers and the promises made to them (see Rom 11:28). The Church loves this people.

Equally, for the first time, *Nostra Aetate* acknowledged Islam as a faith tradition alongside Catholicism, worshipping the same God.

> This sacred synod urges all to forget the past and to work sincerely for mutual understanding and ... to promote together for the benefit of all mankind social justice and moral welfare, as well as peace and freedom.

Although, as might be expected, the language used was carefully chosen, and although one primary purpose of *Nostra* was to facilitate evangelism through greater understanding of Islam, the respect offered to Islam by such a significant document was ground-breaking, and was cemented not long afterwards by the first visit of a Pope to a mosque when John Paul II visited the Umayyad Mosque in Damascus – ostensibly to pay respects at the shrine of John the Baptist but nonetheless crossing the threshold and praying within the precincts of a mosque.

Not to be outdone, the World Council of Churches, which represents mainly the Protestant denominations, published Guidelines on Dialogue with People of Living Faiths and Ideologies in 1979:

In an age of worldwide struggle of humankind for survival and liberation, religions and ideologies have their important contributions to make, which can only be worked out in mutual dialogue.

Partly in response to these developments, a statement 'Dabru Emet' – speak the truth – was issued on 10 September 2000, written by four Jewish scholars and signed by many more:

> We believe these changes merit a thoughtful Jewish response. Speaking only for ourselves—an interdenominational group of Jewish scholars—we believe it is time for Jews to learn about the efforts of Christians to honor Judaism. We believe it is time for Jews to reflect on what Judaism may now say about Christianity. As a first step, we offer eight brief statements about how Jews and Christians may relate to one another.

The statement goes on to affirm that Jews and Christians worship the same God, that Nazism was not a Christian problem, and that a new relationship between Jews and Christians will not weaken Jewish practice.

'Dabru Emet' was welcomed by many Christians, including for example the European Lutheran Commission on the Church and the Jewish people. However, progress in interfaith relations has been tentative and halting. I remember very well the explosion of controversy in 2008 when Archbishop Rowan Williams, in an otherwise unexceptional lecture about the relationship between national and religious law, suggested that sharia law might become part of British jurisdiction, recognising a reality that already existed amongst many Muslim communities in the country. And Pope Benedict XIV's 2006 lecture at Regensburg, quoting from a dialogue between Emperor Manuel II Paleologus and 'an educated Persian' in a way which seemed to suggest that harmony between faith and reason was not present in Islam and that violent conversation seemed to be legitimate, produced a sharp and powerful counterreaction, including riots and several deaths. The lecture was an own goal for the Catholic church, undermining much of the good work which had happened since *Nostra Aetate*. The Pope's subsequent apology and clarification did little to assuage the anger, although it did give direct rise to some new initiatives. The Pope travelled to Turkey about three months after the lecture, where he visited the Blue Mosque and prayed for the first time in front of the *mihrab*, facing towards

Mecca, and a Catholic-Muslim forum was established in 2008, followed by
a visit by the Pope to Jordan in 2009.

Out of the darkness comes light. Another direct result of the Regensburg
lecture was the publication of *A Common Word Between Us and You*. Initially,
an Open Letter was published signed by thirty-eight scholars from
different parts of the Islamic world, in which they gently challenged the
Pope's lecture. In 2008, inspired and led by Prince Ghazi bin Muhammad
of Jordan, a much fuller and more comprehensive letter was published
under the title *A Common Word*. The title was derived from the Qur'an 3.63:

> People of Scripture, come to a common word between us and you, that we
> worship none but God, and ascribe no partner to Him, and take no other lords
> beside God.

The letter received a huge and mainly positive response from Christians,
including a full-page advert in the *New York Times* and a detailed reply from
Rowan Williams, then Archbishop of Canterbury, and it was summed up
by David Thomas of the University of Birmingham as the Muslim
equivalent of *Nostra Aetate*, opening up dialogue in a similar way.

Pope Francis has continued the rapprochement, washing the feet of a
Muslim woman prisoner at his first Maundy Thursday celebration and in
2019 visiting the Arabic peninsular (the first time a Pope had done such a
thing) and signing in the United Arab Emirates a *Declaration on Human
Fraternity*, with the Sheikh of Al-Azar. In the *Declaration* the hope is
expressed that:

> dialogue, understanding and the widespread promotion of a culture of toler-
> ance, acceptance of others and of living together peacefully would contribute
> significantly to reducing many economic, social, political and environmental
> problems that weigh so heavily on a large part of humanity.

However, relations between Islam and Judaism have become massively
more complicated following the establishment of the modern State of
Israel. Initially, Zionism was a predominantly secular movement, led by
political rather than religious Jews seeking a political homeland: 'A land
without people for a people without a land', ran the slogan. And therein
lies the issue, for the Palestinians were already nourishing hopes of an
independent state, an Arabic kingdom, following the collapse of the

Ottoman Empire and the withdrawal of the British in the first decades of
the twentieth century. Sociologist and scholar of Judaism and nationalism,
Alan Dieckhoff, has written:

> It was indisputably the Zionist project of reconstructing a Jewish nation as a
> political state that profoundly transformed relations between Arabs and Jews
> in Palestine. The Arabs had hoped to achieve their national independence on
> the rubble of the Ottoman Empire within the framework of an Arab kingdom.
> They saw their dream of unity obliterated by the Franco-English colonial divi-
> sion of the region.

Since the 1970s the conflict has become increasingly religionised on both
sides. Orthodox and ultra-Orthodox Jews (initially opposed to the
establishment of the State of Israel precisely because of its secular nature)
becoming more and more vocal and determined, refer back to the Hebrew
Scriptures for the justification for their possession of the land. Radical
Muslims increasingly identify the struggle with the state of Israel as a jihad
inspired partly by the verses in the Qur'an quoted above which allegedly
seem to justify the destruction of the Banū Nadīr tribe of Medina.

The complexities of the Israel/Palestine situation are beyond the remit
of this essay. But it is more than noteworthy that what was for centuries a
relatively harmonious co-existence, especially in the Umayyad and the
Ottoman Empires – not without its massacres and pogroms, of course, but
also marked by a recognition of the rights of minority religions – has now
become a deadly minefield of mistrust.

So, where, then, is the hope? How can Jews, Muslims and Christians
work together to make the world a better place?

In posing this question, a number of others are raised. Which Jews,
which Muslims and which Christians? If there is one conclusion to be
drawn from the history of interfaith relations, it is that faith traditions are
absolutely not monolithic: each collection of scriptures, whether it is the
Qur'an, the Hebrew Bible or the New Testament contains within it
passages of immense hope and beauty as well as passages which can be
taken to justify violence and slaughter. Each faith tradition includes and has
always included those who would justify violence in terms of God's will,
as well as those who reach above and beyond cultural, tribal or linguistic
boundaries to celebrate shared humanity.

We have heard much about the violence and mistrust, which arise, to a large extent, because of the objectification of other faiths. Very often, the stranger or alien has been identified as literally demonic, as a threat to stability and to racial or religious purity. The British rabbi, theological and Biblical scholar Jonathan Magonet, in an article on Jewish-Muslim relations, wrote: 'Our individuality and our humanity become lost. We become instead a symbol of the unacceptable other, trapped in someone else's ideological construction of the governance of the universe'. But increasingly, there is a manifestation of a deep desire to do things differently, to break down or cut holes in the walls which divide us. To understand the similarities and points of contact between faiths rather than taking refuge in caricatures of difference. There are also unreported stories of good news – examples of continued *convivencia*, for example in Sierra Leone, where in many villages close and harmonious relations between Muslim and Christian continue to this day.

In the context of *Convivencia*, an interfaith dialogue about how Jews, Christians and Muslims understand their sacred scriptures, is significant. In *The People of the Book* (the second book with the same title), scholars Dan Cohn-Sherbrook, George D. Chryssides and Usama Hasan, describe an in-depth conversation, held over a number of years, on the relations between the three Abrahamic faiths. In the Foreword, Revd Marcus Braybrooke expresses the hope:

> May this book help us to listen more attentively, and as we listen to recognise that the God who assures of divine love has the same love for other people, even if it is expressed in different texts and languages.

The book is wide-ranging and honest, covering questions such as: How did our scriptures come about? Are they divinely inspired or the work of human hands? How do we understand the nature of God, and what guidance do the scriptures offer for social, political issues and for the future – on the earth and in the possible life beyond? There is strong emphasis on the relationship between the legal aspects of the Qur'an and the Hebrew scriptures – Dan Cohn-Sherbrook refers frequently to the 613 laws and regulations which Orthodox Jews are expected to observe and the many volumes of *halakah* (interpretation) which has built up around them. But he is also very clear that Reform and Liberal Jews have a quite different relationship to these laws,

> For non-Orthodox Jews, like me, this heritage of biblical interpretation … is a rich resource of Jewish learning and culture rather than a blueprint for Jewish existence in the modern age.

Similarly, Usama Hasan speaks of how the various Islamic schools of law and jurisprudence reflect the diverse and even conflicting interpretations of disputed passages, and the multitude of hadith traditions on every topic. Much common ground is found between the interlocutors: indeed, the main area of disagreement is, as might be expected, over the status of land of Israel/Palestine.

My own experience of working across faith traditions also gives me grounds for hope. For the last four years I have been involved in a project within the Church of England called *Living in Love and Faith*. The project, instituted by the Archbishops of Canterbury and York, aims to provide resources to help the C of E in its internal struggles over questions of gender, sexuality and identity. It seeks to create the potential for dialogue between conservative and progressive, and I, as someone with a foot in Christianity and more than a toe in Islam, have been involved in conversations about this in both traditions, through Inclusive Church and the Inclusive Mosque Initiative, as well as with Jewish colleagues. In the book *Living in Love and Faith*, published in November 2020, we wrote:

> Concerns about Islamophobia mean that Muslim groups are finding common ground with LGBTI+ activists with regard to equality legislation and hate crimes. These groups … call for a rediscovery of *itjihad* – the notion of using independent reasoning to find a solution to a legal question … Other arguments for an inclusive position are drawn from *tawhid* – the doctrine of God's absolute unity. We are very aware that we in the Church of England do not deliberate and decide alone. Our arguments and decisions are affected by what we see and hear from our friends, relatives, neighbours and colleagues in other communities, and we in turn affect them. We are not islands.

In another capacity, I chair Faith for the Climate (FFTC), an organisation founded in 2014 to encourage more inter-faith work on climate change and to raise awareness of the challenges of climate across all faith traditions. Our Trustees include representatives from Muslim, Jewish,

Christian, Buddhist, Sikh and Hindu umbrella organisations, and the
delight in close interfaith working on an issue of such seriousness is
palpable. We were funded by Religions for Peace UK to build capacity
within the smaller faith traditions. Out of that shared work came a close-
knit group of people who founded Hindu Climate Action, the EcoDharma
Network (within the Network of Buddhist Organisations), and EcoSikh
UK, as well as forming good links with the Bahu Trust, a Muslim charity
with more than 20 centres across the UK. Our conversations developed
into friendships across faith traditions grounded in a belief in God's justice
for all people.

I am reminded of an extraordinary and very public friendship that grew
up in the 1960s between Rabbi Abraham Joshua Heschel and the Revd. Dr
Martin Luther King. They first met in January 1963 at the Religion and
Race conference in Chicago, where Rabbi Herschel delivered a powerful
address that began:

> At the first conference on religion and race, the main participants were
> Pharoah and Moses. The outcome of that summit meeting has not come to an
> end ... In fact, it was easier for the children of Israel to cross the Red Sea than
> for a black person to cross certain university campuses. Let us yield no inch to
> bigotry, let us make no compromise with callousness ... some are guilty [of
> racism] but all are responsible.

King and Heschel bonded at that conference. In March 1965, Heschel
walked alongside King in the march from Selma to Montgomery, declaring
'I felt my legs praying'. They united in their unpopular opposition to the
Vietnam War, working closely with Buddhist monk Thich Nhat Hanh, who
King nominated for the Nobel Peace Prize in 1967. They stressed, together
and separately, that prophetic religion and a just society are inextricably
linked. As King famously said, 'the establishment of justice can only be by
the embodiment of love'.

In 1968 their friendship was shattered by an assassin's bullet: but it
remains a lasting testament to the power of love and the call for justice to
transcend the boundaries of fear and mistrust. Similarly, Muslims,
Christians and Jews worked closely together in South Africa to bring about
the end of apartheid. The close relations built up then have since been
undermined as a result of the Israeli-Palestinian conflict, despite some

strong statements from, for example, Archbishop Desmond Tutu who in 2002 compared the treatment of Palestinians in Israel to the treatment of black people under apartheid. But attempts to rebuild the cooperation in South Africa continue.

Within the North Atlantic region the power and influence of faith traditions is in many places on the wane: while across the world there seems to be an increasing symbiosis between authoritarian faith and autocratic government. For evil to triumph it is only necessary for the good to do nothing. But I draw hope from the many incidences of friendship, dialogue and collaboration between faith traditions which have emerged in the last fifty years. The last word goes to the authors of *People of the Book*:

> We have deliberately used the model of dialogue to present ideas because we believe that it is through such encounter and exploration that true understanding and sympathy can best be achieved.

IMAGINING OTHERWISE

Elhum Shakerifar

I felt the thrill of possibility at the launch of Lola Olufemi's second book, *Experiments in Imagining Otherwise*, at the ICA (Institute of Contemporary Arts) in November 2021, when Hajar Press co-founder and co-publisher, Brekhna Aftab took to the stage to introduce the press as a space that is deliberately and absolutely 'not neutral'. The words came as a breath of fresh air.

Hajar Press crowdfunded their way into existence in 2020, anchoring their work in the promise of plurality and community. Co-founded by Aftab and Farhaana Arefin, both of whom have worked in publishing for a number of years, the independent and 'proudly political' publishing house clearly defines itself and its primary audience as 'run by and for people of colour', thus setting forth its commitment to a complete re-imagination of what publishing can be and do.

Lola Olufemi, *Experiments in Imagining Otherwise*, Hajar Press, London, 2021

Cradle Community, *Brick by Brick, How We Build a World Without Prisons*, Hajar Press, London, 2021

Sarah Lasoye, *Fovea / Ages Ago*, Hajar Press, London, 2021

Heba Hayek, *Sambac Beneath Unlikely Skies*, Hajar Press, London, 2021

Jamal Mehmood, *The Leaf of the Neem Tree*, Hajar Press, London, 2021

Yara Hawari, *The Stone House*, Hajar Press, London, 2021

Hajar Press's crowdfunding campaign outlined a clear-eyed assessment of the publishing landscape it was launching into, yet poised to work differently:

Antiracism is not a commercial trend, an optics trick to look good and cash in. We reject the notion that our worth is market-driven—our stories occasionally tokenised and uplifted to serve white guilt and liberal curiosity, then relegated again to 'special markets' and the back of the list.

As a political press, we are uninterested in increasing 'diversity' while ignoring the oppressive structures that keep us unequal. We cannot talk about 'inclusion' at the expense of racism, white supremacy, and imperialism; nor 'representation' instead of capitalism and exploitation.

But we must also intervene in the left, where for too long people of colour have been asked to legitimise and lend our support to movements that have only sidelined and silenced us in return. We don't have time for politics that erase and leave behind the most marginalised people.

Building on these statements, a sense of engagement and inclusivity permeates Hajar's social channels, and their submission process clearly recognises how the written word can become a potent archive against erasure – as noted on their website: 'We understand that history can reside in stories passed down through generations and want to provide a platform for writing that appreciates social memory and the spoken word.' There is also the distinct aim to create communities around books, authors, and the press itself. To this end, Hajar has developed a subscription model whereby readers will receive each book in advance of publication and are invited to reading groups and events to engage with Hajar authors.

Their first year has given life to six books of expansive positionality and plurality. It's an electric line-up – prose and poetry collide, theory meets speculative fiction, drawings grace several collections, others include a blank space for readers to contribute their own thoughts, several authors step out of the page to ask you direct questions. All of the 2021 publications include a playlist; one book is written by a collective – Cradle Community – with no individual author taking precedence, and in fact no individuals named as authors at all, which is radical in itself.

To understand just how radical this is, look no further than the recent controversy surrounding teacher and writer Kate Clanchy's memoir *Some Kids I Taught*. The book resorted to racist and ableist tropes in staggering frequency when describing the children whose writing Clanchy shares throughout – an approach which does reveal its extractive nature when compared with, say, a book written by a collective. The controversy, disturbingly, was not the content of the book, but that some people dared to question it. It was Clanchy herself who called out an online review for supposedly fabricating racist quotes – except that these were in fact drawn directly from her work. The visibility of this discussion brought more attention and authors into the mix, for instance seventeen-year-old autistic author Dara McAnulty, who received such overwhelming abuse after highlighting two passages in which autistic children were described as 'odd' and living in 'ASD land' that he left social media. Similarly, writers Monisha Rajesh, Chimene Suleyman, and Sunny Singh received a torrent of abuse for calling out racist tropes, and for months following their statements, were accused of censorship and of attacking Clanchy.

Concluding an incisive *Guardian* article about the debacle, Rajesh wrote: 'Publishers have churned out books about race and identity over the last two years, an endeavour that is meaningless if the problem lies deep within publishing itself. Writers, agents, editors, publishers, and literary festival organisers need to accept that there is a lot of learning to do about genuine diversity and inclusion, and that empty platitudes and diversity schemes mean nothing if we're punished for speaking out.'

The harmful irony of the situation, given the media's staunch defence of Clanchy, was that she will have benefited from the visibility, whilst the abuse and resulting trauma experienced by Rajesh, Suleyman and Singh – and any other writers who echoed their criticisms – will be merely absorbed into the ever-growing catalogue of micro and macro aggressions carried by writers of colour, which become either active or absorbed deterrents to writing at all. Against this backdrop and atmosphere, the publications of Hajar's inaugural year stand out for their precious and considered work in enacting the care and openness to enable ground-breaking writing by people of colour in the UK today.

Back at the ICA, Aftab went on to state that as a publisher, Hajar saw 'no either/or between the revolutionary and the beautiful', the two qualities that make this press a vital new platform for incisive, generous and impactful writing. Its resonance is already being validated: by the time of the launch, less than three weeks after its initial publication, Lola Olufemi's *Experiments in Imagining Otherwise* had already sold out its initial print run.

Olufemi's writing is full of possibility, of conjecture, of challenge. 'If I ask you to connect *point A* to *point B* and you inevitably draw a straight line, what do you *think* you think of history?' she asks, in her opening *note on language*. Alongside these confrontations, she also outlines her commitment as a statement of intent. And makes it difficult for you to not join her.

> Most concepts with potential start to droop from overuse. Indulge me! I write to say, I do not wish to box you into the *otherwise*. We are not trying to put our finger on it; I bet you have heard that before. Here, the otherwise is a linguistic stand-in for a stance against; it is a posture, the layered echoes of a gesture. I promise you that no approximations will be made. Only pleas, wishes, frantic screams, notes on strategy, contributions in different registers. Substitute the *otherwise* for that thing that keeps you alive, or the ferocity with which you detest the world.

In the casual, open and expansive talk, Olufemi admits that she was more nervous about this book than her previous work, highlighting clearly the value of the permission that Hajar Press afforded her to delve into uncertainty. What is anything radical and new if not, at some level, a risk? As she writes herself:

> The otherwise requires a commitment to not knowing.
> Are you ready for that?

In between readings and reflections, Olufemi celebrated the potentiality of writing in the realm of the speculative ('timeless time') and underlined that downplaying the importance of imagination is a mistake made in the theoretical realm – statements that recall Mexican intellectual and writer Octavio Paz's suggestion that we should imagine the past and remember the future.

The imagination is a site where Hajar's publications are in clear conversation, whispering to each other. The importance of the imaginary comes to life prominently in Yara Hawari's novella *The Stone House*, a text that inscribes itself into a tradition of Palestinian resistance, of narratives shared to challenge the oppressive dominant story. It draws on stories of Hawari's own family – father (Mahmoud), grandmother (Dheeba) and great-grandmother (Hamda) – and leans into the memories instilled in her from a young age, and the spaces into which imagination had to step to complete the picture.

It was in this ephemeral cognitive realm of inherited stories, personal and collective, that I sought solace and temporary relief from the world around me. I was able to bring the destroyed Palestinian landscape to life and simultaneously blur out the colonisers' infrastructure. I could revive long-lost relatives and imagine our community whole, intact and unfragmented. And I was able to breathe.

Movingly, Hawari's imagination casts her father as a boy, seeing him lean into the imaginaries he builds around facts. In the process, the book becomes a conduit through which we learn names, remember places, people and dates, and understand the story that isn't inscribed in history books, but that is passed down from generation to generation as a vital form of resistance.

He knew details about places that no longer existed, like the villages of Al-Zeeb, Al-Basa and Al-Kabri. Although they were in ruins, he could bring these villages to life in his mind, where he rebuilt them bustling and whole. Mahmoud knew people he'd never met, like Um Adel, whose lemon tree he was under strict instructions from his parents to take care of. Or the Al-Qadi family, in whose abandoned house he and his friends played hide-and-seek.

It also enables the reader to understand, as a child might, how the dominant narrative came to be, making it also an archive of undeniable witness to Palestinian history.

In lessons the children were shown photographs of what appeared to be arid land and destitute people from before the establishment of Israel. Mahmoud asked his father later if it was true. Kamel replied that if the photograph had only been taken from the other direction, it would show the bustling international port of Yaffa. But that history was deliberately erased. 'Don't believe them when they tell you that before Israel there was nothing,' he told Mahmoud.

In writing from the perspectives of three generations, Hawari also reflects on trauma, its intergenerational presence and its omnipresence – the 'devastation that was not visible to the naked eye, the kind that wreaked havoc in minds and hearts'.

The urgency of Hawari's book is compounded by its ongoing relevance; it was written largely in 2021 during the Unity Intifada, which was sparked by resistance against expulsions in the Palestinian neighbourhood of Sheikh Jarrah in Jerusalem. 'As I was putting pen to paper to archive my great-grandmother's struggle to stay in her home over six decades ago, another generation of Palestinians was rising up against displacement and dispossession today', Hawari writes in her author's note, underlining the ongoing destructive horror of settler-colonialism.

Brick by Brick: How We Build a World Without Prisons by Cradle Community is also concerned with dismantling the all-encompassing apparatus of the prison industrial complex, as well as – crucially – building and transforming. Delving into questions of immigration, healthcare, education, housing and food, amongst many other thoughtfully articulated topics, the book reads as a manual or a step-by-step reflection on what needs to change and how to change it. One member of the collective reflected that it was a book seeking to answer the question of 'I know what I believe, I know what I value, I know what I care about, I know what I stand against, but what do I stand *for?*'

In this sense, it is very much built on prominent prison abolitionist and scholar Ruth Wilson Gilmore's statement that 'abolition is not *absence*, it is *presence*. What the world will become already exists in fragments and pieces, experiments and possibilities. So those who feel in their gut deep anxiety that abolition means knock it all down, scorch the earth and start something new, let that go. Abolition is building the future from the present, in all of the ways we can.'

The collaborative nature of the book's writing is powerful in itself. Following a robust reflection on language used, as well as a statement on foundations, co-conspirators, and guides, the collective's introduction notes that 'we have written this as a collective in acknowledgement that individual acclaim is counter to our message, and because none of us could do this alone.' It should be understood from this statement that the work of abolition is not easy but its goals can be achieved in community. By positioning the book itself as an outcome of collaboration, Cradle Community acknowledges its limitations and invites you to join in the conversation – recognising the changing landscape, potential blind spots, and a long-term goal that can only be achieved in community, in collaboration, in ongoing communication. 'Working collaboratively has given us the courage and protection to produce imperfect, opinionated, principled work. We're still growing, and we're growing together.' In short, work that speaks urgently to imagining more, better, otherwise.

At an event for Edinburgh's Radical Book Fair, one member of Cradle asks the audience to reflect on whether they had spoken to someone who was incarcerated in the last week; in the past month; in the past three months; in the past year; in the past three years; in the past ten years… 'They are disappeared. We are not meant to think of them. So what we're doing with abolition is that we're trying to subvert a world in which entire human people can be disappeared to a place where no one is meant to care about them anymore. Or can be relegated to a status… criminal, insurgent, you know, terrorist. To which their humanity becomes second place.' Again, the whispers between publications can be felt. They could have been speaking about the Hawari family in *The Stone House*, or those striking in Olufemi's imagination.

As with all of Hajar's publications, *Brick by Brick* too is about the power of imagination — its aim is not merely to decry the state of the country (for it is clearly anchored in the UK context, whilst drawing on examples of international solidarity and care) but to imagine other ways. 'Abolition motivates us to solve problems, instead of attempting to vanish people for being too complicated. We must work to build institutions that affirm our humanity, rather than deny it.'

In the introductory pages to her dazzling debut poetry collection *Fovea / Ages Ago*, Sarah Lasoye explains the fovea in the eye as both receptacle and receptor — representing 'aspirational acuity, and fundamental receptivity', which she goes on to qualify in terms that bring both past and present into view. 'I used to spend so long yearning for acuity, wanting to know precisely where my body started and ended, to be sharp and deliberate, to make myself solid, to do justice to that watery kid. In more recent years, as I have grown more substantial, my weight has shifted towards the receptivity part — the ability to sit still, open, ready, and with gratitude.'

The collection gleams with clear-eyed, angular reflections on that formative age, where imagination was both malleable and at risk of being stilted by the world's dominant monoliths.

SCHOOL POEM
(FED)
and the spoon was in my mouth when I woke
and I didn't ask why
and maybe I should have, but instead I swallowed it

and the cool metal slid down my throat
and the silver was – at once – within me (like it was
never its own)
and I found that I could be fed by a tool for feeding
and I never hungered again
She expands:

within poetry, imagination offers me an escape from a lot of pressures I
sometimes feel to write in a particular way. I think a lot of poets of colour feel
[like this]. There are some things that I know people will want to hear a black
queer woman write about. And I don't want to do that! I feel it, I feel the
pressure on me. Holding firm to the imaginative potential is my guiding steer.

To speak on your own terms is a recurring subject for Hajar's writers,
many of whom are publishing their first works. Gaza-born, London-based
Heba Hayek says that

I chose auto-fiction because I wanted, first of all, to stop looking at myself as
an anthropological project, which is, again, how the world usually looks at me.
And even to, as Toni Morrison says, lose the white gaze in my imagination. I
did not feel like I had to write for the purpose of publishing and then for the
purpose of Western or English-speaking readers to observe me and absorb me
in a way that's accessible to them and acceptable.

Reflecting both on her girlhood in Gaza and existing now so far from it,
Sambac Beneath Unlikely Skies bristles with the struggle to reconcile two
realities entirely at odds, yet coexisting. In doing so, one also creates a
skewed lens on the other. At the same time, the book is infused with food,
permeated by laughter, compassion, rowdy aunts and ambivalent
matriarchs.

In my kitchen, I whisk all the ingredients together and lick the rest of the
batter as I switch my phone camera on.
'Sho ya helwa? Mnawra ya mama.'
'Ba'ref manzari midh mneeh. Don't pretend.'
She reassures me that I look nice, as long as I don't mention the word anxiety.
I make the syrup as we continue to chat: sugar, orange blossom water, lemon,
water. My house smells like Mama.

The lump in my throat slowly melts, and I feel my heartbeat slow down. Baba joins the video call with his big grin, and I watch them argue about whether I need to add the cream on top or in the middle of the cake.

No one should be this far.

The text's accessibility is notable, and its 'normalcy' something that Hayek has been asked about a lot since its launch. 'I find it ridiculous sometimes, because violence exists in these countries as well, it's just the way slow death and the way we're washed under the systems and capitalism and whiteness — it's very, very different from the death that's happening back home, but people talk about normalcy in such a surprising way as if it shouldn't exist back home and it should exist here. I think there is war everywhere, there's words and there's also normalcy.'

Sambac's writing began to take shape in community with other women in exile, a community being a balm against a surprising level of erasure experienced in Ohio. A place where people 'see you only if they really, really want to (except, of course, when you're wearing an *Occupy Wall Street not Palestine* t-shirt).

Your manager at work looks alarmed when he notices your t-shirt and throws an apron at you.

'I'm with you, but it's like you're asking for trouble.'

You catch it with your right hand, which feels like a victory. You don't argue because you begged him for this double shift.

'It's Ohio, sweetheart,' he adds.

It creeps you out, the way he always calls you pet names. When you say this to a guy from your MFA, he says that this is just the way people speak here. *Midwesterners are known for their kindness*, as if you're being rude about it. You've never felt this invisible your whole life.

Subtle observation, lived and gleaned, is also the heart of Jamal Mehmood's *The Leaf of the Neem Tree*. Poetry and short stories elegantly trace the contours of grief and reflections on death, on place. Elders amble along the pages, imparting the wisdom of humility and care. Mehmood's literary canon is invoked by name — Naguib Mahfouz, Mahmoud Darwish, Faiz Ahmad Faiz, Saadat Hasan Manto. It is in fact a representation of Manto that lends the collection its title, as Mehmood explains in his introductory note, 'in Nandita Das's biopic on Saadat Hasan Manto, the talented Nawauddin Siddiqui says the following phrase: "Neem ke pathe kadwe salih – khoon to saaf karte hain." Roughly translated: "Neem leaves may indeed be bitter, but they do clean the blood." This simple metaphor has never left me.' This opening anecdote also reflects all the sources one might gather meaning from – how one person's imagination of another's reality will impact on others' understandings of the world.

Cultural and linguistic multiplicity is a recurring theme. As in Hayek's writing, not everything is translated, yet much can be understood:

> Shabnam Aunty had sensed how affected I was by her words that day. She slid me a small box of *jalebis* when we were both on tills and apologised in Urdu— for reasons I can't explain, this always makes forgiveness easier. *'Maaf kar do, bete meri baat tumhe buri lago na?'* I could have cried. 'No, no, aunty, it's okay, *koi baat nahi.'* She asked me to forgive her anyway, and I had to comply. She was forgiven.

But it is also a bittersweetness that drives attempts to bridge the gap in between. As Mehmood writes in the poem *Tongue*,

> Translation is among our strangest
> passtimes, both most and less fruitful.

The leitmotiv of permission, of existing on your own terms, is again accentuated when looking at the six publications together – how distinctly each is what it wants to be, what it needs to be.

Otherwise
*Other*wise
Other*wise*

'What would you write, if you could write anything you wanted?' is the question Hajar asks their prospective authors. Suddenly the blank page takes on a different meaning – far from writer's block, it asks what *actually* blocks writers.

The Otherwise
and the Wise Other

In 'This Work Isn't For Us', an important piece of research into diversity and inclusion in the arts, which was published in 2020 freely on Google

Docs, and thereby devoid of association with any single platform, writer and curator Jemma Desai asks: 'why, despite thirty years of sustained professional development programmes, recruitment drives and "mentoring" programmes resulting in a highly qualified, well-networked and credible set of individuals from a range of ethnic backgrounds, the industry in its static nature is still focused on the individuals who are excluded rather than those who do the excluding'. This comment can be applied to any structure that has thrived on systemic racism, sexism, classism and ableism. That is, most likely, just about every industry and institution around us. It also underlines why Hajar's work is so significant – born out of a reflection on who does the excluding, but not stopping to dwell on that place. Instead, building.

In Arabic, the root *h-j-r* means to migrate. Hajar (or Hagar) was the name of the Egyptian handmaiden of Abraham's wife Sarah and mother of Ishmael. Abraham married Hajar so that she might bear him children, but after Sarah later gave birth to her own son, Isaac, she insisted that Hajar and Ishmael be banished into the desert. As such, the press explains on their website, 'Hajar represents the racialised people who perform the hidden labour that maintains society but are then disposed of and cast into the margins, their lives, stories and sacrifices forgotten or co-opted.'

In her seminal 1989 essay 'Choosing the Margin as a Space of Radical Openness', the late cultural theorist and social activist bell hooks wrote:

> I am waiting for them to stop talking about the 'other', to stop even describing how important it is to be able to speak about differences. It is not just important what we speak about, but how and why we speak. Often this speech about the 'Other' is also a mask, an oppressive talk hiding gaps, absences, that space where our words would be if we were speaking, if there were silence, if we were there. This 'we' is that 'us' in the margins, that 'we' who inhabit marginal space that is not a site of domination but a place of resistance. Enter that space.

Two decades on, these words still resonate. And as if in response to hooks's clarion call, Hajar Press has indeed entered that space.

IN-BETWEEN

Nikhat Hoque

'Apa (sister), never fear someone who is *hijra* as we are also human, we are also Allah's *bandas* (people of God)'. I received this advice from a *hijra* sister in April 2015 in Dhaka, Bangladesh. I remember everything about her. She immediately stood out to me – wearing a black salwar-kameez, kohl under her eyes, and a small black *teep* (or *bindi*) on her forehead – in comparison to her more vibrantly adorned counterparts. Our interaction was very different to what I was told to expect from a *hijra* group. She did not see me, a 19-year-old British-Bengali girl with no previous exposure to the *hijra* community, in the same way as she approached my sister-in-law. Growing up with Vitiligo, a skin condition characterised by patches of skin losing its pigment, I had experienced my own share of 'othering', and I did not approach them as 'others' in the same way that society often does. I merely saw them as unacquainted people I was meeting for the first time.

In Leyla Jagiella's *Among the Eunuchs: A Muslim Transgender Journey*, we meet a plethora of *hijras*. The compelling text explores her encounters, as a white transgender Muslim woman, with the *hijra* and *khwajasara* communities in South Asia. It is part memoir and part historical research, weaving together the long-forgotten history of the transgender community in South Asia with Jagiella's own personal and political experiences. Throughout the book, she strives to make her first-hand knowledge accessible to all – 'the uprooted, the in-betweens, the mixed and the misfits.' Jagiella speaks of her experiences of not belonging – in her hometown, her assigned gender, her name; and the book follows how she navigates around the complexities and fragilities of finding her place in the world.

I must admit that initially I was sceptical at the idea of a white European Muslim transgender woman writing about her experiences of living in *hijra* and *khwajasara* spaces in India and Pakistan. I was unfamiliar with Jagiella's work, and was worried about the 'exoticisation' of a marginalised community and being South Asian there was also a sense of protectiveness behind the concern. I was weary at the use of the word 'eunuch' as I (and perhaps many others) have misunderstood it to not include people who are intersex or do not identify with their birth sex. Jagiella traces back the use of the word 'eunuch' to ancient Mediterranean times to show its connection to contemporary transgender identities in order to 'understand the traditional self-image of the *khwajasara* and *hijra* community'. The history of the term becomes increasingly important in understanding the official social category of 'third gender' and its importance to the South Asian trans community. Jagiella urges that in order to fully empower the community it is essential to understand that they already occupy a specific space in their respective societies harboured through a longstanding historical, cultural and religious legacy. Although, this legacy does not always do justice to these communities, it does offer them their own space which does not exist in the West. Despite the view held by Western activists that the queer communities of the Global South are oppressed and need to fit into 'more globalised notions of gender and sexuality,' South Asian *hijra's* and *khwajasara's* have through their own efforts secured their spaces as well as gained legal recognition as a 'third gender.'

Jagiella is aware that many Western activists may feel discomfort with the term 'third gender' as it could imply that transgender women are not 'real

Leyla Jagiella, *Among the Eunuchs: A Muslim Transgender Journey*, Hurst, London, 2021

women'. However, she points out that many in the *hijra* and *khwajasara* communities do not in fact see themselves as women. They have their own complex way of thinking about gender and sexuality which may not complement popular globalised Western concepts on gender. Jagiella believes that one can experience multiple gender identities according to the social and cultural context. She explains how when in Europe she would be offended at the idea of not being considered a woman, in India she has used the more androgynous *hijra* status to enter the inner sanctum of shrines in India (rarely, but when the presence of women is restricted). She notes that identity is not constant, and neither should it be, it is ever-changing and evolving – being in a 'third gender' space does not mean that she is not a woman but that she has many layers of equally important identities.

Jagiella points out that Muslims in the West know next to nothing about the transgender communities of South Asia. Growing up as a South Asian Muslim in the UK, I agree with Jagiella that many Muslims in the West are largely unaware of the existence of queerness within Islam. From court appointed eunuchs, to companions of many well-known saints, to the guards in Makkah and Medina, the presence of trans people is apparent across the Muslim world. Yet, why do so many Muslims today view queerness as a Western concept? In her essay, 'Queer Secularity', Abeera Khan questions the Western positioning of queerness against Islam as inherently colonial. Jagiella shows through a detailed history of eunuchs in Islam that the two are not incompatible but have a long-shared past that is rarely documented. She writes:

> the precolonial Muslim past was not a paradise of sexual freedom and unlimited gender expression. Such ideas, sometimes taught by queer Muslim activists today, are as wrong as ideas of an essentialised Islam that has always been sexually repressive. However, there have been periods when there was indeed a much more widely accepted diversity of sexualities and genders across the Muslim world and when many Muslim societies had space for those who did not fit the gender binary.

That space was ruptured and erased from the Muslim consciousness by colonialism. The 1871 Criminal Tribes Act had a devastating effect on the social, financial and cultural status of the *hijra* community. They were further marginalised by a system of persecution, which from colonial times has relegated them to the outskirts of mainstream society. As opposed to the Western perception that queerness is a contemporary phenomenon, Jagiella shows that queerness, in one form or another, has always existed in the world and within South Asian and Islamic history. We can see the historical relevance of *hijras* and *khwajasaras* in the Islamic world in the works of Ameer Khusrau, the thirteenth century poet and musician of the Delhi Sultanate, and Rumi, the celebrated thirteenth-century poet and Sufi. This does not show, Jagiella suggests, that Islam is completely accepting of non-binary identities, but that during the classical period there was an integral space that they occupied.

The crux of the book critiques the tendency of Western activists and NGO to homogenise transgender experiences by imposing western ideals of transgender sexuality, identity and rights on a context where those ideals are not applicable. In the case of South Asia, it is the failure to fully understand the local traditions of the *hijra* and *khwajasara* communities and the multiple identities that many people of trans communities may embody in a non-Western context. Jagiella challenges the focus on one identity and a single-issue politics, resulting in the disruption and eventual erasure of other oppressive intersections as seen in the younger generation of *hijras* and *khwajasaras*. Queer politics is supposed to be radically intersectional as opposed to the privileging of sexuality over other identity categories. In South Asia the cultural and religious identity of the transgender community is intertwined with their sexual identity. In her essay, 'Punks, Bulldaggers and Welfare Queens: The radical potential of Queer Politics', Cathy Cohen echoes similar concerns of 'individuals who consistently activate only one characteristic of their identity, or a single perspective of consciousness, to organise their politics, rejecting any recognition of the multiple and intersecting systems of power that largely dictate their life chances'. And, in her paper, 'Under Western Eyes', Chandra Talpade Mohanty problematises the category of 'third world women' employed by Western feminist activists and scholars which again homogenises the experiences of all women throughout the global south with different historical, social and economic contexts. She argues that this does not serve to combat the oppression these women face; rather, it implicitly reinforces the superior self-image of western scholars and activists by contrast. Following Cohen and Mohanty's concerns, Jagiella also points out the risk of seeing the *hijra/khwajasara* as a marginal 'third world' group who do not have the knowledge or agency to fight for their rights.

Jagiella admonishes the thinking of those who believe that their own ideas of gender, identity, culture, religion and sexual orientation are right and those of others a delusion. She examines the activism of Trans Exclusionary Radical Feminists, a group which opposes transgender rights legislation and advocates for exclusion of trans women from women's spaces. Jagiella considers the debate around transgender women using men's toilets instead of women's as reductive and violent. In sharp contrast, she points out that many transgender women joined the 'Aurat

March' (women's march), an annual political demonstration in Pakistani cities to observe the International Women's Day, and the 2019/20 Delhi Shaheen Bagh protests in India. 'In the course of these protests', Jagiella notes, it is doubtful that a 'cisgender woman questioned transgender women's use of the female bathroom'. The real strength of feminism, she suggests, is within the intertwining and interconnected margins where people come together instead of excluding each other further.

The strength of Jagiella's book lies in the fact that she does not seek to paint a pretty and uniform picture of the world of *hijras* but creates a well-rounded account of their lives. The *hijras* are beautiful as well as the damned. The *hijra* community provides a shelter to many shunned by their families; it is a space where Jagiella herself belonged and felt at home. But the community is also subjected to stereotypes and sometimes portrayed as violent and dangerous.

My early encounters with queer individuals fell prey to a similar profiling. My first encounter was through the Bollywood film, *Mehendi* (1998), which I saw at the tender age of six. The protagonist, Billu, a cross-dressing gay man, is portrayed as a lascivious sex-crazed rapist. The violent portrayal of Billu disturbed me. I grew up listening to various, mostly negative, stories about the *hijras*. But one of my aunts had a different view of the *hijra* community. 'They *seem* different as they are *hijra*', she would tell me. Her words were never judgmental, unlike other stories I had heard. Her presence was often requested by our neighbours to help manage situations involving *hijra* groups. She had seen both the sweet and not so smooth interactions: the ones that ended in joyful blessings, artistic celebratory dances, and a gratis payment; and others that involved threats, verbal sparring, and sometimes ended in a brawl. Apart from this, I would only see the *hijra* groups walking through the alleys of Dhaka decked in colourful vibrant sarees — but from the safe distance of my veranda. Until my direct contact with a *hijra* group in 2015, I had never really questioned my own position of only viewing the community from the confines of the veranda. Reading *Among the Eunuchs* led me to realise that I may have been at risk of being a '*kupa munduk*', an Adivasi term denoting a frog that resides within a well unaware of the unlimited world outside. The metaphor was popularised in Satyajit Ray's 1991 film *Agantuk* (The Stranger). Jagiella says in the preface of the book that the film influenced her to study anthropology. 'We live in and sustain a global structure of violence', she writes, 'and within such a structure it is ludicrous to expect a marginalised minority in an already struggling society to be free of such violence'.

Among the Eunuchs is much more than a book about Jagiella's personal experience in *hijra* and *khwajasara* spaces. It is also an examination of how these spaces have changed over the course of Islamic, South Asian, and world history, and how they are changing in our times. Jagiella succeeds in her aim of presenting 'a more complicated, but at the same time, much more enjoyable and optimistic analysis of identity'. The book is packed with various references to film and literature, especially Bollywood films, that add a bit of cultural nostalgia (even though the representation of the *hijra/ transgender* community in some of these films is often flawed). It made me question a few of my own beliefs and perceptions of the *hijra* community and transgender issues. Through Jagiella's constant reiterations of her positionality and privilege I was able to reflect on my own; and connect them to the wider discourses on culture, identity and belonging within Islamic history and the Muslim experience. Highly accessible to both researchers and the average reader.

ET CETERA

MY FRIEND, ABDULHAMID ABUSULAYMAN

Anwar Ibrahim

On 18 August 2021, the world shined a little less bright with the loss of AbdulHamid AbuSulayman. Islam teaches us to grapple with the life-long challenge of improving ourselves as individuals while also seeking to better our communities and societies. AbdulHamid personified the true spirit of Islam through his thoughts and actions. He leaves a profound intellectual and institutional legacy designed to improve and reform Muslim societies.

AbdulHamid was born in Mecca, Saudi Arabia, in 1936. He followed most of his contemporaries to Egypt to study political science at the University of Cairo. After finishing his studies in Cairo, he moved to the US, where as a student, he was involved in establishing the Muslim Students' Association of the United States and Canada (MSA) and the Association of Muslim Social Scientists (AMSS). He obtained his doctorate in international relations in 1973 from the University of Pennsylvania. A few years later, he returned to Saudi Arabia to teach at King Saud University in Riyadh, and become the Chair of the Department of Political Science from 1982 to 1984.

I first met AbdulHamid in the mid-1970s, in the heyday of what was then seen as a period of 'Islamic Revival'. Intellectuals, thinkers, academics, activists, modern, and traditional scholars crossed paths and often engaged in furious debates. But we were far from united in our thinking. In fact, the ummah might have been at its most divided, the juxtaposition of ideas was at times overwhelming, and the only unity to be found was in our own individual positions which were inevitably seen as the right cure for our collective sickness. We debated what was to be done amidst the backdrop of turbulence from the siege of Mecca, Soviet encroachment in Afghanistan, the burning of al-Aqsa Mosque, and the Arab-Israeli wars. Many of us came from fledgling nations and hoped to survive past infancy and develop into strong states with new ideas and innovations. Some of us spoke of postcolonial matters, some wanted to embrace modernity, some feared secular democracy, while others were concerned about civilisational interregnum and authoritarianism. There were calls for jihad, reform, and even revolution. A few audacious individuals considered the future. By then, AbdulHamid had become the Secretary General of The World Assembly of Muslim Youth (WAMY), based in Riyadh, and I was with Malaysia's Muslim Youth Movement (ABIM). We had a common friend: the noted Palestinian-American philosopher and scholar of Islam, Ismail al-Faruqi, who was a frequent visitor to Malaysia. Al-Faruqi was a popular speaker and debated with many of the top scholars in Malaysia. Al-Faruqi introduced me to AbdulHamid; and I invited him to come and speak in Kuala Lumpur. My first impression was of an exceptionally gentle and polite person, who displayed unassuming confidence. Eventually, I was invited to join WAMY as a representative of Asia and the Pacific. We became close friends. The conversations al-Faruqi led would bring AbdulHamid, myself, and a brilliant assembly of expat scholars from across the Muslim world together. Our rather intense discussions would lead to the establishment of the International Institute of Islam Thought (IIIT).

AbdulHamid was a brilliant scholar and consummate teacher. Great scholars tend to be great teachers who hold high standards for their students; and do not hesitate to correct them when necessary. His natural aptitude towards education began with the way he used to correct my pronunciation of his name. The Malay language preconditions us towards short cuts and abbreviations. So, when I would introduce him as AbuSulayman, each letter given the same stress, he would object with an aside, 'Brother! Sulay*maan*'. In Malay, we would add an extra 'a' to his name, to extend the sound and ensure this *faux pas* would be avoided; and an extra 'a' would be added to my grandson's name too, so that I would not have to be met with continual reprimand for my impropriety. The details, where it is said the devils tend to hide, mattered to AbdulHamid. He was meticulous in everything he did, paying serious attention to every element.

His main concern was the reform of Muslim society. He wanted to direct our attention to the roots of the problems of the ummah; and the reforms he sought were lived reforms, beyond platitudes and empty promises, ready-made solutions and quick-fixes. His first major work is *Towards an Islamic Theory of International Relations* (1973), which was the result of his doctoral work at the University of Pennsylvania. But it was his second book, *The Crisis of the Muslim Mind* (1986), that turned into a project and propelled his life's work.

AbdulHamid saw the malaise of the ummah both in terms of a deficit of education and an encultured limitation on the mind. He described the later as a breaking from the Qur'anic Worldview, which he would address more fully in his later 2011 work aptly titled *The Qur'anic Worldview: A Springboard for Cultural Reform*. For AbdulHamid, the problem of the Muslim mind arose out of an unconsidered adoption, writ large, of Bedouin Arab culture. He was influenced by ibn Khaldun (1332–1406), who noted the variety of qualities that enabled the Bedouins to survive and thrive in their environment; but when immobilised and removed from such existential threats, these same qualities would lead to a decline of civilisation that inculcated them. AbdulHamid referred to this as the 'Desert Worldview', a mentality that allowed for an exclusivism and chauvinism and gave rise to racist and dictatorial tendencies that thrived in Arab tribal culture, and became dominant within early Muslim civilisation. As this trend rose to prominence, AbdulHamid wrote, 'the Muslim community fell prey, increasingly, to lethargy, stagnation, passivity, superstition, and sophistry. As a consequence, the foundation of knowledge and strength upon which this community had originally been founded began to crumble, while the guiding light of reflection, investigation, creativity, and conscious stewardship steadily died out'.

AbdulHamid traces the roots of this decline to an unreflective embrace of the Prophet's language. The Prophet had to sometimes resort to a discourse of warning, a cultural staple of the desert worldview, 'to bring them out of their primitive social and cultural state into an understanding of the basic starting points for creating a global civilisation based on the Qur'an and its teachings.' Disregarding the changing context of the world, the ummah failed to move forward to something more universal and so the desert worldview superseded the Qur'anic one.

There is an echo here of the criticism of the late Egyptian scholar, Muhammad al-Ghazali (1917–1998), who criticised the *fiqh* mentality adopted by many Muslim thinkers. Fiqh mentality reduces the world down to the convenient simplicity of *halal* and *haram*, right and wrong, particularly in terms of judicial judgement. Al-Ghazali called for a rectification of the heart, where spiritual nourishment and an exploration of ethical values were a greater service to the Sharia and the ummah than the rigid dogma of the fiqh mentality. This mentality reflects AbdulHamid's desert worldview, giving rise to an empty traditionalism where customs are repeated while their relevance and meaning are lost. Life is reduced to going through a set of motions, and spiritual purpose, as well as solidarity and empathy with our neighbours, is forgotten. This uncritical approach to

Islam was the death of faith for AbdulHamid. The resulting fiqh mentality ossifies the lived faith of Islam. Islam become a religion of blind followers, often misguided, and detached from their relationship to Allah. A believer's critical engagement with the Word and the world evaporates. This is precisely the crisis of the Muslim mind that prevents the ummah from realising its civilisational potential.

Ibn Khaldun's analysis traces the way this brought about the decline of the classical Islamic empire. Ibn Khaldun commended the Bedouin for their strong level of *asabiyyah*, the potential for social cohesion, a product of efforts to survive the harsh and unforgiving climate of the desert. While it served well for the expansion and conquest that transformed the early Muslim community into a world civilisation, ultimately, no longer living in such harsh conditions, it turned asabiyyah from a unifying sensibility into a reductive and destructive nationalism – with higher value absent, ransacked with racist undertones, and entrenched within the exclusivist and dictatorial might of the desert worldview. Ibn Khaldun hoped that the asabiyyah could again be revived but as a tool for solidarity and unity. AbdulHamid saw the revival by going forward to the Qur'anic worldview.

AbdulHamid believed that the contemporary neo-conservativism and racist tribalism devoid of critical thought is not some preordained fate of the ummah. Indeed, history provides us with examples of those who broke the chains of the desert worldview and sought reform and return to the Qur'anic worldview. One such figure was the great Salah al-Din al-Ayyubi (1137–1193), who became the first Sultan of Egypt and Syria. He has been somewhat mythologised in an unfair cast of romantic nostalgia by Muslims, but aside from his military prowess as the hero of Jerusalem, AbdulHamid cited Salah al-Din as an example of one whose work to establish robust and sustainable systems of education in the Holy Land was shaped by the Qur'anic worldview. I would also add to this example Salah al-Din's entire administration of Jerusalem. He possessed a natural talent at networking for peace. Without a doubt, Salah al-Din was an exceptional military commander and strategist, but he surpassed himself in his mastery as a diplomat and in maintaining peace in one of the most diverse regions of the world, Palestine – particularly amongst Muslims, Christians, and Jews despite the macroaggressions occurring outside the city walls. His effective leadership and adept approach to events unfolding before him allowed him to maintain trade in Palestine and oversee peace amongst all the diverse communities of the Holy Land. He also nurtured good ties with the Byzantine Orthodox Christians as he held off Crusaders from the West. Moreover, he instilled an awareness and understanding in society and its institutions to ignite a spirit of reform and learning. His example of good governance was forged in a delicate balancing act that saw the construction of new mosques, improvements to the economic situation, as well as physical infrastructure of the region, and social reforms achieved through advancing the state of education.

Salah al-Din's spirit and example informed many of our debates as we endeavoured to build IIIT throughout the early 1980s. To confront the crisis of the Muslim mind, we set out to invigorate an intellectual revival of academic thinking on the basis of AbdulHamid's Qur'anic worldview. This took us through projects of de-westernisation of knowledge to Islamisation of knowledge, and finally nowadays, to the Integration of Knowledge as we set about resisting secularisation and navigating decolonisation of culture and institutions. We would stand against the *taqlid* (conformity to the teaching of others) of misguided fanatics as well as *talfiq*, the imitation found in grafting Western solutions onto our problems. We needed a new way that brought us back to Islamic values and the Qur'an. We need to tear down the desert worldview of dichotomising good and bad so that we could attain a more sophisticated, moral ethics capable of engaging with the complex, chaotic, and contradictory issues of our postnormal times. I think I was the only one who was not a scholar in the group, but we were not simply armchair philosophers or intellectuals confined to the ivory tower. We worked to become agents of the change we desired. And this did not stop AbdulHamid and myself from having our great chicken-or-the-egg debate on how to bring about the social reform we sought.

For me, good governance was the key to curing a society's ills. AbdualHamid fervently disagreed. For him, it was a robust education that must come first in order to heal our civilisation. He argued against any of us getting involved in the nasty enterprise of politics. In contrast, I would retort by saying that without good government there is no one to support our new ideas and efforts. Far too many oppressive regimes have stymied the flourishment of the people's minds and their educational systems. Yet, AbdulHamid persisted, without a good education, you cannot create the ruling class with the capability of empowering educational progress. So, in the end, no resolution could be reached on this debate. But Salah al-Din provided the example whereby we could both have what we needed. As the sun began to set on the 1980s, we would be presented with our opportunity to actualise all that we had been arguing back and forth on for at least a decade: in the form of a university.

I went into politics in the 1980s, much to the chagrin of AbdulHamid. In 1986, when the term of the first president of the International Islamic University Malaysia (IIUM), former Prime Minister Hussein Onn came to an end, I was Minister of Education and was named as his successor. The university had been established but there was much work to be done in turning it into the intellectual centre we had envisioned. Being a minister and a member of parliament, I needed a trusted team to help with advancing IIUM, to live up to the name we had given it, and I had just the person in mind. And I had another point to make in the recurring debate between AbdulHamid and I. As someone in politics who was a minister, I was in a position to take our intellectual and reform agenda forward.

I still remember being in the car, operating one of the bulky, early model, mobile phones and calling AbdulHamid in Washington, DC. Would he accept the position of the new Rector of IIUM? As I went about explaining the situation and the opportunity, he was shocked. He had thought I wanted him to be a visiting scholar with an honorary and temporary post. But, I said, we have had too many guest lectures, it is time that we did something substantial. We have an incredible opportunity with me as the minister and a relatively new university. We can transform it into a bastion of reformist thoughts and ideas. AbdulHamid paused for a thought. 'When do you want me to start? Tomorrow?', he asked. I told him to take at least a week, perhaps consult his wife. But the week had begun and he agreed without hesitation, and this was before we had gotten into the negotiations of salary or the logistics of moving his family half way around the world. This has always stood as a wonderful illustration of the man AbdulHamid AbuSulayman was.

When AbdulHamid arrived in Malaysia, no time for adjustment, even to the tremendous jetlag he must have felt, was needed. Few have possessed the level of commitment and dedication he had for the university. In public he was the perfect example of cordiality. But in private, I was in for one of the greatest battles of my over forty years in public service! There was continuous warfare between us, his passion would have it no other way. 'Brother', he would say, 'this is *the* university, this is where civilisation is made!' As a minister, I had to abide by the budget and had to act fairly to the other universities. But AbdulHamid would ask me if I wanted 'some run of the mill university for the sake of political expediency so that you can show the world what a great product we have, or do you want *the* university, that services its conceptual and institutional purposes to society?' This was not to be a mere centre of excellence, but a civilisational endeavour that saw to the betterment of society, just as we had discussed during all those IIIT meetings.

Eventually, AbdulHamid's meticulous attention to detail saw a major transformation of IIUM. I can confidently say that without AbdulHamid, IIUM would not be the world recognised institution it is today. From the architecture of the buildings to the structure of the Kulliyyah (university departments), he proved himself not only a brilliant academic but also an effective manager as well as a visionary leader. I had let loose a workaholic who would not rest until the good work was done. His wife Faekah even joked that AbdulHamid had two wives, her and the university. He built a new campus for IIUM, transforming a hill in Gombak, Selangor, into a mini city, a sanctuary for thinkers, learners, and those who sought after truth. He brought world class graduates to the university from abroad; and they returned home to take on leading positions in Bosnia, China, Albania, Indonesia, the Philippines, and throughout Africa. And his efforts also lead to the beautiful medical campus in Kuantan. Throughout the 1990s, we had built something truly remarkable.

As someone who has always lived in Malaysia, AbdulHamid had expanded my sense of what home means. His home was the world and his family was the ummah. And while born in Saudi Arabia, he left his mark both in the United States through his university education and work with IIIT and also in Malaysia which will serve future generations of Malaysian and international students at IIUM. He made a faraway land, of infinite diversity and languages he did not speak, into a home by the strictest definition of the term and built bonds with people stronger than those to our own blood-bound family.

Yet, as Ibn Khaldun says, each cycle of history must give way to the next. One of my greatest heartbreaks in life came in the form of a lesson that when you dedicate your life to justice and doing what is right, those who would have it otherwise do not only take you down, they also go after friends and family. But in the hardest of times, we also see the reality of those bonds of friendship. Following my sacking from government in 1998, my home at the time had become a public square of sorts, filled with outraged citizens calling for an end to the toxic politics of Malaysia, and for long overdue (even back then) reforms. Despite being apolitical, AbdulHamid and Faekah would be there every day, giving their support even though they could not understand all that was being said around them. AbdulHamid was a loyal friend.

One day, the cries of the public were interrupted by the Royal Police, who burst into my house, arrested me and took me away, in front of a huge gathering of protesters, to prison. While in solitary confinement, I learned that AbdulHamid had also been removed as Rector of IIUM, and would be leaving Malaysia. I was overwhelmed with grief. AbdulHamid and his family had made Malaysia their home, his children had grown up in the land I call my home. So, with the best handwriting I could muster (which is not particularly good in the most ideal circumstances), with the materials made available to me in my prison cell, I penned something I had intended as an apology that played out more as a call to action. In the end, it was a reassurance to a friend that I would not go quietly into the dark and history may remember it as the most unusual Eid address I have yet given. For Ibn Khaldun also said that cycles of history repeat themselves, after the fall and collapse, a new cycle begins and there is an opportunity for reform and change that could lead a civilisation into a new epoch.

The only things available to me in solitary confinement was my reflections and so I took stock of the lessons my great teacher, friend, and brother, AbdulHamid, had taught me. The reform agenda would not fail, there were too many great minds creating too much knowledge and wisdom for it to all to be for nought. Those who take comfort in ignorance and thrive on the withholding of justice will have their comeuppance. Despotic dictators would burn out and be overthrown. Reform will always win, we had laid the foundations, so we would just have to bide our time. There was always hope; and IIUM was left in good hands while we were away. The letter concluded on the sorrowful note. 'What sort of a Muslim farewell was this!'. No dinner, no presents! Something far too familiar in the midst of the ongoing pandemic. All I can give now is all I could give then. *Al qalb bil qalb!* Heart to heart.

Following the historic 2018 Fourteenth General Election, the flame of hope was once again reignited in Malaysia; and I was happy to bring AbdulHamid back to a global home one more time. While in Malaysia, he endowed an international student fund in his name that, insha'Allah, will continue to secure the education of future students for a long time to come.

AbdulHamid taught us that education was not just about learning, but also about developing. He stood against the rigid dichotomy between the secular and the religious and challenged us to revive the Qur'anic worldview by doing away with the petty cultural differences that do little more than divide us. As a guiding force, education involves going out to the people, improving their insight and foresight, and working to transform their social and economic conditions. Educated people, AbdulHamid had argued, were agents of change, they cultivate the flame of knowledge so that it may burn so bright and not diminish, even after we perish. As I say yet another farewell to AbdulHamid AbuSulayman, I recall the words of the French philosopher and resistance fighter, Roger Garaudy. 'To be faithful to our ancestors is not to preserve the ashes of their fire but to transmit its flame'. And the flame of AbdulHamid will burn on in the thoughts and actions of those he touched through his work with IIIT; and the hundreds of students at IIUM he inspired and sent off to different corners of the world.

Brother AbdulHamid, you have left the ummah and our civilisation in good hands.

ON ZOOMBIES

Shamim Miah

Has the Covid-19 pandemic radically altered your view of employment? Did the rapid shift from in-office to virtual work lead you to re-assess your life and future? If the answer to these questions is yes, then you are not alone. Less, than eighteen months after the first Covid-19 lockdown, a survey from the career site, Monster, revealed that 95 per cent of workers are thinking about applying for a new job, while 92 per cent of workers considered switching professions. Many complained about burn-out and Zoom fatigue arising from new arrangements, which continue to blur the boundary between home and work.

Enter, polyworking! Many people use the new opportunity provided by 'working from home' to undertake two or more jobs. The idea of polyworking, during pre-pandemic, included an element of freedom and emancipation as many managed multiple jobs to escape the world of monotony and boredom. It gave the YOLO (You Only Live Once) generation an opportunity for creativity, self-expression, and authenticity. Polyworking gave people the opportunity to pursue hobbies and passions; it gave teachers the opportunity to do part-time film-making and tech-consultants to pursue professional photography. Thus, it is not surprising to see that a study by the social network Polywork shows 64 percent of employees aged twenty-one to forty are working more than one job or hope to work multiple jobs in the future.

The 'Great Resignation' has accelerated the speed and the desire for polyworking, which has prompted high number of job vacancies, burnout and new working arrangements due to the pandemic. More crucially, Covid-19 has exposed the gender inequality baked into polywork. For men polyworking includes an element of choice, for women it includes completing the double-burden of paid and unpaid work, completing relevant household chores, ensuring that the children are attending virtual learning, whilst maintaining a full-time job. Nevertheless, the new and emerging types of work arrangements arising from the Covid-19 pandemic will continue to shape the future of work, some of this may ultimately be an extension of what the late anthropologist, David Graeber, described as 'bullshit chores'. Thanks to Covid-19, the very nature of time is changing; we are now in corona-time. Corona-time, or 'blursday', is when the day and a week, a weekday and a weekend, the morning and night, the present and the recent past, are all rolled into one. More significantly, the days blend together and the months simply lurch ahead. Covid-19 also transformed the nature of life, as it began to blur the boundaries between the virtual and the real. We see this in how everything from birth, engagement, indeed, the cycle of life, is captured, uploaded, and shared online. As the world suddenly changed beyond recognition, Zoom emerged as the key word of our time.

Zoom, or Zoom Video Communication, Inc, to give it the full name, is a Silicon Valley communication company set up by the former Cisco engineer and executive, Eric Yuan in 2011. In 2019, Yuan was worth just under $4 billion. Thanks to Covid-19, Zoom became a verb and a household name. The company is now worth $18 billion. The meteoric rise of Zoom saw a staggering ten million daily meeting participants in December 2019; rising to more than 300 million in April 2020. Throughout 2020, people complained about *'Zoombombing'* (crashing an online meeting); this was followed by security complaints (due to its undisclosed data mining). Despite this, its popularity continues to rise, as friends and office staff would frequently say, 'Let's Zoom' or 'I'll Zoom you', even if they are using rival video conferencing platforms such as Microsoft Teams or Google Meets. By early 2021, 'Zoom-fatigue' became a clinically diagnosed reality.

Jeremy Bailenson, founding director of the Stanford Virtual Human Interaction Lab, was one of the first academics to publish a peer-reviewed article in the journal *Technology, Mind and Behaviour* examining the impacts of prolonged back-to-back video-conferencing. The health risks and consequences associated with spending long-hours on Zoom is now becoming apparent, shattering some of the many myths associated with the idea of technology as agents of liberation. The causes of Zoom-fatigue are, firstly, excessive amounts of eye-gaze at a close proximity. In fact, at your next face-to-face meeting take time out to see how people behave. You will no doubt notice people taking notes, some will be looking at the speaker, whilst others will take regular glances at their latest social media threads. But with Zoom, all people get non-stop front-on views of all other people. This is similar to being in a crowded lift while being forced to stare at the person you are standing very close to, instead of looking down or at your phone. The rupture of natural patterns of behaviour on Zoom conferences, where we are forced to look at others for a prolonged period of time, can cause dramatic rise in social anxiety.

Secondly, think about the last moment you took a glance at the mirror. How long did that take? If it was a quick glance as you walked past a mirror in the shopping centre, couple of minutes perhaps? Or, if it was first thing in the morning whilst brushing your teeth then naturally it would be five minutes or less. Now imagine, going to work and you were followed around with a handheld mirror, and for every movement and every conversation you were engaged in, you were forced to see your own face in that mirror. Sounds crazy! This is what most video-conferencing medium gets us to do every day. Bailenson reminds us, how, 'Zoom users are seeing reflections of themselves at a frequency and duration that hasn't been seen before in the history of media and likely the history of people'. Zoom-fatigue is such a big issue within the corporate and the public sector that some universities, such as Stanford, have created their own ZEF Scale (Zoom Exhaustion & Fatigue Scale).

Finally, if you observe your colleague having an audio-phone conversation, the chances are that you will find them moving around, stretching their hands, or making notes, or in the case of a mobile phone conversation then no doubt they will walk and talk at the same time. On a Zoom call people are forced to stay within the frustum, or region visible on the screen, in order to be seen by others. In fact, it is the cultural norm to stay within the frustum despite its restriction on movement. The psycho-physiological impacts of reduced mobility has profound impacts on movement and cognitive performance. It can, no doubt, make people look and feel like zombies. Not surprisingly, end-to-end Zoom conferences have changed human behaviour. Zooming has forced people to forget the boundaries between the public and the private. Thanks to the demands of the frustum, we can see Zoombies in action; it is where the social mask slips and the true nature of the zombie is made transparent.

So let us meet our first Zoombie. In fact, this person is not difficult to locate. Countless numbers of friends and colleagues have seen this Zoombie in action. Typically, it involves a college student or indeed a work official participating in an online-class or a virtual business meeting. From a distance you see small images of people all abiding by the protocols of video-conferencing. Suddenly you see some movement: someone picks up their laptop and decides to go for a walk, you think this is an innocent gesture, only for you to realise that they are walking up a flight of steps into the bathroom. Then suddenly, everyone stops paying any attention to the main-speaker and all gazes set upon this person. Does he/she, or doesn't he/she? Before the thought passes through your mind the deed is done. And this basic of all human functions is on public display; and thanks to the record function on Zoom, it's captured and circulated to every Bushra in Bradford and Dorothy in Dorset.

The second Zoombie is a male and often an adult; sometimes, but not always, a mature adult. Unlike, our first Zoombie, he is difficult to locate. However, by sheer miracle, this Zoombie was captured in an online meeting in the US, the video went viral during the peak of lockdown with almost five million views. It involves a young line manager, called Daniel, hosting a meeting with nine other work colleagues. The video starts off as a typical meeting with discussions of graphs and charts on a report. This atypical business meeting is ruptured when Daniel decides to reach out for a bottle of lubricant and tissues. And in full display of the camera, he reaches out to change screens (or switch off his camera, it is unclear) on his computer whilst he is dropping his trousers. The rest of the team are in total shock. His work mate Sophie, shouts 'Daniel' 'Daniel'. Sean calls out: 'turn off your camera Daniel'. In the full commotion of laughter and shock, Channel lambasts, 'call him and tell him to stop'; this forces Chris to reach out for his mobile to call Daniel. Mika and Michael find the unfolding drama very funny, whilst Channel has had enough and exits the meeting. More significantly, nobody is able to turn off the Zoom call because Daniel is the host. Everyone is left in a state of total embarrassment, with the exception of Daniel! Whilst Daniel continues with his teenage antics; Sean is left traumatised, Xelena is quick to exit, leaving Bennet fascinated and amused.

Both of the above Zoombies share similar Zombie traits. Zombies are essentially a paradox as they are dead and also living at the same time. The nature of the zombie is that 'it is human and non-human, living and not living, cultural and non-cultural, natural and supernatural, suspended between fundamental binaries that most definitions presuppose'. There are countless *besharam* (without any shame) Zoombies. One of them even appeared on BBC Wales to discuss job struggles during the pandemic shutdowns only for the viewers to raise their eyebrows at the sight of a pink penis object on a bookshelf, just over her right shoulder. Other examples includes the suspension of the *New Yorker* magazine writer and legal expert, Jeffrey Toobin, after it was reported that he was masturbating whilst on a work call. Such Zoombies have an absent present, they give visible signs of attendance, in reality they are mentally absent and like all zombies they make up the living dead.

The third type of Zoombie gets trapped by video filters. While this is often unintentional, nevertheless the filter acts as a mask that conceals one's true identity. The etymology of 'mask' is rather interesting. Some have argued the term derives from the French *masque,* 'covering to hide' or 'guard the face'; others have pointed out how it may, in fact, have connections to the Arabic word *maskharah,* which means 'buffoon', from the verb *sakhira* 'to ridicule'. This definition is more apt for this variety of Zoombie, especially given the ambiguous nature of the 'buffoon'. In this example, most would think it is the Texas lawyer who is the buffoon, but it can equally be argued that it is the judge that is being ridiculed. The case revolves around a Texas lawyer, Rod Ponton, who appears, as a white fluffy cat before the judge using Zoom. 'I'm not a cat,' the lawyer was forced to clarify during a hearing in Presidio County, south-west Texas, as he and his assistant frantically tried to remove the filter. The filter displayed the image of a cat, instead of the image of Mr Ponton. His eye contact and mouth movement manage to capture the confusion and horror. Forced to continue with the scheduled legal hearing with the 'cat', Judge Roy Ferguson of Texas's 394th judicial district reminded Ponton: 'I believe you have a filter turned on in the video settings. You might want to …'. The panic-stricken cat/Ponton hesitatingly says: 'Can you hear me, judge?'

Judge Ferguson replies: 'I can hear you. I think it's a filter …' 'It is', the cat-faced Ponton reluctantly responds. 'And I don't know how to remove it. I've got my assistant here, she's trying to, but I'm prepared to go forward with it … I'm here live. I'm not a cat.' This incident of the Judge and the cat went viral, especially after Judge Ferguson circulated the video on Twitter, despite the notice on the video, which states 'recording of this hearing or live streaming is prohibited…violation may constitute contempt of the court and result in a fine of up to $500'!

If the verb to Zoom captures the everyday travails of Covid-lockdown, then Zoombies provide an apt metaphor in understanding the nature of the Covid zeitgeist or spirit of the age. The zombie genre continues to inspire and explain the current ongoing world pandemic as we move from one lock-down uncertainty to another. The zombie imagery often starts with civilised life and ends with a post-apocalypse world. It includes the inherent idea of pessimism and death. As such, it provides us with metaphors to make sense of our changing times. The outbreak of zombieism is a twentieth century phenomenon, rooted in the Western imagination, it explodes in the twenty-first century and becomes part of the cultural zeitgeist. Since 1920, over a thousand zombie movies have been produced but over half have been made in the last ten years. The genre was popularised by George Romero's 1968 *Night of the Living Dead*, which established zombies as a cultural phenomenon. It is clear that while there has been much academic discussion of zombie movies there has been little examination of the zombie itself, prompting a number of sociologists to 'analyse the zombie as a symbol in itself'. Zombieism has now become a topic of critical assessment within cultural studies. It is no longer seen simply as a product of Hollywood entertainment. Rather, it has become the basis for 'critical reflection and cultural self-examination'. The culture of Zooming has now brought the living dead into our houses and offices, conference, and meetings. Zoombies may turn out to be the catalyst – the straw that broke the camel's back – for a cultural apocalypse!

TEN FUTURE VESTIGIAL BODY PARTS

Our bodies undergo a tremendous amount of change throughout our life. Music heard in adulthood is never quite as good as that discovered in youth and food never matches the love and comfort of a parent or grandparent's particular method for combining the ingredients of your favourite dish. Yet the speed with which change occurs is, barring certain blunt injuries, mind-numbingly slow. Such is the case that one, observing from the perspective of one human lifetime, could be forgiven for concluding that nothing much *really* changes. What we fail to notice is that our entire aural apparatus, from the ear to neural interpretations of the inner ear bone vibrations in the cerebrum, changes dramatically throughout our life. Ditto our tastebuds, which die and are reborn with micro changes that medical science has not yet conclusively put the lid on. We could chalk this up to normal wear and tear, a phenomenon constantly occurring in our bodies, but that it takes the ownership of property or a vehicle for some of us to truly understand and appreciate. The point is these small changes can eventually lead to major shifts, spanning the whole species.

These major shifts will result in the evolution of a given species if selected from generation to generation. For humans, from our perspective, evolution is also a relatively snail-paced process. And to see this phenomenon in humans requires the consultation of the fossil record. But fortunately, in smaller organisms, we can observe these changes.

In the UK, an all too familiar textbook example of natural selection giving way to evolution is found in the Peppered Moth. Sometimes called Darwin's Moth, one might say the normal peppered moth bears a relatively even pattern of black and white splotches to its hue. That is until the mid-nineteenth century turned Manchester into a smoggy cloud of industrial might. In these dark and dismal times, the peppered moth stood out to its predatory neighbour flycatchers, nuthatches, and European robins, so something needed to change. Peppered moths selected for a higher concentration of dark pigment, allowing them to blend into the Industrial Revolution. To add a cherry on top, after the UK (sort of) got its act together and started regulating its carbon footprint, we witnessed a change back to the familiar peppered moth pigmentation from the good old days. There and back again, the whole process only took 150–200 years. In just over the last year, we have seen evolution on the microscopic level as variants of the Covid-19 virus select their way through our natural immune defences. Thanks to our less than Three Musketeers approach to global vaccination we are filling textbooks with examples that maybe one day a future generation might learn from.

Currently, we are experiencing an unprecedented level of acceleration in numerous systems, so it begs the question as to how humans will change. Since humans have only been a feature on Earth for a relatively minuscule fraction of time it can be difficult to properly study the changes we have undergone since the first *Homo sapiens* walked the earth. But perhaps we need not consult the fossil record (which humans and other primates, at the moment, have not contributed a great deal to) but look within ourselves to see the change that is always with us – for you see, evolution is slow, but is abysmal at covering its tracks!

On many of us, but importantly not all of us, there are parts that tend not to serve a particular purpose, often they are dormant or reduced parts that served a function in our ancestors. We call these vestigial organs. A classic and often dubious example of a vestigial organ is the appendix, that worm like projection that presents at the junction of the small and large intestine. You can locate yours either by the scar where it had been removed in the past (a lifesaving procedure that, until recently, tends to leave a nasty mark) or between your lower right abdominal region and your right hip. Although this little organ has spawned a tremendous debate, it is believed to be a barracks for an important gut bacteria that aids with recovery from episodes of diarrhoea, but without clear evidence showing symptomatic differences between those who have and those who have not had an appendectomy (the procedure for removing the appendix) most consider the organ officially vestigial. Only good for the unpleasant swelling of the organ known as appendicitis which can eventually lead to rupture, shock, and death. When it becomes a problem, it is often removed, for in our contemporary world of the Big C being one of the top three killers, anything that doesn't serve a purpose only becomes a potential harbourer of cancer.

Vestigial organs are nature's organic artefacts, clues that serve as a window into our deep past. And as we are facing extreme changes in the present, many have wondered what vestiges will go the way of the appendix in the future. In this list we explore the possible wonders that future generations will carry with them, signs of when ours will be a bygone era.

1. Wisdom Teeth

'And not a moment too soon' may accompany a note of 'good riddance' to those who have suffered the trauma of wisdom tooth removal (regardless of the amount of ice cream excused during one's recovery!). The wisdom tooth is a common name given to the third, most distal molar on each of the four quadrants of the dentition. Hints at its vestigial nature come in that not everyone develops these four extra molars, meanwhile some can develop more. Beyond three molars may be called extra wisdom teeth, they are more correctly named as supernumerary molars, but this phenomenon is not restricted to molars and can occur with any type of tooth beyond the standard set. The third molar was thought to be a product of our ancestorial development into a hunter-gatherer society – where food such as leaves, nuts, and meats required additional grinding to ensure proper digestion. Though, the beauty of evolution is that nothing is set in stone, so theoretically if the Paleo Diet trend wins the battle of fad dieting, perhaps over a few generations, we can look forward to even more prominence of wisdom teeth. But, at the moment, wisdom teeth in the context of our shrinking jaw size are set on a course for disaster from impact (when the growing pathways of teeth intersect) to the highly dangerous periodontal disease (gum disease) which is on the same tube line, a few stations down from cancer. As is the case with most vestigial organs, a great debate exists between removing them proactively (healthy or not) or if they should be left to be until we can fully understand how their function has evolved into our current *Homo economicus* condition.

2. Ancestorial Muscles and Bones

Can you wiggle your ears? If so, then you are one of a dying breed who has retained some usage of the vestigial auricular muscles that can control the movement of our ears. Largely docile, an elaborate network of muscles attaches your external ear to your skull. In dogs and cats, you can witness the use of these muscles as once our ancestors did to focus our hearing and remain alert for predators. It is believed that as our neck mobility improved, there was no need to be able to move one's ears. These are one of a whole subset of vestigial organs – the retained hardware from our more predatorially preoccupied and tree-bound ancestors. Anyone with little ones at home may have noticed a certain propensity for climbing and those with individuals of a more elderly persuasion may notice that ability rapidly fades with time. One vestigial muscle thought to be used for climbing is the palmaris longus which extends from the wrist to the elbow. You can show yours off by laying your wrist, palm upward, on a table and touching your pinky finger to your thumb, you will notice a cord like protrusion in the middle of your wrist, if not, you may be part of the ten percent of the population that doesn't have this curious muscle. The coccyx, or tail bone, is also one of those vestiges that has gone into dormancy, fusing into a protrusion that when broken makes for a most uncomfortable recovery. The coccyx is all that remains of our ancestral tail that is theorised to have been used for balance, climbing, and mobility. Before and/or after (the debate rages amongst paleoanthropologists) the trees, the subclavius muscle which runs between our clavicle and first rib was more pronounced and helped with walking on all four limbs. The presentation of extra ribs also ties us to certain living distant relatives, extra cervical ribs (in the neck) were a more reptilian feature and are seen in less than one percent of humans, while extra ribs (at the bottom of the rib cage) is a feature of chimpanzees and gorillas, but only turn up in about eight percent of humans.

3. Sinuses

One of life's great mysteries, which seasonally weighs heavy on the heads of many, is why on Earth humans have retained the paranasal sinuses.

These sinuses are essentially cavities in the skull that are lined with mucus as a first line of immune defence, good for draining, or failing too, when under heavy assault. It is believed these sinuses developed as a way to lighten the overall mass of the head, except, of course, for those wonderful times of the year when the pollen count is high.

4. Goosebumps

It goes by many names, goosebumps, goose flesh, goose skin, goose pimples – that phenomenon when the skin bubbles up and body hairs stand on end. Although in our present form, this reflex comes in handy as a natural mode of thermoregulation, a way to shield the body from sudden cold, in our ancestors it is believed this reflex played other roles that have faded with the thickness of our body hair. The phenomenon, also known as piloerection, horripilation, and cutis anserina, presents when small muscles, arrector pili, constrict, pulling hair follicles upwards. The presentation is more pronounced where fine body hair exists, particularly on the arms and legs. As is seen in other animals, this reflex can serve as a method of intimidation but can be triggered by fear, strong emotional experiences, and arousal along with exposure to cold temperatures. The loss of this bodily feature would fade alongside the next future vestigial body part.

5. Body Hair

Habits as well as circumstance can have a profound impact on our evolutionary trajectory. And global warming combined with our general preference for wearing clothes ought to be cause for concern to the industry doing gangbusters on personal grooming appliances. As the need for the additional thermal protection decreases, a gift becomes a burden in a more arid planet. It has often been theorised that the further humans get from their less than human ancestors, the less hair we would possess, but these theories are tainted by modernists and eugenicists' equating evolution to progress, when in actuality it is simply change and would be better served, as such, as a neutral concept. Also, the reality of natural selection and preference may see to human mating rituals, or even religious custom, keeping body hair in the human gene pool a bit longer.

6. Toes

Head, shoulders, knees, and – oh my, the future may see to this old nursery rhyme not aging so well! Feet have undergone quite the transformation which has resulted in the toes losing much of their former function, particularly for grasping and holding objects. In our present, mostly bipedal condition, the need for individual toes wanes, particularly with the influence of shoes where fashion statements have often proven more important than functionality. The importance of toes is maintained on the idea that they are required for balance, which was the case when our walking gate was more focused on balancing along the midline of the foot. Over time it has been noted that our balance has shifted more to the inward side of the big toe, and thus the need for individual toes is less and less necessary for keeping us upright. It is projected that our feet could evolve to resemble how they appear in shoes and webbed feet could come in handy should our need to live in more aquatic environs become necessary.

7. Sex organs

Have you ever wondered why men have nipples? Believe it or not they are fully equipped to perform the same task as female nipples and given the right hormone cocktail, voilà lactation. Embryology shows that we all start as the phenotypic default you might call female, only later in development do our genes tell us to crank up the testosterone or oestrogen to bring on secondary sex characteristics. But before this happens, the nipples have already formed, doomed to remain dormant for some. And while natural selection may have made these an important element in certain mating rituals, it could also be the case that the utter uselessness of male nipples could go the way of the dodo. But who ever said vestigial organs had to be the product of only natural happenings? In our advancing world of genetic manipulation, it is not hard to imagine natural reproduction one day being viewed as archaic and pastiche. And if scientific advancement renders organs useless, then best to be away with them as even today they are critical sights of cancerous metastases. Of course, this simplistic scenario does what we are all too good at doing at the present, ignoring important discussions on sex, gender, and identity that we need to be having.

8. Digestive System

The human digestive tract has been one of the key areas of change in human bodies since our first arrival on the planet. From the biological mechanics to the ecological relationships needed to be maintained with organisms that live or simply pass through us involves a highly adaptable mechanism for homeostasis – balance. Since we started cooking food, our digestive system radically changed (and now we cannot simply eat raw food anymore without serious consequences) and moving into more contemporary times fad diets and new methods for food production (GMOs and lab-produced food products), and even climate change is pushing the uncertain future of our digestive systems to the edge of chaos. Perhaps we will move towards more vegan lifestyles, perhaps the scenario of all food being in the form of a swallowed pill will come to pass, and perhaps we will find a way to sustain ourselves without the consumption of other things. However it turns out, our organs could form new lobes (think of the multiple stomachs required for a cow's digestion) and the whole bacterial ecosystem of our gut could radically change. And that's just speaking in terms of natural evolution, 3-D printed organs and external interventions make the potential futures of the digestive system nearly limitless.

9. Imagination

The human brain can be described by a variety of metaphors from supercomputer to God's house for the soul, but one often forgotten is the brain's semblance to a muscle. Muscles, if left unused, can atrophy and shrink just as quickly as they can be bulked up through overexertion. Similarly, the brain hangs in the balance between bulking its neurological pathways and cerebral atrophy. This is why it is often recommended that as we age, we do brain puzzles, read, and even dedicate ourselves to the lifelong vocation of learning. Yet, like all development, development for development's sake can be fraught with peril. It is not just important to work the brain out, but keep it open to new ideas and approaches to the everyday struggle of life. As we are learning from patterns on social media and have seen in geriatric studies, it is not just lack of use that causes brain atrophy, but the opportunism inherent to all biological systems and the danger of routine that not only minimises the use of our brains in a given day, but allows for the degradation of old pathways and a resistance to change. Targeted and online advertising methods thrive on this to their advantage. The rising intervention of technology and artificial intelligence are the latest and most dangerous cultural development that renders our brains no longer needing to be as sharp as they used to have to be. Generation Z is unfortunately becoming the ultimate guinea pig for how human brains will develop differently with a cradle-to-grave existence assisted by smart machines. Imagination will be one of the first causalities, but this is only the beginning, the more we ask Siri, the less we need that complex organ that separates us from other species in the kingdom animalia.

10. The Lot

But why stop at just the brain? If that organ can be replaced by chips and education replaced by downloads, why not replace the whole body for something better, something more machine like. It's the ultimate sycophantic dream of posthumanism. But, again, why stop with better bodies, why not move beyond bodies. Perhaps human society can thrive in the cybersphere. The metaverse is only the beginning. Evolution is simply a tool to help us cope with the limits of our bodies – the ultimate metaphor of limitation. Without bodies, we no longer need evolution or progress, right? Why simply augment when we can go full transcendence? What's the worst thing that could happen?

Bonus: Unthought Returns

In looking to the futures, we quickly get carried away with the upward, far-reaching ideas, losing sight of the fact that the future is and always will be multidirectional. Our needlessly dichotomised thinking conditions us to see past = back and future = forward, but the future can also go back, while actually taking us towards an advancement. Take the example of the plica semilunaris, it's that little doodad – bulbus fold of flesh – on the inner crevasse of your eye. That little guy is thought to be a vestigial third eyelid that allowed us to, once upon a time, see underwater. Our voice box and lower jaw are thought to be made of the gills we used to bear. Evolution is not necessarily a ladder, perhaps more aptly compared to the Wonkavator – Roald Dahl's fictional elevator that can move in any direction – able to move however our environment and choices see fit. As global warming continues to ravage the planet, for the rowers keep on rowing and they certainly show no signs that they are slowing, what the world looks like in a hundred or two hundred years will certainly have a profound effect on what our bodies consist of. What is lost. What is gained. And even, what might be replayed.

CITATIONS

Introduction: Body Horror by C Scott Jordan

To learn more about the murder of Emmet Till, the Library of Congress's Collection, the Civil Rights History Project provides a remarkable compendium of articles, essays, and further works that can be accessed at https://www.loc.gov/collections/civil-rights-history-project/articles-and-essays/murder-of-emmett-till/; For more on the murder of William Brown, History Nebraska has collected several resources accessible at https://history.nebraska.gov/blog/lest-we-forget-lynching-will-brown-omaha%E2%80%99s-1919-race-riot; For more on abjection see Julia Kristeva's *Powers of Horror: An Essay on Abjection* (New York, Columbia University Press, 1982)/.

This Body: A History by Robin Yassin-Kassab

For a fascinating interpretation of OBE's, lucid dreaming, and 'reality' as a controlled hallucination, see Thomas Metzinger. 'The Ego Tunnel: The Science of the Mind and the Myth of the Self.' Basic Books. 2010.

A news report on the tribes of the Andaman Islands escaping the tsunami: https://www.cbsnews.com/news/ancient-tribe-survives-tsunami/
Ali Bader is a very prolific writer. As far as I'm aware, however, only the novel 'Papa Sartre' is available in English (American University in Cairo Press. 2009).

Shame Again by Samia Rahman

A large part of the analysis for this essay is built around Salman Rushdie's *Shame* (Jonathan Cape, London, 1983); Supplemental insight was provided by Mona Eltahawy's blog Feminist Giant, which can be accessed by clicking https://www.feministgiant.com/ See also: Eltahawy's 2021 interview for *The New Arab*: https://english.alaraby.co.uk/analysis/mona-eltahawy-arab-spring-feminism-and-hope, Sara Ahmed's *The Cultural Politics of Emotions* is published by Routledge, 2007. For her other writings see: https://www. saranahmed.com. *Ain't I A Woman, Black Women and Feminism* by bell hooks is published by South End Press, 1981. And for more on our present melting modernity, see Zygmunt Bauman, *Liquid Modernity*, (Polity, 2000).

Brains Degendered by Jeremy Henzell-Thomas

My essays, 'Simple Stories vs Complex Facts, appeared in *Critical Muslim 28: Narratives,* 2018 (Hurst, London); and 'Hidden Windows' was published in *Critical Muslim 32: Music,* 2019 (Hurst, London).

On gendered differences, I have referred to: Steve Connor, 'The hardwired difference between male and female brains could explain why men are better at map reading, and why women are better at remembering a conversation.' *The Independent,* 3/12/2013. See https://www. independent.co.uk/life-style/the-hardwired-difference-between-male- and-female-brains-could-explain-why-men-are-better-at-map- reading-8978248.html. See also https://neurosciencenews.com/ brain-connectivity-differences-men-women-636/; Bruce Goldman, 'Two minds: The cognitive differences between men and women.' *Stanford Medicine*, Spring 2017. See https://stanmed.stanford.edu/2017spring/ how-mens-and-womens-brains-are-different.html; John Gray, *Men are from Mars, Women are from Venus,* (HarperCollinsPublishersInc, 1992);Madhura Ingalhalikar et al, 'Sex differences in the structural connectome of the human brain.' *Proceedings of the National Academy of Sciences of the USA,* 111(2), 823-828, 14/1/2014. See https://www.pnas.org/ content/111/2/823; Allan and Barbara Pease, *Why Men Don't Listen and Women Can't Read Maps.* (Orion, 2001); Margaret Tarampi, 'A tale of two types of perspective taking: Sex differences in spatial ability.' *Psychological Science,* 27 (11), 1507-1516.

On the refutation of hard-wired sex differences in the brain, I have referred to:Penn Collins, 'A new study claiming men read maps better than women isn't true at all:Results suggest negative reinforcement may have been the sole factor in the gap.'*Good,* 12/12/2016. See https://www.good.is/

Health/women-read-map 12/12/16; Rachel Cooke, 'Review of *The Gendered Brain* by Gina Rippon: demolition of a sexist myth.' *The Observer,* 5/3/2019. See https://www.theguardian.com/books/2019/mar/05/the-gendered-brain-gina-rippon-review; Lise Eliot, 'Neurosexism: the myth that men and women have different brains: The hunt for male and female distinctions inside the skull is a lesson in bad research practice.' *Nature,* 6/3/2019.See https://www.nature.com/articles/d41586-019-00677-x;'You don't have a male or female brain – the more brains scientists study, the weaker the evidence for sex differences.' *The Conversation,* 22/4/2021. See https://theconversation.com/you-dont-have-a-male-or-female-brain-the-more-brains-scientists-study-the-weaker-the-evidence-for-sex-differences-158005; Cordelia Fine, *Delusions of Gender: How Our Minds, Society, and Neurosexism Create Difference* (W.W. Norton, 2010); Genevieve Fox, 'Meet the neuroscientist shattering the myth of the gendered brain: Why asking whether your brain is male or female is the wrong question.' *The Guardian,* 24/2/2019. See https://www.theguardian.com/science/2019/feb/24/meet-the-neuroscientist-shattering-the-myth-of-the-gendered-brain-gina-rippon; Gina Rippon, *The Gendered Brain: The new neuroscience which shatters the myth of the female brain* (The Bodley Head, Penguin Random House, London, 2019); 'The 'female' brain: why damaging myths about women and science keep coming back in new forms.' *The Conversation,* 3/8/2020. See https://theconversation.com/the-female-brain-why-damaging-myths-about-women-and-science-keep-coming-back-in-new-forms-129310; Gina Rippon, Lise Eliot, Sarah Genon and Daphna Joel, 'How hype and hyperbole distort the neuroscience of sex differences.' PLoS Biol 19(5), 2021. Seehttps://journals.plos.org/plosbiology/article?id=10.1371/journal.pbio.3001253; Rebecca M.Young and Evan Balaban, 'Pychoneuroindoctrinology'. Review of Louann Brizendine, *The Female Brain* (Morgan Road, 2006). *Nature,* 443, 634, 2006. See https://www.nature.com/articles/443634a

Other sources consulted comprise: Anne Bolwerk, Jessica Mack-Andrick, Frieder R. Lang, Arnd Dörfler, and Christian Maihöfner, 'How Art Changes Your Brain: Differential Effects of Visual Art Production and Cognitive Art Evaluation on Functional Brain Connectivity.' PLOS ONE 9(12): e116548, 1/7/2014. See https://journals.plos.org/plosone/

article?id=10.1371/journal.pone.0101035; Eric Garcia, *We're Not Broken: Changing the Autism Conversation* (Houghton Mifflin Harcourt, Boston, 2021); Sara Gibbs, *Drama Queen:One Autistic Woman and a Life of Unhelpful Labels* (Headline Publishing, London, 2021); Daniel Kahneman, *Thinking, Fast and Slow* (Penguin Books, London, 2012); Nancy Kline, *Time to Think: Listening to Ignite the Human Mind* (Lock, London, 1999); Joanne Limburg, *Letters to My Weird Sisters*: On Autism and Feminism (Atlantic Books, 2021); Researchers at NYU Langone Medical Center/New York University School of Medicine, 'Sleep after learning strengthens connections between brain cells and enhances memory.' *Science Daily*, 5/6/2014. See https://www.sciencedaily.com/releases/2014/06/140605141849.htm; Thai Nguyen, '10 Proven Ways To Grow Your Brain: Neurogenesis And Neuroplasticity.' *Huffpost,* 6/12/2017. https://www.huffpost.com/entry/10-proven-ways-to-grow-yo_b_10374730; Josh Noel, 'Travel as a health regimen.' *Chicago Tribune*, 28/1/2014. See https://www.chicagotribune.com/travel/ct-xpm-2014-01-28-sc-trav-0128-travel-mechanic-20140128-story.html; Thai Nguyen, '10 Proven Ways To Grow Your Brain: Neurogenesis And Neuroplasticity.' *Huffpost*, 6/12/2017. See https://www.huffpost.com/entry/10-proven-ways-to-grow-yo_b_10374730; Oliver Sacks, *Musicophilia: Tales of Music and the Brain* (Knopf, 2007); Harriet Sherwood, 'We don't need to be cured or fixed': writers speak out on autism'. *Observer*, 27/6/2021. See https://www.theguardian.com/society/2021/jun/27/we-dont-need-to-be-cured-or-fixed-writers-speak-out-on-autism; Nassim Nicholas Taleb, *The Black Swan:The Impact of the Highly Improbable* (Random House, New York, 2007); Thai Nguyen, '10 Proven Ways To Grow Your Brain: Neurogenesis And Neuroplasticity.' *Huffpost*, 6/12/2017. https://www.huffpost.com/entry/10-proven-ways-to-grow-yo_b_10374730

'Lazy' Bodies by Shanon Shah

This essay owes much of its analysis to *The Myth of the Lazy Native* by Syed Hussein Alatas, first published in 1977 and issued in paperback in 2010 by Routledge.

For former Malaysian premier Mahathir Mohamad's unchanged views about 'lazy' Malays, see: https://www.malaymail.com/news/malaysia/2021/12/13/in-2021-dr-mahathir-says-many-young-malays-still-stuck-in-old-ways-resistan/2027950, and for his admonition of allegedly unassimilated, chopstick-wielding Malaysian Chinese, see https://www.thestar.com.my/news/nation/2021/12/13/dr-m039s-039chopsticks039-views-show-a-disconnect-with-society-says-mca-sec-gen-chong

Some of my reflections in this article are also explored in my contributions to *Critical Muslim 13: Race* and *Critical Muslim 36: Destinations*. The remarkable story of the 'discovery' of the Komodo Dragon and its impacts on Hollywood can be found in Timothy P. Barnard (2009), 'Chasing the Dragon: An Early Expedition to Komodo Island', in Jan van der Putten & Mary Kilcline Cody (Eds.), *Lost Times and Untold Tales from the Malay World* (pp. 41–53), National University of Singapore.

A brief introduction to Ngugi wa Thiong'o can be accessed at Postcolonial Studies @ Emory, written by Jennifer Margulis:https://scholarblogs.emory.edu/postcolonialstudies/2014/06/11/ngugi-wa-thiongo/.

My mention of Serena Williams is meant to be provocative. The Australian Press Council ruled that while some people found the *Herald Sun*'s angry-ape cartoon about her 'offensive', it did not amount to racism or misogyny. See https://www.bbc.com/news/world-australia-47352854.

For a systematic introduction to the connections between climate and colonialism, I consulted Martin Mahony & Georgina Endfield, (2018), 'Climate and colonialism', *WIREs Clim Change*, Volume 9, pp. 1–16. A fuller discussion of Lloyd's can be read at Sahar Shah & Harpreet Kaur Paul, (2021, November 29), 'Lloyd's of London's debt', *New Internationalist*: https://newint.org/features/2021/10/07/long-read-lloyds-london-debt

Shah and Paul discuss the Adani coal mine, but for a more in-depth perspective on the indigenous peoples' opposition to it, see John Quiggin,

Kirsten Lyons, & Morgan Brigg, (2017, June 19), 'The last line of defence: Indigenous rights and Adani's land deal', *The Conversation*: http:// theconversation.com/the-last-line-of-defence-indigenous-rights-and -adanis-land-deal-79561

The Malaysian government's admission of the human rights violations suffered by the Penan girls – way back in 2009 – is discussed at https:// thenutgraph.com/penan-girls-and-women-sexually-violated/

Autism, Yusuf and I by Naomi Foyle

A full reading of the Yosef story in relation to Autism Spectrum Condition can be found in Samuel J. Levine's study *Was Yosef on the Spectrum? Understanding Joseph Through Torah, Midrash, and Classical Jewish Sources* (Jerusalem, New York: Urim, 2019), his quotes are form p201-202. In *Letters to My Weird Sisters: On Autism and Feminism* (London: Atlantic Books, 2021), Joanne Limburg offers highly informed reflections on contemporary and historical women and autism; the quote is from p11.

The Secret Life of a Black Aspie: A Memoir (Fairbanks: University of Alaska Press, 2017) by Anand Prahlad is a lyrical exploration of the writer's synaesthetic journey from a plantation in rural Virginia to higher education in the Midwest. The scholarly articles 'The Pathos of Mindblindness: Autism, Science, and Sadness in "Theory of Mind" Narratives' (*Journal of Literary and Cultural Disability Studies*, Jan 2011) by John Duffy and Rebecca Dorner and 'Autistic Disruptions, Trans Temporalities: A Narrative "Trap Door" in Time' (South Atlantic Quarterly, April 2021) by Jake Pyne can be read online at, respectively: https://www.researchgate.net/ publication/254951732_The_Pathos_of_Mindblindness_Autism_ Science_and_Sadness_in_Theory_of_Mind_Narratives and https://www. academia.edu/48903683/Autistic_Disruptions_Trans_Temporalities _A_Narrative_Trap_Door_in_Time.

The *Lancet* Commission on the future of care and clinical research in autism can be downloaded at https://www.thelancet.com/commissions/ autism. More information on autism research can be found at *Spectrum*

News, including the following articles which specifically informed my essay: https://www.spectrumnews.org/news/new-evidence-ties-hans-asperger -nazi-eugenics-program/
https://www.spectrumnews.org/features/deep-dive/history-forgot-woman-defined -autism/
https://www.spectrumnews.org/news/reversing-mutations-in-top-autism-linked-gene-makes -adult-mice-more-social/
https://www.spectrumnews.org/opinion/viewpoint/autism-research-continues -to-stress-basic-science-over-improving-interventions/

NeuroClastic, Autism Collaboration, the National Autism Society, Spectrum News, Autism Mosque and many other websites, including mainstream news media, provide crucial information on diversity within the autistic community, of which the following is just a tiny sample: https://www.autism.org.uk/what-we-do/news/new-data-on-the-autism-employment-gap;　　https://the-art-of-autism.com/24-black-autistic-people-you-may-want-to-know-about/ ; https://chicagoreader. com/news-politics/black-autistic-and-killed-by-police/　; https:// neuroclastic.com/osime-brown-a-life-sentence-for-not-stealing-a-mobile-phone /;
https://neuroclastic.com/white-privilege/;　https://www.islam21c. com/islamic-thought/autism-hour-in-the-mosque/;https:// autismmosque.org/　and　https://www.spectrumnews.org/opinion/ islam-and-autism/.

Enhancements by Wendy L Schultz

To explore further the medical enhancements available discussed in this article, please see the websites of the following medical institutions: Mayo Clinic, Johns Hopkins School of Medicine, National Institute of Health, University of Maryland Medical Center, National Health Service (UK), and Medical News Today, and the blogs found at techmeetups.com;

For more on transhumanist technologies see the Lifeboat Foundation, http://lifeboat.com/ex/transhumanist.technologies;

The following articles were mentioned throughout the article: Annette B. Brühl, Camilla d'Angelo, and Barbara J. Sahakian, 'Neuroethical issues in cognitive enhancement: Modafinil as the example of a workplace drug?' *Brain and Neuroscience Advances*. 15 Feburary 2019. https://journals. sagepub.com/doi/full/10.1177/2398212818816018; Melinda Wenner Moyer, 'A Safe Drug to Boost Brainpower,' *Scientific American*. 1 March 2016, https://www.scientificamerican.com/article/a-safe-drug-to- boost-brainpower/; Hayley Thair, et al. 'Transcranial Direct Current Stimulation (tDCS): A Beginner's Guide for Design and Implementation,' *Frontiers in Neuroscience*. 22 November 2017, https://www.frontiersin.org/ articles/10.3389/fnins.2017.00641/full; Diego Salinas, 'The 5 Coolest Companies Changing Neuroscience in 2021 Other Than Neuralink,' *Medium*. 12 June 2021, https://medium.com/artificial-intelligence-and-cognition/the-5-coolest-companies-changing-neuroscience-in-2021-other-than-neuralink-b0aa12f58183; Rob Gilhooly, 'Wearable muscle suit makes heavy lifting a cinch,' The New Scientist, 18 April 2012, http://www. newscientist.com/article/mg21428614.800-wearable-muscle-suit-makes-heavy-lifting-a-cinch.html; James Gallahger, 'Will we ever grow replacement hands,' *The BBC*. 21 March, 2012. http://www.bbc.co.uk/ news/health-16679010; Editors '3D-printed sugar network to help grow artificial liver,' 2 July 2012. http://www.bbc.com/news/ technology-18677627; David Whitehouse, 'Genetically altered babies born,' *The BBC*, 4 May 2001. http://news.bbc.co.uk/1/hi/sci/ tech/1312708.stm; Ed Yong, 'Single protein can strengthen old faded memories,' *Discover,* 4 March 2011. http://blogs.discovermagazine.com/ notrocketscience/2011/03/03/single-protein-can-strengthen-old-faded-memories/#more-3963; Tibi Puiu, 'Stem cells treatment dramatically improves vision of the blind,' *ZME Science,* 27 October 2017. http://www. zmescience.com/research/stem-cells-treatment-improve-vision-321213/; Cedars-Sinai Medical Center 'Stem cells boost heart's natural repair mechanisms,' *Science Daily,* 30 January 2013. http://www.sciencedaily. com/releases/2013/01/130130101820.htm; and Tenzin Kyizom et al., 'Effect of pranayama & yoga-asana on cognitive brain functions in type 2 diabetes-P3 event related evoked potential (ERP), *Indian Journal of Medical Research*, 131:636-40. May 2020. http://www.ncbi.nlm.nih.gov/ pubmed/20516534.

Normal Indian Wives by Chandrika Parmar

The stories shared in this article are from my own field work and newspaper reports. A couple of interviews cited were conducted by Vasundhra Narang and Bindra Guru as part of their social internship (Development of Corporate Citizenship) at SPJIMR. They interned in CORD and El Shiddai respectively. In the essay I have anonymised the responses of the women I spoke with. Pooja Priyamvada's tweets can be accessed by her twitter handle @SoulVersified. The story of Vismaya Nair and related stories from Kerala are available in all new reports during that period.

Several write ups are available on Domestic violence complaints during COVID. These include Vignesh Radhakrishnan, Sumant Sen, and Naresh Singaravelu, 'Domestic violence complaints at a 10-year high during COVID-19 lockdown,' *The Hindu*, 22 June 2020. https://www.thehindu.com/data/data-domestic-violence-complaints-at-a-10-year-high-during-covid-19-lockdown/article31885001.ece; Sushmitha Ramakrishnan, 'All doors shut: When home is not the safest place…,' *The New Indian Express*, 7 April 2020. https://www.newindianexpress.com/cities/chennai/2020/apr/07/all-doors-shut-when-home-is-not-the-safest-place-2126681.html

For commentaries and some of the data in public press see Himanshi Dhawan, 'Not rape, domestic violence is top crime against women,' *The Times of India*, 5 October 2020. https://timesofindia.indiatimes.com/india/not-rape-domestic-violence-is-top-crime-against-women/articleshow/78494876.cms; Swagata Yadavar, 'Indian Women Facing Domestic Violence Find Succour At Government Hospital Crisis Centres,' *India Spend,* 5 October 2018. https://www.indiaspend.com/indian-women-facing-domestic-violence-find-succour-at-government-hospital-crisis-centres/; Editors, '10 Years of Domestic Violence Act: Dearth of Data, Inadequate Implementation, Delayed Justice,' *India Spend,* 9 August 2017. https://www.indiaspend.com/10-years-of-domestic-violence-act-dearth-of -data-inadequate-implementation-delayed-justice-85613/

Reports on judgement and the commentaries on marital rape can be found on the internet. These include but are not limited to: Avantika Mehta, 'No, the Chhattisgarh court was not offering up its opinion on marital rape. It was reiterating the law,' *News Laundry*, 3 September 2021. https://www.newslaundry.com/2021/09/03/no-the-chhattisgarh-court-was-not-offering-up-its-opinion-on-marital-rape-it-was-reiterating-the-law; Editors, 'Denying sex to spouse is a ground for divorce: Delhi HC' *LiveLaw News Network*, 10 September 2016. https://www.livelaw.in/denying-sex-spouse-ground-divorce-delhi-hc/

Interviews with Meena Kandasamy can be accessed at https://www.theguardian.com/books/2019/nov/25/meena-kandasamy-interview-exquisite-cadavers. For her article see Meena Kandasamy, 'I Singe The Body Electric,' *Outlook*, 19 March 2012. https://www.outlookindia.com/magazine/story/i-singe-the-body-electric/280179

Slapstick Tragedy by James Brooks

All quoted dialogue and descriptions of scenes from these DVD versions of Harmony Korine's films: *Gummo* – Metropolitan Film & Video, France, 2013; *Julien Donkey-Boy* – Tartan Video, UK, 2001; *Mister Lonely* – Underground Pictures, Spain, year of issue unknown; *Trash Humpers* – Filmfreak Distributie, Netherlands, 2011; *Spring Breakers* – Universal Studios, UK, 2014; *The Beach Bum* – Universal Studios, UK, 2019.

Roger Ebert quote from review of *Julien Donkey-Boy*, 5 November 1999, https://bit.ly/3EjOJll; and Korine discussing casting choices from 'Hidden Treasure: Harmony Korine on *Gummo*', Chris Darke, *Vertigo Magazine*, Summer 1998, https://bit.ly/3H7IWkO

Quotes on Keystone Studios films from Alan Bilton, *Silent Film Comedy and American Culture*, (Palgrave Macmillan, 2013); quotes on *Fight Harm* from 'Harmony Korine's Real-Life *Fight Club*', Adam Heimlich, *New York Press*, 29 September 1999, https://bit.ly/3Jb8E9S and 'All Korine's Transgressions', Domenico Monetti, *Venice Film Festival Review*, 7 September 1999, https://bit.ly/3FkmAfa; Wes Hill quote from 'Harmony Korine's *Trash Humpers*: From Alternative to Hipster', *M/C Journal*, Vol. 20, No. 1, 2017, https://doi.org/10.5204/mcj.1192; Diane Arbus quote can

CRITICAL MUSLIM

be found in 'Oxford Essential Quotations (4th edition)', Susan Ratcliffe, editor, (Oxford University Press, 2016);and *Spring Breakers* analysis quotes from 'The Life Lessons of *Spring Breakers*', Richard Brody, *The New Yorker*, 15 March 2013, https://bit.ly/33QJoFD

A Woman in God's Land by Themrise Khan

The opening quote was from Guy Delisle's *Jerusalem. Chronicles from the Holy City*, Drawn and Quarterly, 2012; The quote that began the section "Resisting Submission" was from the Lady Evelyn Cobbold's *Pilgrimage to Makkah*, First Edition, London, 1934; Other references and discussion in this piece came from Afiya S. Zia, *Faith and Feminism. Religious Agency or Secular Autonomy*, University of Toronto Press, 2018; Fatima Seedat, "Islam, Feminism, and Islamic Feminism: Between Inadequacy and Inevitability", Journal of Feminist Studies in Religion, Volume 29, Number 2, Fall 2013, pp. 25-45; Mona Eltahawy, *Headscarves and Hymens.Why the Middle East Needs a Sexual Revolution,* Farar, Straus and Giroux, 2015; and Saba Mahmood, *Politics of Piety: The Islamic Revival and the Feminist Subject*, Princeton University Press, 2005.

Allah, Asè and Afros by Adama Juldeh Munu

For more information on the websites and articles mentioned in this article see: Adama Munu, 'Are Black Muslim Women Part of the Natural Hair Conversation?', *Huffington Post*, September 2016 which can be accessed at https://www.huffingtonpost.co.uk/adama-juldeh-munu/are-black-muslim-women-pa_b_12103344.html

I X Kendi, 'The Renaissance is Black,' *Time*, 3 February 2021 at https://time.com/5932842/ibram-kendi-black-renaissance/; S J Rasmussen, 'Veiled Self, Transparent Meanings: Tuareg Headdress as Social Expression.' *Ethnology*, *30* (2), 101–117 1991: https://doi.org/10.2307/3773404; 'Respect Our Roots: A brief history of our braids', *Essence*, December 2020 https://www.essence.com/hair/respect-our-roots-brief-history-our-braids-cultural-appropriation/; and K Mtshali, 'The radical history of the headwrap', *Timeline*, May 2018 at timeline.com; Wheeler, Kayla Renée.

'The black Muslim female fashion trailblazers who came before model Halima Aden': https://www.theblackamericanmuslim.com/kayla-rene-wheeler; and H J Spillers, 'Mama's Baby, Papa's Maybe: An American Grammar Book,' *Diacritics*, 17 (2), 65–81 1987: https://doi.org/10.2307/464747; and Imani Bashir, 'Muslim Women Break Down The Myths Around Hair and Hijab,' *Huffington Post*, September 2021: https://www.huffpost.com/entry/muslim-women-hair-hijab-myths_l_5e419b 8dc5b6b708870599c0; ; Doeks: mark of a good woman – or a bad hair day? https://www.timeslive.co.za/sunday-times/opinion-and-analysis/2016-01-31-doeks-mark-of-a-good-woman-or-a-bad-hair-day/

The books mentioned are: Dawn-Marie Gibson and Jamillah Karim, *Women of the Nation: Between Black Protest and Sunni Islam*, New York University Press, July 2014; E Dabiri, *Don't Touch My Hair*, Penguin Books, 2019; Khadijah Abdul-Haqq, *Nanni's Hijab*, Djarabi Kitabs Publications, 2018; and Dalila Baruti, *How to Look After Your Natural Hair in Hijab*, self-published Kindle edition, 2015.

Bonding in Abrahamic Faiths by Giles Goddard

On the Jewish-Muslim tensions, see Alain Dieckhoff, 'The Mobilization of Religion in the Israeli-Arab Conflict' in Abdelwahab Meddeb and Benjamin Stora, editors, *A History of Jewish-Muslim Relations*, Princeton University Press 2013. See also: Jonathan Magonet, *Talking to the Other: Jewish Interfaith Dialogue with Christians and Muslims*, I. B. Tauris, London, 2003.

The 'Dabru Emet' declaration can be found at: https://www.ccjr.us/dialogika-resources/documents-and-statements/jewish/dabru-emet; and Desmond Tutu comments on Israel can be found at:http://news.bbc.co.uk/1/hi/1957644.stm

Imagining Otherwise by Elhum Shakerifar

The website of Hajar Press is at: https://www.hajarpress.com. To find out more about Hajar Press's crowdfunding visit: https://www.crowdfunder.

co.uk/support-hajar-press. To read about the Kate Clanchy controversy, visit https://www.theguardian.com/books/2021/aug/13/pointing-out-racism-in-books-is-not-an-attack-kate-clanchy   and   https://www.thebookseller.com/blogs/lessons-clanchy-1282047; Also see http://roarnews.co.uk/2021/in-conversation-with-poet-sarah-lasoye-part-1/; For Novel Voices, Heba Hayek in Conversation with Ellah P Wakatama, see https://www.youtube.com/watch?v=zKuJsObYVzg; Also see https://www.youtube.com/watch?v=KDi0MLbTNek and https://heystacks.org/doc/337/this-work-isnt-for-us--by-jemma-desai

In-Between by Nikhat Hoque

The papers mentioned in the review are: Abeera Khan, 'Queer Secularity' *Lambda Nordica* 4 133-139 2020; Cathy J Cohen, 'Punks, Bulldaggers, and Welfare Queens: The Radical Potential of Queer Politics' *GLQ* 3 437-465 1997; and Chandra Talpade Mohanty, 'Under Western Eyes Revisited: Feminist Solidarity through Anticapitalist Struggles' *Sign: Journal of Women in Culture and Society* 28 (2) 499-535 Winter 2003. All three papers can be easily located online.

Last Word On Zoombies by Shamim Miah

Reference in order as they appear in the text: David Graeber, *Bullshit Jobs: A Theory* (Simon & Schuster, London, 2018); the definition of corona-time is taken from Arielle Pardes, 'There are no hours or days in Coronatime', *Wired*, 8 May 2020, available at: https://www.wired.com/story/coronavirus-time-warp-what-day-is-it/

Zoom's data mining concerns highlighted in the *New York Times* analysis by Aaron Krolik and Natasha Singer (April, 2020) '*A Feature on Zoom Secretly Displayed Data From People's LinkedIn Profiles,* available at: A Feature on Zoom Secretly Displayed Data From People's LinkedIn Profiles - *The New York Times* (nytimes.com).

Jeremy Bailenson, article on 'Non-Verbal Overload: A Theoretical Article on the Causes of Zoom-Fatigue', *Technology, Mind and Behaviour*, is available

CITATIONS   273 ———————

on open access:Nonverbal Overload: A Theoretical Argument for the Causes of Zoom Fatigue · Volume 2, Issue 1 (apaopen.org)

If you are interested in determining your ZEF scale, details can be accessed via: Online Survey Software | Qualtrics Survey Solutions

Crazy Zoom calls, especially the clip of Daniel, can be located via: CRAZIEST/FUNNIEST ZOOM FAILS OF 2021 SO FAR – YouTube (accessed 20 December 2021).

See also: C M Moreman, 'Dharma of the Living Dead: A Meditation on the Meaning of the Hollywood Zombie', *Studies in Religion/Sciences Religieuses* 39 (2): 263-281 2010; and J Vervaeke, C Mastropietro and F Miscevic, *Zombies in Western Culture: A Twenty-First Century Crisis* (Open Book Publishers, Cambridge, 2017)